PROJECTING EMPIRE

Cinema and Society series
GENERAL EDITOR: JEFFREY RICHARDS

Best of British: Cinema and Society from 1930 to the Present
    Anthony Aldgate & Jeffrey Richards
Brigadoon, Braveheart and the Scots: Distortions of Scotland in Hollywood Cinema
    Colin McArthur
The British at War: Cinema, State and Propaganda, 1939–1945
    James Chapman
British Cinema and the Cold War
    Tony Shaw
Children, Cinema and Censorship: From Dracula to the Dead End Kids
    Sarah J. Smith
The Crowded Prairie: American National Identity in the Hollywood Western
    Michael Coyne
An Everyday Magic: Cinema and Cultural Memory
    Annette Kuhn
Film and Community in Britain and France
    Margaret Butler
Film Propaganda: Soviet Russia and Nazi Germany
    Richard Taylor
From Moscow to Madrid: Postmodern Cities, European Cinema
    Ewa Mazierska & Laura Rascaroli
Hollywood Genres and Post-War America
    Mike Chopra-Gant
Hollywood's History Films
    David Eldridge
Licence to Thrill: A Cultural History of the James Bond Films
    James Chapman
Past and Present: National Identity and the British Historical Film
    James Chapman
Powell and Pressburger: A Cinema of Magic Spaces
    Andrew Moor
Projecting Empire: Imperialism and Popular Cinema
    James Chapman & Nicholas J. Cull
Propaganda and the German Cinema, 1933–1945
    David Welch
Shooting the Civil War: Cinema, History and American National Identity
    Jenny Barrett
Spaghetti Westerns: Cowboys and Europeans from Karl May to Sergio Leone
    Christopher Frayling
Spectacular Narratives: Hollywood in the Age of the Blockbuster
    Geoff King
Typical Men: The Representation of Masculinity in Popular British Cinema
    Andrew Spicer
The Unknown 1930s: An Alternative History of the British Cinema, 1929–1939
    Edited by Jeffrey Richards

PROJECTING EMPIRE

Imperialism and Popular Cinema

James Chapman and Nicholas J. Cull

I.B. TAURIS

LONDON · NEW YORK

Dedicated to Jeffrey Richards and Tony Aldgate,
whose collaboration and scholarship inspired this volume

Published in 2009 by I.B.Tauris & Co Ltd

6 Salem Road, London W2 4BU
175 Fifth Avenue, New York NY 10010
www.ibtauris.com

Distributed in the United States and Canada
Exclusively by Palgrave Macmillan
175 Fifth Avenue, New York NY 10010

ISBN: 978 1 84511 940 9

A full CIP record for this book is available from the British Library
A full CIP record is available from the Library of Congress

Library of Congress Catalog Card Number: available

Printed and bound in Great Britain by
CPI Antony Rowe, Chippenham

FSC
Mixed Sources
Product group from well-managed
forests and other controlled sources
Cert no. SGS-COC-2953
www.fsc.org
© 1996 Forest Stewardship Council

Contents

Illustrations

The illustrations in this book were provided by the Stills, Posters and Design Division of the British Film Institute; the Cinematic Arts Library, University of Southern California; and the Margaret Herrick Library, Academy of Motion Picture Arts and Sciences. They are included for the purpose of criticism and review.

Abbreviations

BBFC	British Board of Film Censors
BFI	British Film Institute
CIA	Central Intelligence Agency
EMB	Empire Marketing Board
FBI	Federal Bureau of Investigation
GPO	General Post Office
MOI	Ministry of Information
MPAA	Motion Picture Association of America
MPEA	Motion Picture Export Association
OWI	Office of War Information
PCA	Production Code Administration
SEAC	South East Asia Command
USIA	United States Information Agency

General Editor's Introduction

The birth of cinema coincided with the high noon of the British Empire. Cameras were on hand to record the great ceremonial events of that era, such as the Diamond Jubilee of the Queen-Empress Victoria in 1897 and the Delhi Durbar of the King-Emperor Edward VII in 1903. Fragmentary visual images of troops on the march in the key imperial events of the time, the Boer War and the Boxer Rebellion, survive, thanks to the medium. At the same time fictional episodes from the same conflicts were being staged and filmed. Together these early manifestations of imperial cinema embodied the elements that were to constitute the enduring appeal of the subject: spectacle, action, drama and exotic locations.

Ever since those early days, empire has featured regularly in the filmmaking schedules of both Britain and America. In this fascinating, wide-ranging and insightful book, James Chapman and Nicholas Cull take 13 productions from the cinema of empire, ranging from the 1930s to the present, and subject them to close critical analysis. They deal not only with the cinematic texts themselves but also the production and reception histories of the films. Their examples are drawn from a wide variety of genres, from imperial action-adventure (*Gunga Din*) to colonial melodrama (*Elephant Walk*), from wartime documentary (*Burma Victory*) to historical epic (*Lawrence of Arabia*), from knockabout comedy (*Carry On Up the Khyber*) to reverential biopic (*Gandhi*), revealing how widely and deeply the imperial experience has impacted on the popular consciousness.

Frequently the behind-the-scenes stories they have to tell about the often tortuous and eventful process of producing the films is as intriguing and revealing as the narratives of the finished films themselves. Issues of race, gender, hegemony and identity run like binding threads through the films as they react, each in their own way, to the rise and fall of the British Empire and its replacement by American imperialism. This book therefore constitutes a major examination of the cinema's reaction to and involvement with a global phenomenon that dominated the twentieth century and continues on into the twenty-first.

JEFFREY RICHARDS

Preface

This book originated in discussions at the 22nd Congress of the International Association of Media and History (IAMHIST) on *Media and Imperialism* at the University of Amsterdam in July 2007 and was mapped out during the authors' day trip to the town of Arnhem to visit the war museum and cemetery and walk the battlefield. It comprises eleven case studies of key films, British and American, in the history of the cinema of empire. These have been chosen according to several criteria, including the availability of primary sources documenting their production, their narrative and visual representations of empire, and their significance in shaping the genre. The book has been written according to a set of agreed principles and themes. The preface and chapters 1, 2, 4, 6, 10 and 11 are written by James Chapman, while chapters 3, 5, 7, 8, 9, 12 and the afterword are the work of Nick Cull.

We have selected films from different periods and genres – adventure, documentary, melodrama, biopic, comedy – which are broadly representative of the main trends and themes in the Anglo–American cinema of empire. *The Four Feathers* and *Gunga Din* were made at the height of popular cinema's investment in the British Empire and imagine it as a site of heroic masculine adventure. They exemplify the thematic and ideological strategies of British and American film-makers, respectively, in their promotion of an imperial worldview during the 1930s. The Second World War is represented by *Burma Victory*, an official documentary of the British campaign against the Japanese in the Far East. It is included here because its production history maps the political tensions between the British and their American allies over strategic policy in Southeast Asia.

The post-war period is represented by *Elephant Walk*, one of Hollywood's colonial melodramas of the 1950s which is significant both for its representation of a feminine perspective and for the hidden hand of the CIA in its production. This film demonstrates a more equivocal attitude towards the empire informed by the process of decolonization that was underway by the 1950s. The critique of colonialism becomes more overt in David Lean's magisterial epic *Lawrence of Arabia*. This film marked a watershed for the cinema of empire, which can be divided into pre-*Lawrence* and post-*Lawrence* cycles. This is reflected in the film itself, which divides into a heroic first part, told through the eyes of Lawrence himself, and an anti-heroic second half, a study in imperial hubris, told from the perspective of an American journalist.

The changing attitude towards imperialism signalled by *Lawrence of Arabia* is further evident in the cult film *The Naked Prey*, Cornel Wilde's savage allegorical tale of the hunter hunted, and in the *Carry On* parodies of the late 1960s which spoofed the conventions of the imperial adventure movie. Those conventions are restored in John Huston's *The Man Who Would Be King*, which reinterprets Kipling for Vietnam-era America. *Raiders of the Lost Ark*, the first of the enormously successful Indiana Jones movies, is on the surface a nostalgic homage to the adventure serials of the 1930s and 1940s but beneath is an imperialist narrative of the projection of American power into the Third World. *Gandhi*, Sir Richard Attenborough's long-cherished biopic of the Indian martyr, marks a return to the imperial biopic, this time exploring the perspective of the colonized as well as the colonizers. We conclude with the 1999 Gulf War action movie *Three Kings*, a liberal critique of US policy which represents a lost moment of self-awareness before America committed itself to another imperial folly in Iraq.

Projecting Empire is based largely on the fruits of our researches in British and American archives. We would like to record our thanks to the staff of the following institutions for their support and assistance: the British Film Institute Library, especially Janet Moat of the Special Collections Unit who retired in 2008; the National Archives (formerly the Public Records Office) at Kew; Barbara Hall and the Margaret Herrick Library, Academy of Motion Picture Arts and Sciences, Los Angeles; Becky Cape and the Lilly Library, University of Indiana, Bloomington; Ned Comstock and the Cinematic Arts Library, University of Southern California; and the New York Public Library.

For advice, information and criticism, our thanks are due to Tracey Alexander; Dr Guy Barefoot; Philippa Brewster at I.B.Tauris; Dr Sally Dux; Dr Chris Gittings; Dr Mark Glancy; Nilufa Junaideen; John Milius; Bruce Raymer; Corinne Roosevelt; Professor Jeffrey Richards; David O. Russell; Dr Jack G. Shaheen; and Dr Jonathan Stubbs. It goes without saying, of course, that any faults are entirely the responsibility of the authors.

An earlier version of chapter 3 appeared as 'America's Raj: Kipling, Masculinity and Empire', in C. E. Gittings (ed.), *Imperialism and Gender: Constructions of Masculinity* (Hebden Bridge: Dangaroo Press, 1996), pp.85–97. Chapter 10 uses some material previously included in 'Camping on the Borders: History, Identity and Britishness in the *Carry On* Costume Parodies, 1963–74', in Claire Monk and Amy Sargeant (eds), *British Historical Cinema* (London: Routledge, 2002), pp.92–109. Both have been substantially revised here.

1
IMPERIALISM AND POPULAR CINEMA: A SURVEY

From its outset cinema has been a vehicle for disseminating images and ideologies of empire. Some of the earliest 'topicals' – short film records of newsworthy events – were of imperial spectacles such as the Diamond Jubilee of Queen Victoria in 1897 and the Delhi Durbar of 1903. Imperial subjects were a natural for the travelogues, or 'scenics', that provided a staple of early film exhibition. They impressed audiences with their images of imperial splendour and brought pictures of exotic lands and customs to the patrons of the cinematograph. At the same time early cinematographers were involved in the propagation of imperial propaganda. The Spanish–American War (1898) and the South African War (1899–1902) were the first to be covered by film cameramen. G. W. Bitzer of the Biograph Company and Alfred E. Smith of American Vitagraph were amongst the pioneer cinematographers who travelled to Cuba as America first flexed its imperialist muscles against the Spanish. And William K.-L. Dickson of the British Mutoscope and Biograph Company sailed to South Africa in October 1899. He shot footage of troops in camp and staged re-enactments with British soldiers dressed in Boer uniforms. Dickson's published memoir, *The Biograph in Battle*, recorded that the British commander-in-chief, Lord Roberts, 'consented to be biographed with all his Staff, actually having his table taken out into the sun for the convenience of Mr Dickson'.[1]

It is significant that the advent of cinema in the 1890s coincided both with the zenith of British imperialism and with the first stirrings of America as an imperial power. It was only natural that early film-makers would reflect the popular mood of jingoism. The Edison Manufacturing Company's *The Monroe Doctrine*, released in April 1896, was probably the first propaganda film. It referred to a boundary dispute between Venezuela and the colony of British Guiana: it was nothing less than a warning to Britain to keep out of America's back yard. The *Boston Globe* reported that the film 'shows

John Bull bombarding a South American shore, supposedly to represent Venezuela. John is seemingly getting the better of the argument when the tall lanky figure of Uncle Sam emerges from the back of the picture. He grasps John Bull by the neck, forces him to his knees and makes him take his hat off to Venezuela'.[2] Similarly, early British films of the South African War included staged allegorical dramas such as the Warwick Trading Company's *The Set-to between John Bull and Paul Kruger* (1900) and R. W. Paul's *Kruger's Dreams of Empire* (1900).

The Spanish–American War occurred at an opportune moment for the fledgling US motion picture industry. The novelty value of moving pictures was waning by 1898 but the war created a demand for topical films ranging from actualities of American troops to staged dramatic re-enactments. This gave a boost to exhibitors and stimulated competition between producers. The role of press magnates such as William Randolph Hearst in precipitating the US intervention in Cuba is well known, but less attention has been paid to the part played by the cinematograph. As the early cinema historian Charles Musser has written: 'It would be a gross exaggeration to say that the cinema launched a new era of American imperialism. But cinema had found a role beyond narrow amusement, and this sudden prominence coincided with a new era of overseas expansion and military intervention.'[3]

In Britain, too, the cinematograph played an important role in supporting the British Empire in its war against the Boers. The evidence would suggest that actuality films from the front were well received by cinema audiences. A review of a programme of topical films at the Empire Theatre, Leeds, in January 1900, for example, records that the 'audience cheered wildly when the presentment of Lord Roberts was shown on the screen ... One and all of these patriotic pictures stirred deeply the emotions of the crowded audience'.[4] When actuality material was not available, however, enterprising film-makers were not averse to dramatic reconstruction. The Gaumont Company produced a 'ludicrously imaginative' film *Signing of the Peace at Vereeniging* (1902) with actors playing Lord Kitchener and Jan Smuts. Gaumont's Colonel A. C. Bromhead later recalled: 'We included Lord Roberts and only found out afterwards that he had not been there.'[5]

Early film representations of empire took a variety of different forms. Some, such as James Williamson's *Attack on a China Mission* (1900), adopted the conventions of Victorian stage melodrama. This short film (actually shot in Williamson's back yard) was a distillation of events during the Boxer Rebellion in China with the rebels killing a European missionary and laying siege to the mission station until the arrival of the Bluejackets. It is an embryonic version of the rescue narrative later perfected by D. W. Griffith in his Biograph shorts such as *The Lonely Villa* (1909), *The Lonedale*

Operator (1911) and *The Battle of Elderbush Gulch* (1913). Other films, consistent with the theatrical tradition of early cinema, drew upon the imperial
pageant. W. G. Barker's *The Pageant of Empire* (1911), produced for the coron-
ation of George V, for example, 'shows Britannia on her throne, supported
by John Bull, his bull-dog and sisters, and before whom the Colonies pay
obedience'.[6] The most spectacular of these pageants was Charles Urban's
film of the Delhi Durbar of 1911 – a great Orientalist extravaganza wel-
coming George V as Emperor of India – which was shot in Kinemacolor
and premièred at the Scala Cinema in London accompanied by a 24-piece
orchestra.[7]

These early films of empire need to be understood in the context of a wider
popular culture of imperialism during the late Victorian and Edwardian
periods. As social historians of imperialism such as John MacKenzie have
shown, imperialism was a core element of the British historical experience.
MacKenzie identifies an 'ideological cluster which formed out of the intellectual, national, and world-wide conditions of the late Victorian era, and
which came to infuse and be propagated by every organ of British life in
the period'.[8] The British Empire was celebrated in popular fiction, theatre,
music hall, cigarette cards and postcards. It represented a force for political stability and moral improvement. Nowhere was this more evident than
in the field of juvenile literature where the works of W. H. G. Kingston,
R. M. Ballantyne, Manville Fenn and, pre-eminently, G. A. Henty imagined the empire as a site of heroic adventure for their schoolboy protagonists. While novels may have been aimed at a predominantly middle-class
readership, the working classes were catered for by the story papers such
as *Marvel, Union Jack, Chums, Captain* and *Young England* – cheaper rivals
to the decidedly middle-class *Boy's Own Paper*.[9] The working classes were
amongst the most avid consumers of such fiction and also provided the
core audience for the cinematograph.

The relationship between early cinema and the popular culture of
imperialism can be seen on several levels. Early film shows, for one thing,
were part of a multimedia experience which also included lectures, slide
shows and novelty acts. The influence of juvenile fiction, furthermore, can
be seen in the production of series films featuring similarly square-jawed
imperial heroes. The British and Colonial Kinematograph Company, for
example, produced a series of 13 *Lieutenant Daring* films between 1911 and
1914 relating the adventures of a naval officer who saved Great Britain from
the plots of assorted spies and anarchists. In the United States the 1910s
were the heyday of the 'serial queen' melodrama as plucky heroines such as
Pearl White (*The Perils of Pauline, The Exploits of Elaine, Pearl of the Army*) and
Ruth Roland (*The Red Circle, The Adventures of Ruth, Ruth of the Rockies*) took

on all manner of foreign villains in narratives of American intervention and overseas expansion.

It was during the First World War, however, that the cinematograph came of age as a medium of propaganda. The British War Office was initially sceptical of the value of film and refused to allow cameramen access to the front. Consequently the early films of the war were staged melodramas, with a particular vogue for atrocity stories about the 'beastly Hun'. It was not until 1915 that the Topical Committee for War Films was set up under Sir William Jury to liaise between the government and the trade. The first official cinematographers were allowed in British sectors of the Western Front in November 1915 and the first newsreels of the front line were shown publicly in London in January 1916. The first feature-length film produced by the Topical Committee was *The Battle of the Somme* (1916), compiled from material shot by two British official cameramen, Geoffrey Malins and J. B. McDowell. It was a critical and commercial success and was followed by two more long documentaries: *The Battle of the Ancre and the Advance of the Tanks* (1917) and *The German Retreat and the Battle of Arras* (1917). In 1917 the War Office took over the production of the newsreel *Topical Budget* which included items from other fronts. Amongst the events covered by *War Office Official Topical Budget* were General Allenby's entry into Jerusalem on 11 December 1917 and the signing of the peace treaty in the Hall of Mirrors at Versailles on 28 June 1919.[10]

The growing acceptance of the cinematograph by military authorities was indirectly responsible for the creation of one of the most enduring myths of the war. T. E. Lawrence has been described as 'the only old-style hero of the first World war'.[11] Lawrence came to prominence largely through the efforts of Lowell Thomas, an American journalist, who, with cameraman Harry Chase, covered the British campaign in the Middle East in 1917–18. There was already an official British cinematographer in Palestine, Harold Jeapes, who, along with his Australian colleague Frank Harvey, shot *General Allenby's Entry into Jerusalem*. Lawrence, then a major, can be seen taking part in the parade and is visible amongst a group of officers standing around Allenby.[12] The fact that other cinematographers were allowed in the theatre – Ariel Varges, another American, was shooting in Mesopotamia at the same time – suggests that the War Office attached considerable importance to the propaganda value of the Middle East campaign at a time when the Western Front was still deadlocked.

Thomas's arrangement with the War Office prevented him from showing any of his material publicly until after the war. In August 1919 he brought his travelogue *With Allenby in Palestine* from New York to London where he presented it to packed houses at the Royal Opera House, the Albert Hall and the Queen's Hall. Thomas was a showman rather than a historian: his account of the war in the Middle East owed more to the tradition of imperial adventure fiction than it did to history. Even the title was redolent of juvenile fiction: in 1918 Captain F. S. Brereton had published a novel entitled *With Allenby in Palestine*, one of a series of books that also included *With French at the Front* and *Under Hague in Flanders*.[13] The authenticity of Thomas's filmic material has also been called into question. The Imperial War Museum catalogue describes *With Allenby in Palestine* as 'a typical Lowell Thomas mishmash' and questions how much of it he actually shot.[14]

The part of Lowell Thomas's lecture that attracted most attention was his account of Lawrence and the Arab Revolt. He reflected this when he changed the title of his show to *With Allenby in Palestine and Lawrence in Arabia*. It played in London for several months before touring the provinces. Thomas then took it overseas to other major cities of the British Empire. It was seen by an estimated four million people.[15] Lawrence was the first celebrity whose image was created by the mass media. 'Lawrence of Arabia', as he quickly became known, was the latest in the lineage of great imperial heroes who also included Clive of India and Gordon of Khartoum. Lawrence's own attitude to this image, however, was ambivalent. He is known to have attended the London lectures, writing afterwards to Thomas: 'I saw your show last night and thank God the lights were out.'[16]

The popularity of Lawrence would suggest that the First World War did not, after all, destroy the romantic allure of empire. Historians such as Paul Fussell have argued that the bloody attritional battles and mechanized slaughter of the Western Front exposed the myth of 'King and Country' once and for all.[17] The evidence usually cited in support of this view is the bitter, disillusioned poetry of Wilfred Owen and Siegfried Sassoon and the grim accounts of trench warfare in memoirs and novels such as Robert Graves' *Goodbye to All That* and Erich Maria Remarque's *All Quiet on the Western Front* – the latter filmed as an early talking picture by Universal Pictures in 1930. In fact the war provoked different responses. On the one hand there was shock and revulsion at the killing fields of the Somme and Passchendaele and a sincere desire that it should be the 'war to end wars'. On the other hand, however, there was also a genuine sense of pride in the achievement of Britain and her empire in weathering the storm. The British Empire emerged from the war strengthened and united. The role of the self-governing dominions (Australia, New Zealand, Canada, South Africa) was celebrated in compilation films such as *The World's Greatest Story* and *Our Empire's Fight for Freedom* in 1918–19. And in the 1920s a cycle of reconstructed documentaries – *The Battle of Jutland, Ypres, Mons* and *The Battles of Coronel and the Falkland Islands* – was produced by British Instructional Films under the supervision of 'ardent imperialist' Harry Bruce Woolfe.[18]

By the interwar period there was a growing recognition of the potential of film for the promotion of British commercial and cultural interests. This was reflected in the formation of the Empire Marketing Board (1926) and the British Council (1934). The aim of the EMB was to promote trade throughout the British Empire through exhibitions, posters and pamphlets. Its greatest success, however, came in the production of documentary films through the EMB Film Unit, set up in 1930 under the Scots documentarist John Grierson. Grierson argued that the role of the unit was to promote a new vision of empire based on trade and commerce rather than territorial expansion: 'For the old flags of exploitation it substituted the new flags of common labour; for the old frontiers of conquest it substituted new frontiers of research and world-wide organisation.'[19] The EMB itself was wound up in 1933, but its film unit was transferred to the General Post Office. The origins of the British documentary film movement are to be found, therefore, in the work of an official agency of imperial propaganda.[20]

It was the feature film, however, that became the primary vehicle of what, following Jeffrey Richards, we may term 'the cinema of empire'.[21] In the 1930s the cinema of empire emerged as a major genre in the film industries of Britain and Hollywood. Between 1934 and 1939 most of the major Hollywood studios contributed to a cycle of British Empire films that included *Clive of India*, *The Lost Patrol*, *Lives of a Bengal Lancer*, *The Charge of the Light Brigade*, *Wee Willie Winkie*, *Four Men and a Prayer*, *Storm Over Bengal*, *Stanley and Livingstone*, *The Sun Never Sets*, *Beau Geste* and *Gunga Din*.[22] Paramount's *Lives of a Bengal Lancer*, loosely based on the book of the same title by Francis Yeats-Brown, became the prototype of the Northwest Frontier film for the next 25 years. Its success prompted Warner Bros. to locate most of *The Charge of the Light Brigade* in India, moving the action to the Crimea for the rousing action climax.[23] This cycle of 'Hollywood British' films prompted *The Times* to remark in 1937: 'The Union Jack has in the last few years been vigorously and with no little effect flown by Hollywood.'[24]

How can we explain the emergence of empire cinema in Hollywood in the 1930s? One reason is cultural. John Fraser has pointed to the existence of a shared Anglo–American culture of chivalry that exerts a strong hold on the popular imagination on both sides of the Atlantic. He writes:

> The family of chivalric heroes has been by far the largest and most popular one in twentieth-century American culture, and its members, in whole or in part, have entered into virtually everyone's consciousness. They include, naturally, the legion of

knightly Westerners in print and celluloid sired by Owen Wister's *The Virginian* and their Indian counterparts ... They include the officers and gentlemen of *Lives of a Bengal Lancer*, and the gentleman rankers of *Beau Geste*, and the First World War aviators of *Dawn Patrol* ... They include gentlemanly English actors like Ronald Colman and George Sanders, and gentlemanly American ones like Douglas Fairbanks Jr and William Powell, and all those immortals, Gary Cooper, Spencer Tracy, and the rest, who have epitomized native American gallantry and grace.[25]

It is this shared sense of Anglo–American values that explains how actors such as Gary Cooper (American but educated at an English public school) and Errol Flynn (born in Tasmania, and educated in Australia and England) could move effortlessly between British Empire films and Westerns. Cooper starred in *The Virginian* (1929) and also in *Lives of a Bengal Lancer* and *Beau Geste*, while Flynn made the transition from *The Charge of the Light Brigade* to reprise much the same role in the cavalry Western *They Died with Their Boots On* (1942) in which he played George Armstrong Custer. The absence of major 'A' feature Westerns in the 1930s has sometimes been seen as another reason for the ascendancy of the British Empire film. The two genres share common ground – the narrative of expansion, the taming of the frontier, the clash between civilization and savagery – and both feature outdoor action and spectacle. It is no coincidence that the end of the empire cycle in 1939 coincided with the revival of the 'A' Western: *Stagecoach, Dodge City, Union Pacific, Jesse James*.

Yet there was also a hard-nosed economic reality behind Hollywood's British Empire films. Approximately half of the US film industry's total revenues came from outside North America and for the more expensive productions (which included the empire films) overseas revenues could mean the difference between profit and loss. Furthermore, the British market was by far the most lucrative of all foreign markets. In the 1930s Britain accounted for some 50 per cent of all Hollywood's overseas revenues. There are several reasons for this. For one thing there was no language barrier to the export of American films to Britain and therefore no need for costly dubbing or subtitling. American films also benefited from the relative instability of the British production sector, which was hit by a cycle of boom and bust. Above all, however, the British were very frequent cinema-goers. There were some 5000 cinemas in Britain – the same number in one small densely populated country as in the whole of Latin America.[26] Moreover, as other markets, such as Nazi Germany, were closed to American films from the late 1930s, the British market assumed even greater significance. In his study of Hollywood's 'British' films, Mark Glancy argues persuasively 'that Hollywood's love for Britain stemmed primarily from box-office consider-ations rather than ardent Anglophilia'.[27]

The first major cycle of empire cinema ended with the outbreak of the Second World War. The propaganda imperative of the war, exemplified in both British and American films, was to promote the idea of Britain as a progressive liberal democracy in contrast to the highly ideological totali-tarian regime of Nazi Germany.[28] British feature films such as *49th Parallel* (1941) focused on the idea of a democratic British Commonwealth, while historical films such as *Lady Hamilton* (1941) and *The Young Mr Pitt* (1942) mobilized the past for propaganda by drawing parallels between Napoleon and Hitler. The British Empire was conspicuously absent, except in docu-mentaries produced by the newly instituted Colonial Film Unit largely for consumption in the colonies themselves.[29] The ideological demands of the war, however, made the cinema of empire redundant at a time when films were promoting the war effort of the United Nations. India, where the nationalist cause was boosted by the war, represented a particularly thorny problem. In 1942 the US Office of War Information prevailed upon RKO not to re-issue *Gunga Din* and in the same year MGM abandoned its production of *Kim*.[30]

When the cinema of empire returned in the 1950s it took on a very different hue. The pervading theme of British-made empire films of this period is the idea of the empire under threat. This is evident in a brace of colonial police films produced by Ealing Studios (*Where No Vultures Fly*, *West of Zanzibar*) and in melodramas set against the background of colonial insurgencies in Malaya (*The Planter's Wife*, *The Seventh Dawn*) and Kenya (*Simba*, *Safari*).[31] The colonial melodrama was also a favourite of Hollywood in the 1950s: *The Snows of Kilimanjaro, Mogambo, Elephant Walk, The Rains of Ranchipur, Bhowani Junction*.[32] These films displaced political tensions around the rise of nationalism onto romantic dramas involving European and American ex-pats. They are significant in that they tend to privilege the female perspective: women become the focus of tension in the tropics rather than native uprisings. Their characterizations are drawn from the romantic melodrama: essentially they are soap operas set in the colonies. The tradi-tional imperial adventure film returned in the 1950s, though with the excep-tion of MGM's *King Solomon's Mines* and its long-delayed *Kim*, most of these were routine programmers: *Soldiers Three, King of the Khyber Rifles, Khyber Patrol, Bengal Rifles, Storm Over Africa, Storm Over the Nile, Zarak, The Bandit of Zhobe, Killers of Kilimanjaro*.[33] The last, glorious flowering of the *Boy's Own* imperial adventure film came in 1959 with the Rank Organization's *North West Frontier* – an 'elegiac farewell to Empire' that both harks back to the empire cinema of the 1930s and anticipates the more critical examination of the imperial project that would emerge in the 1960s.[34]

From the 1960s the cinema of empire has been a less consistent presence in Britain or Hollywood. To an extent this might be attributed to the winding up of the British Empire: the cinema of empire no longer possessed the ideological currency it had enjoyed in the 1930s when it had been a vehicle for the promotion of imperialism. But it also reflects the trend across the film industry as a whole as it shifted from the continuous production of bread-and-butter genre films to concentrating on fewer but bigger films intended to reap rich box office rewards. This 'blockbuster' mentality can be traced back to the 1950s when Hollywood had responded to declining cinema attendances and the emergence of television as a rival mass entertainment medium by turning to spectacular Biblical and Ancient World epics produced on a scale that television could never match. This trend continued into the 1960s with a cycle of major empire films including *Lawrence of Arabia* (1962), *55 Days at Peking* (1963), *Zulu* (1964) and *Khartoum* (1966). These were international epics shot on location by independent producers – Sam Spiegel (*Lawrence of Arabia*), Samuel Bronston (*55 Days at Peking*), Joseph E. Levine (*Zulu*) and Julian Blaustein (*Khartoum*) – backed by Hollywood studios.

At the same time as the British Empire was disappearing from the map, however, another was emerging to take its place. The United States emerged from the Second World War as the leading industrial and military power in the world. Since 1945 the United States has abandoned its traditional isolationism and has looked to assert its influence on a global scale. The American empire is not a formal empire of territorial acquisition but an informal empire of political and economic influence. Americans might not always acknowledge their role as new imperialists, but since the middle of the twentieth century there is no question that the United States has acted like an imperial power in enforcing its strategic interests in South America, the Middle East and Southeast Asia through a combination of diplomacy and military power. Like the rise and fall of the British Empire, moreover, the United States has had to contend with a shifting geopolitical landscape and to face the consequences of global over-reach as its imperial pretensions were exposed first in Vietnam and again in Iraq.[35]

Hollywood became one of the prime vehicles for the projection of US imperialism. In part this was an extension of the economic hegemony that the US film industry enjoys around the world. After the Second World War the newly formed Motion Picture Export Association – the foreign division of the principal trade body, the Motion Picture Association of America (MPAA) – spearheaded an aggressive campaign to re-establish American domination of those markets lost during the war. The primary motive was economic and the US film industry was undoubtedly helped by the devastation wrought upon the domestic film industries in Europe by the war. But there was also a powerful cultural motive. As Eric Johnston, president of the MPAA, declared in 1947: 'The American motion picture will carry the ideas of Canton, Ohio, to Canton, China; the point of view of Paris, Maine, to Paris, France.'[36]

Projecting Empire, then, examines the changing representation of imperialism in the cinemas of Hollywood and Britain between the 1930s and the present. It is the first study of the cinema of empire in over 35 years.[37] We have focused on films that, in the main, were popular with audiences on the grounds that this provides most insight into changing attitudes towards imperialism. We have considered films by major producers and directors – Alexander Korda, David Lean, John Huston, Steven Spielberg, Richard Attenborough – as well as the work of lesser-known or cult film-makers such as Cornel Wilde and the producer–director partnership of Peter Rogers and Gerald Thomas.

As cultural historians our methodology is that of empirical investigation and analysis. We have been concerned to locate the films in their various contexts – industrial, economic, political, social, cultural – and to document their production and reception histories. To this end we have drawn upon a wide range of primary sources including government archives, studio records, personal papers, scripts, censors' files, diaries, autobiographies, trade papers, and contemporary newspaper and journal reviews. Our approach has been influenced by the work of Jeffrey Richards and Anthony Aldgate, especially in their book *Best of British*.[38] That is to say that we treat the films as social documents which speak of and for the times in which they were produced and consumed.

A crude version of social film history, influenced by Siegfried Kracauer's pioneering but methodologically flawed *From Caligari to Hitler: A Psychological Study of the German Film* (1947), understands films as a reflection or mirror of their social context.[39] This is no longer widely accepted as a reliable methodology. A more useful metaphor, we believe, is to see films as the residue of the production process. The finished film is the outcome of a range of factors including, but not limited to, the intentions of the producer and/or director, the commercial interests of the production company, the interventions of censors and in some cases the hidden hand of government agencies. We will see, for example, how the Foreign Office colluded with the British Board of Film Censors to prevent Alexander Korda from making *Lawrence of Arabia* in the 1930s, and how the CIA influenced the script of *Elephant Walk* to reflect a more positive view of America for overseas consumption. We will see how the British and American propaganda agencies clashed over the representation of colonial policy in Southeast Asia during the making of *Burma Victory*. We will also see how the content of films is determined by external factors. Several of the films included here – *Lawrence of Arabia*, *The Man Who Would Be King*, *Gandhi* – were in development over many years. The many treatments and scripts of *The Man Who Would Be King*, in particular, reveal how the film developed over nearly a quarter of a century.

The limitations of space prevent us from discussing all the films we would have liked to include. In particular we regret the absence of the different versions of *King Solomon's Mines* and of interesting films such as *The Wind and the Lion*, *Greystoke* and *White Mischief*. We have not included the progressive documentary-drama *Men of Two Worlds* or the perennial popular favourite *Zulu* because those films have been adequately covered elsewhere.[40] However, we do believe that our selection is representative of the main themes and trends in the cinema of empire. Above all we hope that *Projecting Empire* provides new insights into what has become a somewhat neglected genre. For too long the cinema of empire has been unfashionable for its perceived ideological reaction and cultural conservatism. What we hope to demonstrate here is that popular cinema has been a vehicle both for supporting and for contesting imperialism and that the cinema of empire has been a historically significant trend in the film industries of Hollywood and Britain. At a time when the legacy of imperialism is still being felt, it is high time that the cinema of empire came under the microscope.

Notes

1 Preface to W.K.-L. Dickson, *The Biograph in Battle: Its Story in the South African War* (London: T. Fisher Unwin, 1901), p.xiii.

2 Quoted in Luke McKernan, 'The American Invasion and the British Film Industry', in Alan Burton and Laraine Porter (eds), *Crossing the Pond: Anglo–American Film Relations before 1930* (Trowbridge: Flicks Books, 2002), p.7.

3 Charles Musser, *History of the American Cinema Volume 1. The Emergence of Cinema: The American Screen to 1907* (Berkeley: University of California Press, 1990), p.261.

4 Quoted in Simon Popple, '"But the Khaki-Covered Camera Is the *Latest* Thing": The Boer War Cinema and Visual Culture in Britain', in Andrew Higson (ed.), *Young and Innocent? The Cinema in Britain 1896–1930* (Exeter: University of Exeter Press, 2002), p.24.

5 Quoted in Rachael Low and Roger Manvell, *The History of the British Film 1896–1906* (London: George Allen & Unwin, 1948), p.69.

6 Quoted in Rachael Low, *The History of the British Film 1906–1914* (London: George Allen & Unwin, 1949), p.148.

7 Luke McKernan, 'Putting the World before You: The Charles Urban Story', in Higson, *Young and Innocent?*, p.73.

8   John M. MacKenzie, *Propaganda and Empire: The Manipulation of British Public Opinion* (Manchester: Manchester University Press, 1984), p.2.

9   Ibid., pp.199–226; and Michael Paris, *Warrior Nation: Images of War in British Popular Culture, 1850–2000* (London: Reaktion, 2000), pp.49–82.

10 See Nicholas Reeves, *Official British Film Propaganda during the First World War* (London: Croom Helm, 1984); Luke McKernan, *Topical Budget: The Great British News Film* (London: British Film Institute, 1992); Gary S. Messinger, *British Propaganda and the State in the First World War* (Manchester: Manchester University Press, 1992); and M. L. Sanders and Philip M. Taylor, *British Propaganda during the First World War* (London: Macmillan, 1982).

11 A. J. P. Taylor, *English History 1914–1945* (Oxford: Oxford University Press, 1965), p.49.

12 See Luke McKernan, '"The Supreme Moment of the War": *General Allenby's Entry into Jerusalem*', *Historical Journal of Film, Radio and Television*, 13: 2 (1993), pp.169–80.

13 See Michael Paris, *Over the Top: The Great War and Juvenile Literature in Britain* (Westport CT: Praeger, 2004), pp.75–99.

14 Roger Smither (ed.), *The Imperial War Museum Film Catalogue Volume 1. The First World War Film Archive* (Trowbridge: Flicks Books, 1994), p.422.

15 Graham Dawson, *Soldier Heroes: British Adventure, Empire and the Imagining of Masculinities* (London: Routledge, 1994), p.168.

16 Quoted in Joel C. Hodson, *Lawrence of Arabia and American Culture: The Making of a Transatlantic Legend* (Westport CT: Greenwood Press, 1995), p.39. In Michael Wilson's second draft screenplay of *Lawrence of Arabia* (British Film Institute Unpublished Script Collection S15680, 27 September 1960) an early scene has Lawrence attending one of Thomas's lectures in *mufti* and slipping out quietly during the performance.

17 Paul Fussell, *The Great War and Modern Memory* (Oxford: Oxford University Press, 1975).

18 Michael Paris, 'Enduring Heroes: British Feature Films and the First World War, 1919–1997', in Michael Paris (ed.), *The First World War and Popular Cinema* (Edinburgh: Edinburgh University Press, 1999), p.55.

19 John Grierson, 'The EMB Film Unit', in Forsyth Hardy (ed.), *Grierson on Documentary* (London: Collins, 1946), p.99.

20 On the EMB Film Unit, see Ian Aitken, *Film and Reform: John Grierson and the Documentary Film Movement* (London: Routledge, 1990), pp.90–126; and Paul Swann, *The British Documentary Film Movement, 1926–1946* (Cambridge: Cambridge University Press, 1989), pp.21–48.

21 Jeffrey Richards, *Visions of Yesterday* (London: Routledge & Kegan Paul, 1973), p.2.

22 *Clive of India* (Twentieth Century, dir. Richard Boleslawski, 1934); *The Lost Patrol* (RKO, dir. John Ford, 1934); *Lives of a Bengal Lancer* (Paramount, dir. Henry Hathaway, 1935); *The Charge of the Light Brigade* (Warner Bros., dir. Michael Curtiz, 1936); *Wee Willie Winkie* (Fox, dir. John Ford, 1937); *Four Men and a Prayer* (Fox, dir. John Ford, 1938); *Storm over Bengal* (Republic, dir. Sidney Salkow, 1938); *Stanley and Livingstone* (Fox, dir. Henry King, 1939); *The Sun Never Sets* (Universal, dir. Rowland V. Lee, 1939); *Beau Geste* (Paramount, dir. William Wellman, 1939); *Gunga Din* (RKO, dir. George Stevens, 1939). While not strictly a British Empire film, *The Real Glory* (Goldwyn, dir. Henry Hathaway, 1939) belongs in ethos to the same tradition and is an interesting early example of a film about US imperialism: the action is set in the Philippines in 1898.

23   Richards, *Visions of Yesterday*, p.3.

24   *The Times*, 12 April 1937.

25   John Fraser, *America and the Patterns of Chivalry* (Cambridge: Cambridge University Press, 1982), p.12.

26   H. Mark Glancy, *When Hollywood Loved Britain: The Hollywood 'British' Film 1939–45* (Manchester: Manchester University Press, 1999), p.29.

27   Ibid., p.6.

28   See Anthony Aldgate and Jeffrey Richards, *Britain Can Take It: British Cinema in the Second World War* (London: I.B.Tauris, 3rd edn, 2007); James Chapman, *The British at War: Cinema, State and Propaganda, 1939–1945* (London: I.B.Tauris, 1998); Jo Fox, *Film Propaganda in Britain and Nazi Germany: World War II Cinema* (Oxford: Berg, 2007); Clayton R. Koppes and Gregory D. Black, *Hollywood Goes to War: How Politics, Profits and Propaganda Shaped World War II Movies* (London: I.B.Tauris, 1988).

29   See Rosaleen Smyth, 'The British Colonial Film Unit and Sub-Saharan Africa, 1939–1945', *Historical Journal of Film, Radio and Television*, 8: 3 (1988), pp.285–98.

30   Glancy, *When Hollywood Loved Britain*, pp.190–92; Richards, *Visions of Yesterday*, p.216.

31   *Where No Vultures Fly* (Ealing, dir. Harry Watt, 1951); *The Planter's Wife* (Rank, dir. Ken Annakin, 1952); *West of Zanzibar* (Ealing, dir. Harry Watt, 1954); *Simba* (Rank, dir. Brian Desmond Hurst, 1955); *Safari* (Warwick, dir. Terence Young, 1956); *The Seventh Dawn* (United Artists/Charles K. Feldman, dir. Lewis Gilbert, 1964). British cinema's response to decolonization is discussed in Jeffrey Richards, 'Imperial Heroes for a Post-imperial Age: Films and the End of Empire', in Stuart Ward (ed.), *British Culture and the End of Empire* (Manchester: Manchester University Press, 2001), pp.128–44; and Wendy Webster, *Englishness and Empire 1939–1965* (Oxford: Oxford University Press, 2005), pp.122–48.

32   *The Snows of Kilimanjaro* (Fox, dir. Henry King, 1952); *Mogambo* (MGM, dir. John Ford, 1953); *Elephant Walk* (Paramount, dir. William Dieterle, 1954); *The Rains of Ranchipur* (Fox, dir. Jean Negulesco, 1955); *Bhowani Junction* (MGM, dir. George Cukor, 1956).

33   *King Solomon's Mines* (MGM, dir. Compton Bennett, 1950); *Kim* (MGM, dir. Victor Saville, 1950); *Soldiers Three* (MGM, dir. Tay Garnett, 1951); *King of the Khyber Rifles* (Fox, dir. Henry King, 1953); *Khyber Patrol* (United Artists, dir. Seymour Friedman, 1954); *Bengal Rifles* (Universal, dir. Laslo Benedek, 1954); *Storm over Africa* (Allied Artists, dir. Lesley Selander, 1954); *Storm Over the Nile* (London Films, dir. Zoltan Korda & Terence Young, 1955); *Zarak* (Warwick, dir. Terence Young, 1956); *The Bandit of Zhobe* (Warwick, dir. John Gilling, 1959); *Killers of Kilimanjaro* (Warwick, dir. Richard Thorpe, 1959).

34   Raymond Durgnat, *A Mirror for England: British Movies from Austerity to Affluence* (London: Faber & Faber, 1970), p.82.

35   The parallel between the British Empire in the nineteenth century and the USA in the twentieth century is suggested in Paul Kennedy, *The Rise and Fall of the Great Powers: Economic Change and Military Conflict from 1500 to 2000* (London: Fontana, 1988). A more sympathetic understanding of the generally benign influence of 'this most decent, honest, generous, fair-minded and self-sacrificing *imperium*' informs Andrew Roberts, *A History of the English-Speaking Peoples since 1900* (London: Weidenfeld & Nicolson, 2006). For a highly subjective response to the cinematic representation of the American empire, see Gore Vidal, *Screening History* (London: André Deutsch, 1992).

[36]   Quoted in Kerry Segrave, *American Films Abroad: Hollywood's Domination of the World's Movie Screens* (Jefferson NC: McFarland, 1997), p.141.

[37]   There has, of course, been much recent interest in film-making in Africa, Asia and South America, often heavily influenced by postcolonial theory. Studies of the relationship between US and European cinemas and colonized subjects have been fewer. See Prem Chowdhry, *Colonial India and the Making of Empire Cinema* (Manchester: Manchester University Press, 2000); and Martin Stollery, *Alternative Empires: European Modernist Cinemas and Cultures of Imperialism* (Exeter: University of Exeter Press, 2000).

[38]   Jeffrey Richards and Anthony Aldgate, *Best of British: Cinema and Society 1930–1970* (Oxford: Basil Blackwell, 1983). A new edition was published under the revised title *Best of British: Cinema and Society from 1930 to the Present* (London: I.B.Tauris, 1999). Other examples of this approach include Peter C. Rollins (ed.), *Hollywood as Historian: American Film in a Cultural Context* (Lexington: University Press of Kentucky, 1983); John E. Connor and Martin A. Jackson (eds), *American History/American Film* (New York: Ungar, 1979); and K. R. M. Short (ed.), *Feature Films as History* (London: Croom Helm, 1981).

[39]   'What films reflect,' Kracauer argued, 'are not so much explicit credos as psychological dispositions – those deep layers of mentality which extend more or less below the dimension of consciousness.' Siegfried Kracauer, *From Caligari to Hitler: A Psychological Study of the German Film* (Princeton: Princeton University Press, 1947), p.6. For a critique of Kracauer's methodology, see Paul Monaco, *Cinema and Society: France and Germany during the Twenties* (New York: Elsevier, 1976). Fuller methodological discussion of social film history can be found in Robert C. Allen and Douglas Gomery, *Film History: Theory and Practice* (New York: McGraw-Hill, 1985), pp.153–86; and the Introduction to James Chapman, Mark Glancy and Sue Harper (eds), *The New Film History: Sources, Methods, Approaches* (Basingstoke: Palgrave Macmillan, 2007), pp.1–10.

[40]   On *Men of Two Worlds*, see Jeffrey Richards, *Thorold Dickinson: The Man and His Films* (London: Croom Helm, 1986), pp.109–36. *Zulu* is a case study in James Chapman, *Past and Present: National Identity and the British Historical Film* (London: I.B.Tauris, 2005), pp.199–227. See also Sheldon Hall, *Zulu: With Some Guts Behind It – The Making of the Epic Movie* (Sheffield: Tomahawk Press, 2005).

TECHNICOLOR EMPIRE

The Four Feathers (1939)

In the 1930s Alexander Korda became the leading propagandist of the British Empire. Korda, a Hungarian-born Anglophile producer, had established himself as a major presence in the British film industry with *The Private Life of Henry VIII* (1933), a populist historical biopic that was a major box office hit on both sides of the Atlantic.[1] Its success propelled Korda into an ambitious if highly profligate production programme and the building of a modern new studio complex at Denham. Korda pursued an international production strategy, with films aimed at the world market; he was prepared to take financial and aesthetic risks, though his flair for judging popular taste was as inconsistent as it was instinctive. He also believed strongly in the role of the feature film as a medium of national projection and cultivated relationships with members of the political classes in his efforts to put Britain on the screen. This was never more apparent than in the cycle of British Empire films he produced in the late 1930s: *Sanders of the River* (1935), *The Drum* (1938) and *The Four Feathers* (1939).

British cinema of the 1930s is typically characterized as a cinema of containment and consensus.[2] Film producers worked within the constraints imposed upon them by a variety of external factors that were economic, political and ideological. The production sector of the British film industry was chronically unstable and prone to a cycle of boom and bust: overproduction in the mid-1930s, following Korda's success with *The Private Life of Henry VIII*, precipitated a disastrous slump in 1937 when several studios closed. British films had to compete with American imports for a share of their home market and the general view was that audiences preferred Hollywood fare to the domestic product. British producers therefore followed one of two strategies: making either modestly budgeted genre films intended for the domestic market (mostly low-brow comedies and thrillers) or more prestigious and expensive films produced with an eye on the international market (particularly America).

The content of films was heavily regulated. The principal agency for the control of film content was the British Board of Film Censors (BBFC). This nominally independent body had been set up by the film trade itself in 1913 to put its own house in order, but its president was appointed by the Home Office and its membership demonstrated impeccable establishment credentials. Its long-serving secretary Joseph Brooke-Williamson was 'a man of Victorian principle and stern moral rectitude' and its examiners included Miss Nora Shortt, daughter of former Home Secretary (and BBFC President) Sir Edward Shortt, and a retired army colonel, J. C. Hanna, the chief script reader whose comments reveal a Blimpish attitude towards social change.[3] The BBFC saw its role as the preservation of the status quo: it would permit no criticism of institutions such as the monarchy, church, judiciary, police or armed forces, and frowned upon discussion of politics and foreign affairs. Lord Tyrrell of Avon, who became President of the BBFC in 1935, once declared proudly that there was 'not a single film shown today in the public cinemas of this country which dealt with any of the burning questions of the day'.[4] The arrival of talking pictures in the late 1920s had instituted a voluntary process of pre-production censorship whereby producers would submit scripts for vetting and the board would advise on their suitability. This extended to American as well as British films: Britain was by some measure Hollywood's most important overseas market and American producers wanted to ensure their films would be acceptable to the censors.

The BBFC was particularly active when it came to films about the British Empire. It would allow only those films that endorsed British rule and blocked any scripts that reflected badly on the institutions of colonial government, or that were deemed likely to inflame native opinion or offend foreign governments. For example, it blocked a film of Hall Caine's novel *The White Prophet*, about an Islamic uprising in the Sudan, on the grounds that it demonstrated 'a tendency to bring the British army into contempt and ridicule'. It raised a similar objection to Lewis Robinson's novel *The General Goes Too Far*, featuring murder and adultery in a British garrison in West Africa – 'A thoroughly objectionable story showing officers of the British Army in a most offensive and objectionable light' – though the film was made, with the objectionable elements removed, as *The High Command* (1936). The same thing happened to *East Meets West* (1936). The BBFC disliked the first screenplay, entitled *The Scarlet Sultan*, 'because it is far too involved with political intrigue and the different incidents between white men and black men are impossible'.[5] When the offensive elements were removed,

however, the film was allowed. Colonel Hanna, whose background qualified him as something of an expert in imperial matters, was scathing about
the factual inaccuracies of Hollywood's British Empire films. He thought
the dialogue of *Lives of a Bengal Lancer* 'is American and very un-English
throughout', while *Storm over India* was 'written by an American with no
knowledge of geography and a complete ignorance of the British army'. The
latter film remained unmade. It was not just Hollywood scribes, however,
who were ignorant of imperial affairs. In 1934 United Artists submitted
a synopsis for *Gunga Din* adapted by British writer R. J. Minney. Hanna
declared: 'There is no justification for connecting this story with Kipling's
poem. It is obviously written by a man who knows nothing about the service or about India.'[6] United Artists did not proceed with the film.

Films about India and Ireland caused the BBFC most concern. Two scripts
set during the Indian Mutiny – *Fifty Seven* and *The Relief of Lucknow* – were
refused in 1936 and 1938 respectively. Both were referred by the BBFC to the
India Office for advice – examples of the collusion between the censors and
Whitehall. The case of *The Relief of Lucknow* was raised during the course
of a parliamentary debate on film censorship in 1938. Home Secretary Sir
Samuel Hoare said that 'it was the kind of film that would create the worst
kind of feelings in India between the Indians and ourselves' and that 'to
produce a film depicting scenes of the Indian Mutiny would be undesirable
at this time when we are just embarking upon a new chapter in the consti-
tutional development of India'.[7] This was a reference to the Government of
India Act (1935) which had introduced a limited degree of autonomy for the
Indian provinces. The board was equally sensitive to films about Ireland.
It rejected a scenario for *The Man with a Gun*, set during the civil war in the
early 1920s, because it was 'too recent history to be a suitable subject for a
film ... No matter how the subject is treated, one side or the other will be
angered and much harm might result'. *Irish Story* was also rejected because
it would be 'quite unpopular with the Free State Government'.[8] John Ford's
The Informer (1935) did eventually make it past the censor, though only after
significant cuts.

Yet, despite the political constraints on the making of films about the
British Empire, producers persisted in doing so, especially during the second
half of the decade. As well as Korda's empire trilogy, for example, there were
three films from the Gaumont British Picture Corporation: *Rhodes of Africa*
(1936), *The Great Barrier* (1937) and *King Solomon's Mines* (1937). How can
we account for these films? One reason, certainly, was economic. Imperial
adventures tended to be successful at the box office. Paramount's *Lives of
a Bengal Lancer* was the most popular film released in Britain in 1935; two
other empire films, *Sanders of the River* and *Clive of India*, were sixth and

ninth. *The Charge of the Light Brigade* was fifth in 1937.[9] Many of the empire films were based on stories by popular writers such as Sir Henry Rider Haggard (*King Solomon's Mines*), Edgar Wallace (*Sanders of the River*) and A. E. W. Mason (*The Drum, The Four Feathers*). Audiences would therefore be familiar with the stories, which had already proved their popularity in other media. *Daily Express* journalist Paul Holt recognized the popular appeal of imperial subjects in 1938: 'Mr Korda plans to make a lot of films about the Empire in the future ... He knows that films about the Empire make money. He knows that films of his like *Sanders of the River* and *Elephant Boy* and *The Drum* have been far more successful at the box office of the country than any equal amount of sophisticated sex nonsense. Patriotism goes with profit.'[10] This requires some qualification. It is not strictly true that empire films were more successful than other genres, though individual films were amongst the most popular. But box office receipts did not necessarily trans-late into profits: production costs also need to be taken into account. *Sanders of the River* and *Elephant Boy*, for example, each cost around £150,000; but while the former made a small profit the latter returned only two-thirds of its production cost. The British market alone was insufficient for the more expensive films to recover their costs.

The economic uncertainty of film production would suggest, therefore, that there were other motives for making relatively costly empire films. Korda's biographer Karol Kulik describes him as 'a confirmed Anglophile who saw the Empire builders as the embodiments of all the most noble traits in the English character and spirit'.[11] Producers such as Korda, Michael Balcon, head of production at Gaumont British, and Herbert Wilcox, who made two biopics of Queen Victoria, *Victoria the Great* (1937) and *Sixty Glorious Years* (1938), were patriots who believed in the value of film as a medium of national projection. This view was shared by film critics. As Winifred Holmes wrote in the journal *Sight and Sound* in 1936: 'It is essential for continued unity and goodwill within the Empire that more and better British films should be distributed everywhere, and that these films should add to England's prestige and show more of her ideals and epic qualities than before.'[12]

The British government, for its part, was also alert to the role of cinema as a means of promoting the national image. In 1927 it had introduced a 'quota' to protect British films from Hollywood competition: the value of a British cinema that reflected British life and values featured prominently in the parliamentary debate over the Cinematograph Films Bill. Sir Philip Cunliffe-Lister, the President of the Board of Trade, declared that 'the cin-ema is today the most universal means through which national ideas and national atmosphere can be spread ... Today films are shown to millions of people throughout the Empire and must unconsciously influence the ideas and outlook of British people of all races'.[13] A similar point was made by Sir Stephen Tallents in his book *The Projection of England* (1932), where he argued that 'for the sake of our export trade; in the interests of our tourist traffic; above all, perhaps, in the discharge of our great responsibilities to the other countries of the Commonwealth of British peoples, we must master the art of national projection and must set ourselves to throw a fitting presentation of England upon the world's screen'.[14] Tallents was secretary of the Empire Marketing Board (1927–33) and had been instrumental in setting up the EMB Film Unit, which upon the demise of its parent body transferred to the GPO. The sponsorship of documentary film, however, was as far as the government was prepared to go in promoting the projection of Britain, preferring to leave the film industry to its own devices.

That film producers could be relied upon to promote a positive image of Britain was due not only to the formal regulation of content by the BBFC but also to the various informal relationships between the 'leaders' of the film industry and members of the political classes. Sir Robert Vansittart, the Permanent Under-Secretary of State at the Foreign Office between 1930 and 1938, was interested in the film industry and friendly with Korda, Wilcox and Basil Dean of Associated Talking Pictures. Vansittart advocated setting up a national film council and, when it failed to materialize, set to work as a propagandist in his own right. Vansittart opposed the National Government's policy of appeasement towards Germany and Italy: he is known to have contributed to the scripts of *Sixty Glorious Years* and *The Four Feathers* which both include strong anti-appeasement speeches. Korda also cultivated the friendship of Winston Churchill, then a backbencher out of favour with the Conservative Party, and even put him on the payroll to script several films that, in the event, were never made. The most ambitious of these was a film to mark the Silver Jubilee of King George V in 1935 for which Churchill prepared a detailed scenario. It displayed a characteristically Churchillian view of history that emphasized links between Britain and the empire. It ends with the direction: 'Role and uplift of drums into Rule Britannia ... breaking into God Save the King.'[15]

There is a sense, indeed, in which Korda's empire films reflect official attitudes. That *Sanders of the River* received official sanction is suggested by a credit acknowledging 'the valuable assistance extended to them in Africa by His Excellency Sir B. Bourdillon KCMG, KBE, and all Government Officials during the making of this picture'. Sir Bernard Bourdillon was Governor of Uganda, where location work for the film was undertaken. There are no equivalent credits on either *The Drum* or *The Four Feathers*, though the location shooting of the latter in the Sudan would have necessitated the cooperation of the Colonial Office. In 1936, for example, when Korda had planned to make a film of T. E. Lawrence's *Revolt in the Desert*, he had approached the Colonial Office for assistance as he wanted to shoot on location in Palestine and Transjordan.[16]

Korda's empire trilogy – all three films were directed by his brother Zoltan – exemplify most of the narrative and geographical possibilities within the British Empire film. Although invariably grouped together, there are in fact significant stylistic differences between the films. *Sanders of the River*, adapted from the popular stories of Edgar Wallace, was, unlike the other two, shot in black and white and was relatively sober in its visual style. Its aim was the endorsement of British colonial administration in West Africa. The prologue declares: 'Sailors, soldiers and merchant adventurers were the pioneers who laid the foundations of the British Empire. Today their work is carried on by the civil servants – the Keepers of the King's Peace.' *Sanders of the River* promotes consensus between the British and their African subjects through the friendship between the strong-but-fair commissioner Sanders (Leslie Banks) and loyal native chieftain Bosambo (Paul Robeson).[17] The threat to this status quo comes from gun-runners and from the treacherous renegade King Mofalaba who attempts to usurp Bosambo. Sanders is characterized as a progressive colonial governor representing the 'white man's burden' who has improved the lot of the natives, for example in ending slavery and the gin trade. The relationship between Sanders and Bosambo is akin to that between a father and a child – a view that accurately reflects prevailing British attitudes towards the subject races of the empire, particularly in Africa, at this time.

The Drum, while also concerned to support British governance, marked a departure from the somewhat pious moralizing of *Sanders* in favour of a tale of the 'Great Game' of empire played out on the Northwest Frontier. Based on a short novel by A. E. W. Mason, it was a starring vehicle for Sabu, the stable-hand discovered by Robert Flaherty in Mysore during the filming of *Elephant Boy* (1937). There is a parallel between *The Drum* and Kipling's *Kim* in the tale of a boy-prince who becomes involved in political intrigue and helps the British, represented by Captain Carruthers (Roger Livesey), defeat the treacherous Ghul Khan (Raymond Massey). The use of Technicolor and location shooting (in North Wales) opened up the visual possibilities of the genre. *The Drum* provoked mixed reactions. *The New York Times* was not blind to the ideological contradictions of a film that it described as 'a gorgeously High Anglican sermon for peace in the inconsistent but swirlingly dramatic terms of Imperialist warfare'.[18] However, the British critics E. W. and M. M. Robson were scornful of a film they thought 'might have been lifted intact out of the *Boy's Own Weekly* of 1888, down to

the last gallant officer, the last soldier caught in an ambush, the last fluttering flag. Psychology and ethical standards also fit in with the same date'.[19]

It was *The Four Feathers*, however, that represented Korda's supreme
achievement in the cinema of empire. To an extent it was a companion piece
to *The Drum* in so far as it was also based on a novel by A. E. W. Mason
and was again shot in sumptuous three-strip Technicolor. Korda's film
was in fact the fourth version of the story, which had been filmed twice
as a silent – in America in 1915 by J. Earle Dawley and in Britain in 1921
by the Stoll Film Company – and again in Hollywood in 1929 by Merian
C. Cooper and Ernest B. Schoedsack. The 1929 version was released with
synchronized music but no dialogue and featured extensive locations in the
Sudan and Tanganyika. It is Korda's film, however, that is the definitive version. It was an ambitious and spectacular film, demonstrating that British
cinema was capable of matching the technical standards and production
values of Hollywood at its best. This point was recognized by *The New York
Times*, which described it as 'an imperialist symphony ... a fine, stirring,
gorgeously Technicolored job ... Mr Korda has managed to plant the British
flag higher than all the rest'.[20]

The production of *The Four Feathers* reveals the cultural and ideological
processes at work in making the cinema of empire. The screenplay, by playwright R. C. Sherriff, made a number of significant alterations from the
source. Some of these were for reasons of dramatic coherence: the main
protagonist Harry Faversham is afforded greater prominence in the film
and the number of supporting characters is reduced. More significantly,
however, the œdipal dimension of Mason's story is removed. In the novel
Harry's decision to resign his army commission on the eve of Kitchener's
campaign to recapture the Sudan in 1898 is presented as much as a rejection
of the authority of his father than as an expression of his revulsion for militarism. In the film, however, it is revealed that Harry's father is dead before
he resigns his commission and the paternalistic authority figure is transferred to the character of General Burroughs, the Blimpish father of Harry's
fiancée Ethne. (Burroughs was a part seemingly written for C. Aubrey
Smith, who excelled at playing old-school army types.) As in the novel
Harry is presented with four white feathers – the symbol of cowardice – by
three fellow officers and his fiancée. He sets out to redeem himself by trav-
elling in disguise to the Sudan, where he saves the lives of his three comrades. Sherriff adds the Battle of Omdurman and the relief of Khartoum to
the end of the film to provide a suitably spectacular climax.

There are some significant differences between the shooting script
and the finished film.[21] The script includes more of a political context
for the Sudan campaign. It opens with the Mahdi's uprising as 'terror

1. From Resignation ... Harry Faversham (John Clements) incurs the wrath
of General Burroughs (C. Aubrey Smith) and Ethne (June Duprez) in
The Four Feathers (1939).

spreads throughout the Sudan'. This is intercut with a speech to the
House of Commons by Prime Minister William Gladstone which
expresses a distinctly anti-imperialist position: 'It is not the policy of Her
Majesty's Government to extend our Empire. It is already far too big ...
England would be far happier and far stronger if she could rid herself of
half her Colonies. We propose to take no steps in Egypt that might lead
us into further unwieldy and unprofitable possessions.' This is immediately followed by a sequence of the death of Gordon at Khartoum.
It seems reasonable to speculate that this was one of the contributions
made by Vansittart given its similarity to a scene in *Sixty Glorious Years*
where Gladstone's refusal to relieve Gordon functions as an allegory of
appeasement: the parallels being drawn are Gladstone/Chamberlain and
Khartoum/Munich.[22] The scene is absent from the finished film, however, which begins with the death of Gordon. The deletion of the scene
is indicative of the ideology of a film that does not question the imperial project: it is taken for granted that the campaign to avenge Gordon's
'murder' is morally justified.

The pro-imperialist ideology of the film was consistent with Korda's views about the British Empire. As producer he was the dominant figure and imposed his own views onto his brother Zoltan, who was more sympathetic to the point of view of the colonized subjects. Michael Korda (son of the third Korda brother Vincent) averred that previous films 'had been struggles between Zoli's own desire to show the reality of the Africans' lives and aspirations in the bondage of colonialism and Alex's determination to make films that would present the Empire to the British audience in a positive and patriotic light'. *Sanders of the River* and *The Drum* 'had been compromises between Alex's view and Zoli's'.[23] There is no such compromise in *The Four Feathers*, however, which shows events entirely from the British perspective and represents the Dervishes as tyrants and savages. In Sudanese history, in contrast, the Mahdi is seen as a national hero and liberator of the Sudanese people.

The production also revealed a tension, evident throughout Korda's films, between a desire for visual authenticity on the one hand and the need for spectacle on the other. Korda was one of the first British producers to employ historical and technical advisers, though he frequently disregarded their advice. Like *The Private Life of Henry VIII*, *The Four Feathers* based some of its compositions on existing visual records: the brief shot of Gordon's death at the beginning of the film, for example, is modelled on the contemporary painting by G. W. Joy. An appendix to the shooting script contains a detailed props list that insists on authenticity down to the smallest detail including 'telegram (War Office pattern 1894)' and 'service revolver (1897)'. However, visual spectacle took precedence over a strict adherence to military authenticity. Korda was prepared to abandon carefully (and expensively) planned sequences if he felt they did not work visually. Famously he insisted that the dress uniforms worn by the officers at a regimental ball should be changed from navy blue to red. When told by his military advisers that blue was correct, Korda simply replied: 'This is Technicolor!'[24]

The Four Feathers represents the British Empire as a site of spectacle and adventure: the desert landscapes and lavishly staged action sequences are easily the equal of any Hollywood film of the time. The imperial adventure film, like the Western, demands an expansive landscape: *The Four Feathers* is particularly effective in its representation of space as the protagonists are positioned precariously in the vast and inhospitable spaces of the desert. The film features some of the best location cinematography (by Osmond Borradaile and Jack Cardiff) in British cinema until *Lawrence of Arabia* in 1962. Unlike many adventure epics, however, the visual spectacle does not overwhelm the narrative but is fully integrated with it. As C. A. Lejeune, the film critic of the *Observer*, put it: '*The Four Feathers* keeps the screen packed with movement, spectacle, and excitement. Beyond these obvious box-office virtues, however, it has another quality. It tells a thumping good personal story. I suppose you might describe its thesis as the conquest of fear.'[25]

The Four Feathers is structured on a classical model of the disruption and restoration of order in which 'the rebellious army of cruel Dervishes' are the forces of chaos and anarchy and the British army is the instrument of stability and control. The theme of the army's role as peace-keeper is a recurring theme of empire cinema in Britain and Hollywood: *Lives of a Bengal Lancer*, *The Charge of the Light Brigade*, *The Drum* and *Gunga Din* all advance the same idea. The British presence, it is suggested, protects the native peoples from oppression: the Dervishes have 'enslaved and killed many thousands of defenceless natives in the Sudan'. Otherwise the film offers a didactic representation of 'good' and 'bad' natives in which moral values are mapped onto imperial politics. Thus the Khalifa is unequivocally evil and motivated by an irrational hatred of the British, whereas the pro-British chieftain Karaga Pasha, imprisoned for 13 years, helps Faversham and his comrades at Khartoum. This didactic characterization was a consistent feature of imperial fictions, such as Bosambo and Mofalaba in *Sanders of the River* or Umbopa and Twala in *King Solomon's Mines*.

The Four Feathers also explores the codes of honour and chivalry that form such an essential part of the imperial ideal. Harry (John Clements) is the son of a military family with a long tradition of service. 'First time in a hundred years there hasn't been a Faversham in the army and look at the mess they make!' declares Harry's father when he hears the news of the fall of Khartoum. Harry rationalizes his decision to resign his commission by citing what he sees as his social duty to manage the family's estate and to protect the interests of its tenants. He tells Ethne (June Duprez): 'I believe in our happiness. I believe in the work to be done here to save an estate that's near to ruin – to save all those people who've been neglected by my family because they preferred glory in India, glory in China, glory in Africa.'[26] Ethne, however, believes in a code of duty they must abide by: 'Some people are born free, they can do as they like without concern for consequences. But you are not born free, Harry, and nor was I. We were born into a tradition – a code which we must obey even if we do not believe. And we must obey, Harry, because the pride and the happiness of everyone surrounding us depends upon our obedience.' Ethne's belief in and commitment to this sense of duty shames Harry, who faces up to the real reason for his resignation – his fear that he is a coward at heart who will let his comrades down in the face of danger. *The Four Feathers* therefore questions but ultimately affirms an ethic of duty: it is essentially a narrative of heroic redemption.

It is also a narrative of self-sacrifice and loss. This is seen through the characterization of Harry's comrade Captain John Durrance (Ralph Richardson). Durrance is in love with Ethne but realizes that she does not love him. Durrance is blinded by sunstroke in the desert, but rescued by Harry in disguise as a mute Svengali native. Returning to England, Durrance becomes engaged to Ethne, but when he learns that it was Harry who saved his life, he once again steps aside to allow their union. Durrance is a genuine tragic hero: he loses the woman he loves twice and his eyesight but maintains a stoical outlook.

The Four Feathers was a great popular success. It was admired both for its technical qualities and for its Britishness. *Film Weekly* thought it 'a spectacular, thrilling and sometimes moving tribute to the British Army and the British spirit' and felt that 'it equals anything that Hollywood has given us, and, in the beauty of its colour photography, surpasses Hollywood's best'.[27] *Kinematograph Weekly* called it a 'spectacular period adventure melodrama, brilliantly adapted from A. E. W. Mason's famous novel ... Outstanding general booking, and British at that'.[28] *Catholic Film News* declared that it was

2. ... To Redemption: A disguised Faversham rescues Durrance (Ralph Richardson), blinded by Sunstroke, in *The Four Feathers* (1939).

'our finest and most successful British film' and felt that it 'succeeded in striking the right national note of the moment'.[29] A more nuanced assessment was offered in *Sight and Sound*:

> A thoroughly British film with a fine British cast and a glorious British war waged and won against the rotter the Khalifa and his fuzzy-wuzzies in the Technicolor Egyptian Sudan. It has all been done before, but never with such a good script and such a wealth of exciting battle scenes. The war, too, comes in for some hard knocks and although there are many scenes of bloodshed and cruelty calculated to rouse the fiercest passions of patriotism, the hero's pacifism puts the other side of the picture very fairly.[30]

Harry's pacifism is suggested in a scene where he remarks upon 'the futility of this idiotic Egyptian adventure – the madness of it all'. This can probably be attributed to Sherriff, who had written the celebrated anti-war play *Journey's End*, filmed as an early talking picture by James Whale in Hollywood in 1930.[31]

The Four Feathers marked the apotheosis of the empire cinema of the 1930s. It was a triumphalist epic celebrating the heyday of popular imperialism and the building of the British Empire. Yet it would also be the last film of its particular kind. The outbreak of the Second World War in September 1939 brought the cycle of empire films to an abrupt halt. There were a number of reasons for this. Wartime conditions forced British producers to implement a policy of strict economy and retrenchment: personnel were called up for national service, some studios were closed and the profligate expenditure that had characterized the 1930s was curtailed. Korda moved his base to Hollywood, where he made the sublime Arabian Nights fantasy *The Thief of Bagdad* (1940), the historical propaganda epic *Lady Hamilton* (1941) and an adaptation of Kipling's *The Jungle Book* (1942) as another starring vehicle for Sabu. In 1942 he was knighted for his contribution to British cinema.

Another reason for the eclipse of empire cinema was that it became ideologically problematic at a time when Britain was fighting against German expansionism in Europe and Japanese imperialism in the Far East. Its two major allies from 1941, the Soviet Union and the United States, were both suspicious of Britain's imperial ambitions. British propaganda during the war preferred to focus on the idea of the democratic Commonwealth – exemplified in films such as *49th Parallel* (1941) – and shied away from celebrating territorial conquest by British arms. The changing political context was demonstrated by the re-issue of *The Four Feathers* in 1943. While it received positive reviews in the trade press, a change of attitude toward its subject matter was apparent in the response of *The Times*: 'This film, with its glib Imperialism and its juvenile attitude to war, although it was made only a few years ago, seems to belong to another age.'[32] It was also condemned by the Robsons, who complained to the Foreign Office about the decision to re-issue the film: 'I am exceedingly sorry to see that Korda is again about to make a film for MOI [Ministry of Information] and that MGM are going to reissue "Four Feathers". This again portrays the "sadistic Englishman" idea so prevalent on the Continent and it calls our protagonists at Omdurman the fuzzy warriors (to say the least) ... it is as inept and blundering about Egypt as his film about India'.[33]

However, *The Four Feathers* has remained a favourite story for filmmakers. To date there have been no fewer than three further versions, each demonstrating in their different ways the changing ideological climate. The first, entitled *Storm Over the Nile* (1955), was based on the same screenplay as Korda's film and included its battle scenes topped and cropped into CinemaScope. Zoltan Korda produced for London Films and was credited as co-director with Terence Young. *Storm Over the Nile* starred Anthony Steel as Faversham and Laurence Harvey as Durrance. It was part of a revival of empire cinema in the 1950s, but its narrative of imperial expansion was now out of step with the times. Penelope Huston in the *Monthly Film Bulletin* felt that 'the material appears not so much dated as fossilised within its period: the flag-waving, the stiff upper-lip dialogue, the whole background of confident Edwardian imperialism belong irrevocably to the past'.[34]

The title of the remake would prove ironic: within a year Britain faced another storm over the Nile when the Egyptian government of Colonel Nasser nationalized the Suez Canal and Britain's attempt to enforce its strategic interests in the Near East through military power led to a humiliating withdrawal. The production of *Storm Over the Nile* pre-dated the Suez Crisis (1956), but it coincided with renewed political tension in the region as the rise of Arab nationalism brought increasingly vociferous demands for British withdrawal. Independence for the Sudan – which since 1898 had been governed as an Anglo–Egyptian joint protectorate – had been agreed in 1954. *Storm Over the Nile* refers to the impending British withdrawal from the region when Dr Sutton remarks: 'You tell me, Harry, that you left the army because we have no right to be in the Sudan – no right to impose what we call decency and order on the people there. Perhaps that's so. But I tell you this. If we have no right to be there, one day, sooner or later, we'll leave it – and we'll leave it better than we found it.' The theme of British administration bringing improvement is also expressed in an opening voice-over, which asserts the social and material benefits of imperialism by highlighting the building of railways, roads and schools ('Today the Sudan is a land of peace – tranquil, thriving').[35] In truth, however, this is an extremely rose-tinted description of a land that has been continually beset by political turmoil, civil war and chronic famine.

The next remake of *The Four Feathers*, reverting to its original title, came in 1978. Produced by Norman Rosemont and directed by Don Sharp, for American television, it had a cinema release in Britain. This version is chiefly notable for restoring the œdipal dimension of the novel: Harry's father disowns him when he burns a telegram summoning him to active service, and his exploits in the Sudan are presented as a way of regaining his father's respect. Another change, entirely unwelcome, is that in this version Durrance learns it was Harry who rescued him and caddishly keeps it to himself rather than telling Ethne. It is a workmanlike production, anticipating the vogue for 'heritage' dramas in the 1980s with its lovingly recreated period atmosphere and its mostly British cast including Robert Powell (Durrance), Jane Seymour (Ethne), Simon Ward (William) and Harry Andrews (General Faversham). Unfortunately it is fatally weakened by the casting of Beau Bridges as Harry. Clearly intended to appeal to American audiences, Bridges is insufferably bland and his attempt to psychoanalyse Harry's cowardice is pitiful to say the least.

Critical response was lukewarm, the film being seen as a dated artefact that failed to imbue the familiar story with any modern relevance. Gordon Gow in *Films and Filming* saw a tension in the film around 'an ambiguous moral element that wavers between reactionary zeal and an effort to keep abreast of latterday trends'.[36] And John Pym in the *Monthly Film Bulletin* called it 'a museum piece, brought up from the vaults, dusted down and carefully mounted: an object which makes one wonder what use anyone could ever have had for it'.[37]

The most recent version of *The Four Feathers* in 2002 was also the most revisionist. A co-production between Paramount Pictures and Miramax International, it was the first Hollywood studio picture by the Indian director Shekhar Kapur. Kapur had come to attention with *Bandit Queen* (1994), a controversial biopic of the female outlaw Phoolan Devi, which he had followed with *Elizabeth* (1998), a visually sumptuous costume drama which provoked outrage amongst some British historians for suggesting that the 'Virgin Queen' was nothing of the sort. Kapur's film was based on a screenplay by Michael Schiffer (*Crimson Tide*) and Hossein Amini (*The Wings of the Dove*) and was shot in Morocco and England. The fact that its production followed in the wake of the terrorist attacks on New York and Washington DC on 11 September 2001 inevitably led to the film being seen as a commentary on the 'War on Terror'. What were the Dervishes if not a nineteenth-century manifestation of the Islamic extremism now represented by Al-Qaeda? This reading was overlaid onto the film by its production discourse. Thus, according to cinematographer Robert Richardson: 'It's about a Western culture that tackles a jihad, not unlike what is happening in current events today.'[38]

Kapur's *The Four Feathers* is a visually spectacular but ideologically confused film. It attempts to nuance the suppression of an uprising by 'an army of Mohammedan fanatics' with some anti-imperialist sentiments. The ideology of racial and cultural superiority asserted by an army chaplain ('God has endowed the British race with a worldwide empire that they may execute His sovereign purpose in the world') is contrasted with Harry's scepticism about the imperialist project ('I sometimes wonder what a god-forsaken desert in the middle of nowhere has to do with Her Majesty the Queen'). The film's ideological revisionism is also evident in its critique of militarism and the class system that marks a radical departure from earlier versions. The tone is set by an opening caption: 'By 1884 over a quarter of the earth's surface had been conquered by the British Army. There was no greater honour than to fight for Queen and Country. Those that refused the call to arms brought shame and humiliation on their friends and families. The symbol of their disgrace was the white feather of cowardice.' Harry's resignation from the army is here presented as a stubborn assertion of his individualism rather than an act of cowardice.

The film therefore seeks to distance itself from the idea of a military caste born to serve Queen and Country. It focuses instead on the theme of comradeship between ranks and across classes. This is made explicit in a closing address by Durrance at a memorial service: 'In the heat of battle it ceases to be an idea or a flag for which we fight. We fight for the man on our left. We fight for the man on our right. And when the armies have scattered and the empires fallen away, all that remains is the memory of those precious moments we spent side by side.' This focus on the comradeship of battle is very much a feature of modern American treatments of war such as *Saving Private Ryan* (1998) and the mini-series *Band of Brothers* (2002). To this extent, it might be argued, Kapur's film detaches the narrative from its original British context and refashions it for a classless American audience.

Kapur demonstrates the visual flair that he had previously displayed in *Elizabeth*: the film is characterized by its fluid camera movement and by the director's trademark overhead shots. The battle sequences are expertly staged and do not seem to have been embellished by CGI. Where the film is let down, however, is in its casting and performances. Heath Ledger (Harry), Kate Hudson (Ethne) and Wes Bentley (Durrance) are all contemporary actors who fail to convince either as Victorians or as English. Consequently this version of *The Four Feathers* becomes an example of presentism in which the characters act and behave as if they are in a contemporary drama rather than a period piece. This may reflect the need to make the story acceptable for modern audiences, though, if so, it rather begs the question of why the film-makers turned to the property in the first place.

If Kapur's *The Four Feathers* failed to be the blockbuster attraction that its producers hoped – its release was delayed by almost a year and was overshadowed at the box office by the nautical epics *Master and Commander: The Far Side of the World* and *Pirates of the Caribbean: The Curse of the Black Pearl* – this was due at least in part to the ideological confusion within the film itself. One reviewer, for example, remarked that the film's attempts at revisionism 'remain half hearted ... subsumed by Kapur's spirited, and old-fashioned, Boy's Own treatment of the novel'.[39] Ultimately, the source material itself is resistant to outright revisionism: perhaps it is simply not possible to refashion a story glorifying the British Empire and its values into an outright critique of imperialism. And this is why it is Korda's 1939 film, and not Kapur's or any other version, which remains the definitive version of this archetypal tale of heroic imperialist adventure.

Notes

1   On Korda see Charles Drazin, *Korda: Britain's Only Movie Mogul* (London: Sidgwick & Jackson, 2002); Michael Korda, *Charmed Lives: A Family Romance* (London: Allen Lane, 1980); and Karol Kulik, *Alexander Korda: The Man Who Could Work Miracles* (London: W. H. Allen, 1975). On *The Private Life of Henry VIII* see James Chapman, *Past and Present: National Identity and the British Historical Film* (London: I.B.Tauris, 2005), pp.11–44; and Sue Harper, *Picturing the Past: The Rise and Fall of the British Historical Film* (London: British Film Institute, 1994), pp.20–3. On the empire films see Jeffrey Richards, 'Korda's Empire: Politics and Film in *Sanders of the River, The Drum* and *The Four Feathers*', *Australian Journal of Screen Theory*, 5: 6 (1978), pp.122–37; and Richards, ' "Patriotism with Profit": British Imperial Cinema in the 1930s', in James Curran and Vincent Porter (eds), *British Cinema History* (London: Weidenfeld and Nicolson, 1983), pp.245–71.

2   See Tony Aldgate, 'Comedy, Class and Containment: The British Domestic Cinema of the 1930s', in Curran and Porter, *British Cinema History*, pp.257–71; Aldgate, 'Ideological Consensus in British Feature Films, 1935–1947', in K. R. M. Short (ed.), *Feature Films as History* (London: Croom Helm, 1981), pp.94–112; Rachael Low, *The History of the British Film 1929–1939: Film Making in 1930s Britain* (London: George Allen & Unwin, 1985); and Jeffrey Richards, *The Age of the Dream Palace: Cinema and Society in Britain 1930–1939* (London: Routledge & Kegan Paul, 1984).

3   Jeffrey Richards, 'British Film Censorship', in Robert Murphy (ed.), *The British Cinema Book* (London: British Film Institute, 1997), p.168. See also Richards, 'The British Board of Film Censors and Content Control in the 1930s (1): Images of Britain', *Historical Journal of Film, Radio and Television*, 1: 2 (1981), pp.97–116; 'The British Board of Film

Censors and Content Control in the 1930s (2): Foreign Affairs', *Historical Journal of Film, Radio and Television*, 2: 1 (1982), pp.39–48; and James C. Robertson, *The British Board of Film Censors: Film Censorship in Britain, 1896–1950* (London: Croom Helm, 1985).

4　Quoted in Nicholas Pronay, 'The First Reality: Film Censorship in Liberal England', in Short, *Feature Films as History*, p.124.

5　BBFC Scenario Reports: 1933 no.90; 1936 no.69; 1936 no.30. These are held by the Special Collections Unit of the British Film Institute, London (hereafter BFI).

6　BBFC Scenario Reports: 1934 no.263; 1939 no.41; 1934 no.35.

7　*Parliamentary Debates: House of Commons*, 5th series, vol.342, col.1306–7.

8　BBFC Scenario Reports: 1933 no.128; 1939 no.28.

9　John Sedgwick, *Popular Film-Going in 1930s Britain: A Choice of Pleasures* (Exeter: University of Exeter Press, 2000), pp.269–76.

10　Quoted in Richards, *The Age of the Dream Palace*, p.136.

11　Kulik, *Alexander Korda*, p.135.

12　Winifred Holmes, 'British Films and the Empire', *Sight and Sound*, 5: 9 (Autumn 1936), p.74.

13　*Parliamentary Debates: House of Commons*, 5th series, vol.23, col.2039.

14　S. G. Tallents, *The Projection of England* (London, 1932), p.40.

15　The full scenario can be found in Martin Gilbert (ed.), *Winston S. Churchill, Volume V: Companion – Part 2* (London: William Heinemann, 1985), pp.989–1031.

16　Jeffrey Richards and Jeffrey Hulbert, 'Censorship in Action: The Case of *Lawrence of Arabia*', *Journal of Contemporary History*, 19: 1 (1984), pp.153–70.

17　Robeson appeared in several British films, including *King Solomon's Mines* as the 'noble savage' Umbopa. He was later critical of these films for their representation of Africans as simpletons. See Jeffrey Richards, 'Paul Robeson: The Black Man as Screen Hero', in Charles Barr (ed.), *All Our Yesterdays: 90 Years of British Cinema* (London: British Film Institute, 1986), pp.334–40.

18　*The New York Times*, 30 September 1938, p.24

19　E. W. and M. M. Robson, *The Film Answers Back: An Historical Appreciation of the Cinema* (London: The Bodley Head, 1939), p.174. The Robsons are one of the curiosities of British film culture, a husband and wife team whose views on cinema were often quite eccentric. They are best known for their vitriolic attacks on the films of Michael Powell and Emeric Pressburger in *The Shame and Disgrace of Colonel Blimp* (London: The Sidneyan Society, 1944) and *The World Is My Cinema* (London: The Sidneyan Society, 1947).

20　*The New York Times*, 4 August 1939, p.11.

21　BFI Unpublished Script Collection S6288: *The Four Feathers*. Final Shooting Script by R. C. Sherriff, 14 July 1938.

22　Chapman, *Past and Present*, pp.83–6.

23　Korda, *Charmed Lives*, p.306.

24　Kulik, *Alexander Korda*, p.214.

25　*Observer*, 23 April 1939.

26　This theme is more fully explored in the script in lines that were cut from the film. Upon resigning his commission Harry tells his commanding officer: 'My duty towards my country is here and not in Egypt. When my father died I took over an estate on the verge of ruin because every man of my family had neglected it to fight in India and Africa – in every country but his own. If I do my job here I may save my home with a dozen farms and a hundred good men who are starving through my family's neglect, if I go to Egypt I shall be away for years and the ruin will be complete.' John Clements would also play a tenant farmer struggling to maintain his crumbling estate in *This England* (British National, dir. David Macdonald, 1941).

27 *Film Weekly*, 29 April 1939, p.31.

28 *Kinematograph Weekly*, 20 April 1939, p.20.

29 *Catholic Film News*, 1: 8 (June 1939), pp.8–9.

30 Alan Page, 'Death Always Wins', *Sight and Sound*, 8: 30 (Summer 1939), p.76.

31 See Andrew Kelly, *Cinema and the Great War* (London: Routledge, 1997), pp.65–75.

32 *The Times*, 31 August 1942, p.8.

33 National Archives, Kew, London, FO 371/36921: Mary M. Robson to 'The Ministry for Foreign Affairs', 18 August 1943. In the film the Dervishes are called 'fuzzy wuzzies' in both captions and dialogue. Robson's letter was prompted by the release of Korda's *Lady Hamilton* in Moscow: 'If there is one thing in evidence, it is that the Russians do not trust us and "Lady Hamilton" is the very film to reinforce that distrust among the ruling class.'

34 *Monthly Film Bulletin*, 22: 268 (December 1955), p.177.

35 BFI Unpublished Script Collection S6287 *None But the Brave*, no date (The original title has been scored out and 'The 4 White Feathers' and 'The Four Feathers' added by hand.)

36 *Films and Filming*, 24: 6 (March 1978), p.32.

37 *Monthly Film Bulletin*, 45: 530 (March 1978), p.46.

38 Quoted in 'Desert Storm', *American Cinematographer*, 83: 10 (October 2002), p.63.

39 *Sight and Sound*, New Series 13: 9 (September 2003), p.50.

AMERICA'S KIPLING
Gunga Din (1939)

The posters for *Gunga Din* promised much: 'Thrills for a thousand movies, plundered for one mighty show.' Audiences agreed. *Gunga Din* became one of the American box office triumphs of 1939, beaten only by *Jesse James. Box Office Digest* estimated its gross earnings well over $3 million in its first year alone and leaving *Mister Smith Goes to Washington* and *The Wizard of Oz* in its wake.[1] With a massive production cost of nearly $2 million RKO had gambled, they seemed to have won.[2] The film was, of course, blatantly racist. It was a valentine to the British Raj, in which three sergeants (played by Cary Grant, Victor McLaglen and Douglas Fairbanks Jr) defeat marauding hoards of 'natives' with the aid of their 'Uncle Tom' water bearer, Gunga Din (Sam Jaffe), whose sole ambition in life is to become a bugler in the British army. Audiences loved it. Its racism notwithstanding, even an astute viewer like Bertolt Brecht confessed, 'My heart was touched ... I felt like applauding and laughed in all the right places.'[3]

Outwardly the film had little to do with the United States. Most of the cast were British-born and its screenplay claimed to be 'from the poem by Rudyard Kipling'. Yet the film was neither British nor particularly faithful either to Kipling's poem or his understanding of empire. *Gunga Din* was solidly American: directed by George Stevens for RKO, with a screenplay by Oxford-educated writer Joel Sayre and Stevens's regular collaborator Fred Guiol,[4] who in their turn were building on a fast-paced wisecracking script by Charles MacArthur and Ben Hecht with additional material by Dudley Nichols and the original director for the project, Howard Hawks. The screenplay also included a few uncredited touches from the first writer asked to adapt the project: William Faulkner – the climax in which Gunga Din and his bugle save the day in the manner of *Song of Roland* and subsequent scene in which the British gather at his grave and solemnly intone the famous line 'You're a better man than I am, Gunga Din'.[5]

That Americans could produce such a film raised few eyebrows at the time. *Gunga Din* stood at the end of a long-standing American interest in Kipling and the British Empire and a highly successful series of big budget Hollywood films with imperial themes. British imperialism clearly struck a lucrative chord with the democratic, historically anti-imperial, American public. However, the gap between what Kipling wrote and America's read-ing of his work – exemplified in *Gunga Din* – is highly significant. It reveals much about the country's psychological needs as it struggled to define its role in the world during the first half of this century. Similarly, the later car-eer of the British Empire film genre offers a commentary on America's own experience of empire.

Kipling in America

From the beginning, Kipling fascinated America. Like Mark Twain, his work was published simultaneously on both sides of the Atlantic. In 1892 Kipling married an American and lived in the United States for the next four years. Accordingly his work touched on North American themes, most obviously in poems such as 'An American: 1894' or 'Great-Heart (Theodore Roosevelt)', his maritime novel *Captains Courageous* and account of his American travels *From Sea to Sea*.[6] Often the American connection has been forgotten. His notorious verse 'The White Man's Burden' of 1899 was written for Americans and subtitled 'The United States and the Philippine Islands'.[7]

Kipling was appreciated at all levels of American society. President Theodore Roosevelt maintained a long correspondence with Kipling, and nicknamed his second son Kermit Roosevelt 'Kim' as a result.[8] The doomed American explorer Leonidas Hubbard quoted great chunks of Kipling to his starving companions during their ill-fated expedition to Labrador and named a range of mountains in his honour.[9] A generation of young American boys with militaristic ambitions found their home in the pages of Kipling. He was a boyhood favourite of both Douglas MacArthur and George S. Patton. Patton even wrote his own, quite dreadful, poems in the style of Kipling.[10] With Kipling's poems regularly appearing in the American newspapers, the Irish–American satirist Finley Peter Dunne pointed to the excesses of the Kipling cult and had his comic creation Mr. Dooley proclaim that 'Roodyard [*sic*] Kipling' wrote 'the finest pothry [*sic*] in the wurruld [*sic*]'.[11] But Kipling had caught the spirit of the age.

Kipling filled a niche in the American imagination at the turn of the century as no indigenous writer could. His novels and poems seemed to offer a lively portrait of military life and Imperial Destiny that did not fit with the old American mistrust of standing armies or the work of the likes of Mark Twain or Stephen Crane, but that played directly to a country charged with the brazen rhetoric of men like Senator Albert Beveridge or Theodore Roosevelt himself. The USA responded to the strategic and economic uncertainties by embracing an empire of its own. The western frontier had ended and Americans now looked to a new frontier in the Pacific and a new manifest destiny to democratize the world. The pattern of imperial culture echoed that of Edwardian Britain. Both had their jingoistic popular press; the American empire marched to the strains of Sousa rather than Elgar and enjoyed the paintings of Remington in the place of the battlescapes of Lady Butler, but Kipling was taken ready-made. He became propaganda off-the-peg.

Yet it would appear that in the midst of their enthusiasm for Kipling, Americans neglected a key element in Kipling's work: the element of warning. The most obvious misreading was of Kipling's poem: 'The White Man's Burden'. This bitter verse carried within it a clear statement of the futility of empire in which 'the best ye breed' could expect only thankless suffering and the 'savage wars of peace'. Nevertheless the poem immediately became part of the American language, surfacing in numerous imperial tracts and parodies.[12] However, the United States soon learned to think of its involvement in the world as something other than a parallel to a European 'White Man's Burden'. Americans justified their empire in terms of anti-imperialism and promoting democracy. They assumed that their higher motives would also be understood by their colonized subjects. The United States had to learn of the 'savage wars of peace' the hard way, in the jungles of the Philippines and Central America.[13]

Kipling's Empire in 1930s Hollywood

The massive trauma of the Great War forced a radical reassessment of American foreign policy. In the aftermath of the war, as anti-war novels and films abounded, the US government turned its back on both alliances and Kiplingesque military forays to right the wrongs of Asia. This was clear from the Hoover administration's approach to the Manchuria Crisis. Hollywood, however, felt differently. Throughout the 1930s the empire prospered in film. The genre had much to offer. First of all the films took place far away and long ago and thus offered a welcome escape from the Depression. Moreover, they offered welcome reassurance at a time of renewed challenges to the old certainties of race, class and gender. The hegemony of the white American male was challenged as never before by the collapse of American industry and agriculture. The post-war years had brought new competitors in the job market – most visibly the wave of African–American migrants from the South – and new challenges closer to home, as women rejected their old position of vote-less subordination. In such a world it was no wonder that a genre of films in which the common white man consistently triumphed should prosper. It is, however, surprising that Hollywood was unable to meet these psychological needs with its traditional fare: the Western.

Western films and novels had flourished in the 1920s; when flushed with the post-war boom, a newly urban generation of Americans seemed eager to celebrate the rural epic of their collective past. Zane Grey outsold all other authors during that decade. Yet during the 1930s the genre went into relative decline, the big budgets drained away and Westerns became the staple of 'B' movies and serials, surviving largely because such films were so cheap to make.[14] It is easy to see why. The agricultural depression sat uneasily alongside narratives of triumph in the West. With refugees streaming to California from the dust bowls of the Prairies, it was hard to sing a hymn to Kansas. By translating the action to the British Empire, Hollywood was able to retain the same themes of horsemen and natives and to use the same locations in the California Sierras.[15] An empire setting also enabled the studios to employ their roster of British stars, recruited with the advent of talking pictures because of their trained voices,[16] and to tap the steady market for army pictures without evoking unpleasant memories of the trenches. Finally, Hollywood needed to make a profit. With the additional cost of 'talkies', the studios found that they could break even only on the US release of a film. Profits required a lively export market. It soon became apparent that Europe had no objection to seeing its imperialism restaged by Americans.[17] Having found a formula that would sell internationally, Hollywood stuck to it.

By the mid-1930s the success of the empire picture was obvious. Henry Hathaway's *Lives of a Bengal Lancer* (1935) unleashed a barrage of imitators. The empire shifted from place to place, from the deserts of Arabia in John Ford's *The Lost Patrol* (1934) and French Sahara in *Beau Geste* (1939),[18] but it was British India more than any other location that captured the American imagination. Americans flocked to see films like *The Black Watch* (1929) or *Four Men and a Prayer* (1938) both directed by John Ford; *Clive of India* (1934), *Storm Over Bengal* (1938) or *The Charge of the Light Brigade* (1936), which claimed to be 'based on the poem by Alfred Lord Tennyson' but played more like a remake of *Bengal Lancer*.[19] The British themselves were able to export the imperial product back to the United States with a string of films culminating in Korda's *The Four Feathers* (1939). Soon the setting of British India was familiar enough to be satirized by Laurel and Hardy in *Bonnie Scotland* (1935) and safe enough to be the basis for a Shirley Temple vehicle: *Wee Willie Winkie* (1937).[20] While only the latter was actually based on a Kipling story, the memory of Kipling's India was never far below the surface in these films.[21] Kipling's death in 1936 leant further topicality and soon plans were afoot to remake *The Light That Failed*, and film *Captains Courageous, Kim* and two episodes from *The Jungle Book*.[22] At the time of his death Kipling himself had been working on treatments of his story 'Thy Servant a Dog' and *Soldiers Three*.[23] In this atmosphere it is hardly surprising that first MGM and then United Artists should embark on an epic film based on Kipling's poem 'Gunga Din'. RKO finished the job.[24]

The Movie

Gunga Din makes an immediate claim to its origins in Kipling. The film begins with a narrator reading the second half of the opening stanza of the poem, perhaps the best known of his *Barrack-Room Ballads* of 1892. In the finale Kipling himself is portrayed writing his poem in response to events that he has witnessed. It is then read at Gunga Din's graveside. The opening of the film also claims historical veracity, with titles reading: 'the portions of this picture dealing with the worship of the goddess Kali are based on historic fact' and acknowledging three British army technical advisers.[25] Such credits are misleading. The notion of a Thug revival in the 1880s is fantasy and Kipling's poem provides little more than the character of Din. The body of the film is a free wheeling adventure very loosely based on the characters of Kipling's cycle of military short stories, the 'Soldiers Three': Privates Mulvaney, Ortheris and Learoyd.[26]

Little of the original 'Soldiers Three' survived into the final screenplay. They are promoted to become Sergeants and their names changed to Cutter, Ballantine and McChesney (played by Grant, Fairbanks and McLaglen respectively). In the original they are wry anti-heroic figures, ironic inversions of Dumas' *Three Musketeers*.[27] They represent both working class and regional foundations of the British Empire – and speak in thick Irish, Cockney and Yorkshire dialects.[28] While the names of the movie characters suggest regional diversity, in order to be comprehensible to an American audience, all three speak with an uneven Hollywood cockney. Unlike the original 'Soldiers Three' and the narrative voices used in *Barrack Room Ballads*, the Hollywood soldiers only rarely use words from Indian languages in their speech. As part of the effort to add an 'authentic flavour' to the script, the Hindi vocabulary of the original poem is sprinkled like curry powder throughout. But the half-dozen words gleaned directly from the two-page poem are lost in the 90-minute film. Din is referred to (and refers to himself) as a *bhisti* (water bearer) and Cutter tells Din to fetch help *julde* (quickly). Ballantine acts as a translator when necessary but English and Hindi are rigidly separated in his speech. Generally, only Indian characters use Indian words. Hollywood preferred to avoid the hybridity that Kipling found at every turn in India.[29]

The adventures of the three are both 'up-graded' and sanitized for Hollywood. Rather than just weathering hearty scrapes around the barracks, the three now hold the fate of India in their hands as they battle to avert its re-conquest by the Thugs. Similarly the tragedy that pervades their lives in Kipling's stories is utterly absent. One does not see in RKO's version of British India the 'madness, alcoholism, self-doubt, and suicide' that, as Zoreh Sullivan has written, 'haunt the characters' in Kipling's Indian short fiction. Victor McLaglen's McChesney has none of the 'inextinguishable sorrow' that marked Kipling's Private Mulvaney.[30]

The plot interweaves three stories. The first is the challenge to British India from a revival of the Thug murder cult. The second is the desire of

3. Hollywood Heroes: Cary Grant, Victor McLaglen and Douglas Fairbanks Jr Save British India in *Gunga Din* (1939).

the loyal water bearer Gunga Din to become a fully fledged member of the Regiment. The third is the struggle to preserve the team of three, in the face of Ballantine's decision to leave the army to get married. These three stories overlap playfully. It becomes clear that McChesney and Cutter find Ballantine's marriage as distasteful as being prisoners of the Thugs. All three strands of the film deliver powerful affirmation of the white working man's race, class and gender. Accents and manners establish the heroes as working class, but it is in the areas of race and gender that the film really goes to work.

Like many films of this era, *Gunga Din* elevates male friendship above all other human bonds.[31] The opening barracks fist fight and first battle with the Thugs show the three sergeants working together. They co-operate instinctively like members of a first-rate cricket team. The three-man friendship lends itself well to exploring the love between men. There is safety in Kipling's triangle of the 'Soldiers Three' that is absent from his other stories dealing with close male friendship, such as *The Light That Failed* or 'The Man Who Would Be King'. Here at least the screenplay of *Gunga Din* reflects Kipling. The protagonists of his short story 'The Man Who Would Be King' acknowledge at the beginning of their adventure that the intrusion of a woman could threaten their plans to conquer a kingdom beyond the Himalayas and write a prohibition on marriage into their contract with each other. The breaking of this clause in the contract shatters their partnership and costs them their kingdom. Ballantine's marriage in *Gunga Din* is hardly less threatening.[32]

The scenes in which Ballantine (Fairbanks) courts his fiancée Emmy (Joan Fontaine) are oddly ambiguous. Close-ups dominated by teeth establish their relationship as rather grotesque, animalistic and oddly un-natural. Ballantine's desire for marriage is cast as un-masculine. He is humiliated when his comrades meet him in a draper's shop, choosing curtains for his 'den' with his wife-to-be. When Ballantine marches away dragging a skein of cloth behind him, Cutter and McChesney joke that his 'petticoat is showing'. Joseph Breen at the Production Code Administration was sufficiently perturbed by the written version of this scene to caution the studio: 'The reaction to Ballantine appearing with drapery must not be suggestive of a "pansy" gag'.[33] Yet once Cutter has fallen into the hands of the Thugs, Ballantine acts, and tells Emmy:

The trouble is you don't want a man for a husband. You want a coward who'll run out on his friend when he's in danger. Well that's not me, and never has been, and never will be. I don't care how much I love you – and I do, very much – I'm a soldier ... I mean I'm a man first.

With manhood defined, Emmy effectively disappears from the film. Ballantine resolves to remain in the army and the joyful reunion at the end of the film is wholly male.[34]

The racial message of the film is equally clear. It takes a horde of Thugs to overpower a single white man. The Indians die without dignity. Their efforts to run from sticks of dynamite are presented comically as though in a cartoon. Although the Thug Guru (played by Edward Ciannelli in heavy black-face) is allowed to explain his cause, he is nevertheless represented as a madman, and is photographed so as to highlight glinting teeth, fanatical eyes and an exaggeratedly black face. His chief warrior – called Chota in the screenplay (Abner Biberman) – is merciless but obsequious to lull his victims into a false sense of security. In contrast, Gunga Din cringes before the white characters. He initially appears only as comic relief, like McChesney's pet elephant, Annie. Yet while Annie is nurtured as 'Daddy's little elephant girl', Gunga Din is merely patronized. Cutter (Cary Grant) discovers him secretly drilling and attempts to help him to master the basic moves including the salute. The scene is played for laughs as the man, dressed only in a *dhoti*, is urged to place his thumbs down the seams of his trousers. When he

4. The Faithful Servant: Sam Jaffe, in the title role, takes a lesson from cutter (Cary Grant) in *Gunga Din* (1939).

manages a vigorous salute Cutter quips: 'That's better ... nearly blew your turban off!' Yet Gunga Din is shown to be making choices throughout the film. He declares to the Guru that he is supporting the British of his own free will, and is a soldier and not a slave. Ultimately he sacrifices his life to raise the alarm.

Although the figure of Gunga Din sits awkwardly in the midst of the triad of sergeants, he is the catalyst who advances the action.[35] Hoping to become a soldier, he tells Cutter of the existence of a golden temple in the hills ripe for plunder, he frees Cutter from prison, summons Ballantine and McChesney to his aid and then raises the alarm to avert a massacre of an unsuspecting British regiment. Yet he is implicitly less of a man than the British. He is diminished both by the camera angles, by his limited ambition (he tells Cutter that he has no wish to be a Maharajah: 'Bugler would be very satisfactory'), and by the visual humour of the film which depicts him as symbolically impotent. In the first battle he mimics the sergeants by waving a broken sword. Later he offers Cutter a small table fork to dig his way out of prison. It could be argued that the film seeks to move the audience into the same position as the narrator of Kipling's poem, and to question the certainties of white supremacy with the line: 'You're a better man than I am Gunga Din', but given that the overwhelming racial thrust of the film, the compliment is rendered meaningless.

While the antics of the three sergeants challenge military discipline, the climax of the film affirms military virtues. A column of British troops, led by the Black Watch, march towards an ambush singing. They seem magnificent and, until Gunga Din raises the alarm, doomed. But Din's sacrifice and their discipline saves the day. They assume formations and sweep the enemy from the field, bringing up Gattling guns on the backs of elephants and then sending in the Bengal Lancers to finish the job. Needless to say there are none of the casualties or cowardice that Kipling himself discussed in such stories as 'Drums of the Fore and Aft' in which a regiment flees and leaves its drummer boys alone in the path of an Afghan charge.[36]

Gunga Din has its own ethical framework, and it is here that the script flirts with a critique of imperialism. Cutter (like Dravot in *The Man Who Would Be King*) is undone by greed, which is exaggerated to an absurd degree with much hand-rubbing and groans of longing. As the film opens Cutter is trying to get redress after purchasing a fake treasure map, and later his eagerness to plunder a golden temple leads him straight into the arms of the Thugs. Cutter's lust for booty is accompanied by an insensitivity towards India. For Cutter, India is just the venue for his jolly army life, to be exploited or manipulated according to his desires. He considers blowing up the Taj Mahal and starting a war just to keep his friend Ballantine in the army. Cutter's motives and assumptions about India are humorously exposed as he over-interprets Thug behaviour. When, during the climax of the film, Cutter finds himself pinned down for hours by Thug snipers a few feet from the treasure for which he lusts, complains: 'is there no limit to the torture that the oriental mind can devise'. The screenplay is reluctant to endorse such positions. He survives the film only by a whisker.[37] But such potentially anti-imperial messages are diluted by the portrayal of the Indians. They are sneaky. They attack from behind. They torture their captives. They are fanatical followers of a blood-thirsty religion. They feign obsequiousness, plot ambushes and only attack in strength. The British, in contrast, are open. They march along singing loudly and are prepared to face terrible odds. At one stage, to allow Gunga Din to escape, Cutter marches into the midst of a Thug ritual singing 'The Roast Beef of Old England' and tells the entire gathering that they are all under arrest. The British are also oddly discriminating in battle. The three sergeants use their fists on unarmed Thugs, but shoot at Thug snipers. Fair play wins the day.

In writing such scenes into their screenplay the American screenwriters give a fair idea of the elements in Kipling's work which they find appealing. Their omissions are no less telling. The ambiguities of Kipling's empire are missing altogether. In such poems as 'Piet' or 'Fuzzy-Wuzzy' Kipling gives his soldiers a grudging respect to their enemies.[38] Moreover, the original Gunga Din was admired by the British narrator not for rescuing the regiment at the cost of his own life, but for the more mundane act of risking his life by attending to the wounded under fire.[39] It should also be said that Kipling consistently presents his soldiers as unappreciated by their country. In 'Tommy' we have the lines:

> For it's Tommy this, an' Tommy that, an', Chuck him
> Out, the brute!
>   But it's 'Saviour of his country' when the guns begin
> to shoot.[40]

The darker underside of Kipling's poem 'Gunga Din,' which emerges in the very final stanza that is read – as though freshly penned by the author – in the closing moments of the film is revealing:

> So I'm meet 'im later on,
> At the place where 'e is gone –
> Where it's always double drill and no canteen.
> 'E'll be squattin' on the coals,
> Givin' drink to poor damned souls,
> An' I'll get a swig in hell from Gunga Din![41]

The bleak implications of 'a swig in hell' for the career of soldiering and the underlying morality of the imperial cause are, however, negated by the images that accompany them. As Gunga Din is piped to rest now posthumously appointed to the rank of Corporal, he appears in an ellipse in the centre of the screen as a contented ghost/heavenly figure dressed in full uniform, and salutes. Unlike the apparently damned Din of Kipling, the Hollywood incarnation is clearly redeemed.[42]

In sum the film that appeared in 1939 was a virtual negation of Kipling's work. Where Kipling found complexity, tragedy, hybridity and futility, *Gunga Din* presents simplicity, facile masculine posturing and easy answers in violence. Moreover, the entire travesty is founded on racial and cultural distortions that make Kipling's own highly problematic writing seem like the most carefully balanced ethnography. As *Gunga Din*'s box office success makes clear, no one in the United States minded. In Britain, Kipling's widow, Caroline, had her reservations. She claimed, a little fancifully, that the representation of her husband in the final reel exposed his memory to ridicule. RKO obligingly cut the offending scenes from later released prints.[43] The film was, however, banned in Japan, Malaya and British India.[44]

The Later Career of *Gunga Din*

The release of *Gunga Din* in January 1939 coincided with the deepening crisis in Europe; audiences, doubtless, relished its shameless escapism. Yet the political situation had already left its mark on the film, and its fate and the future of the cinema of empire were both profoundly affected by the war that followed. *Gunga Din* appeared at a time of considerable delicacy in Anglo–American relations. Britain stood at the brink of war which the United States had absolutely no intention of joining. For at least one participant in the film, the film and its political context were not wholly unconnected. Douglas Fairbanks Jr later claimed that he used his film career specifically to combat Anglophobia and promote Anglo–American co-operation in the face of the Nazi threat. He had been converted to the dream of building an Anglo–American world order by Lord Tweedsmuir (better known as the novelist John Buchan), who he thought of as his 'prophet, guide and friend'. *Gunga Din* seemed a natural outgrowth of these hopes. As the great debate over America's role in war gathered momentum, Fairbanks moved explicitly into the political sphere, playing a leading role in the pro-British Committee to Defend America by Aiding the Allies. Similarly two of the film's writers, Ben Hecht and Charles MacArthur, worked with the Fight for Freedom Committee, scripting that organization's 1941 propaganda stage spectacular: 'Fun to Be Free'.[45] But although Hollywood was keen to support the British cause in such films as Alfred Hitchcock's *Foreign Correspondent* (1940) and William Wyler's *Mrs Miniver* (1942), the old empire genre sat uncomfortably with the emerging politics of the war.[46] By 1942 *Gunga Din* had outlived its political usefulness. The United States joined the war with the expectation that the peace would include decolonization. India was a co-signatory of the United Nations declaration of 1 January 1942 in its own right, and the US government's Office of War Information took care not to offend the sensibilities of that country. As Clayton Koppes and Gregory Black have noted, the Office of War Information prevailed on RKO not to re-release *Gunga Din* and persuaded MGM to abandon their plans to film Kipling's *Kim*.[47]

The empire film also suffered by default from the revival of the Western. The year 1939 saw the release of two seminal Westerns: John Ford's *Stagecoach* and George Marshall's *Destry Rides Again*.[48] The genre seemed an ideal vehicle to celebrate America's newfound self-confidence of the war-years and after. Steinbeck's dust bowl was transformed back into the land of opportunity in Rogers and Hammerstein's runaway stage hit *Oklahoma!* (a reworking of a play from the last flowering of the Western genre in the 1920s). Now Westerns could be packaged as Westerns, and empire movies became Westerns too. John Ford now filmed the Seventh Cavalry as once – to the pain of his Irish soul – he been obliged to film the Khyber Rifles and the Bengal Lancers.[49] The British-born Victor McLaglen also remained on hand as a stalwart Irish Sergeant. George Stevens continued to explore the theme of male friendship and used the Western genre. But the friendship at the core of *Shane* was far more dangerous than that of *Gunga Din* for now there were only two protagonists.[50] Empire films were remade directly as Westerns. As Jeffrey Richards has noted, *Lives of a Bengal Lancer* became *Geronimo* (1939), *Four Men and a Prayer* became *Fury at Furnace Creek* (1948) and *Gunga Din* itself resurfaced as a Western *Sergeants Three* in 1961, remade by John Sturges (who edited the original) with Frank Sinatra, Dean Martin, Peter Lawford and Sammy Davis Jr as their faithful bugler.[51]

Kipling and the empire bubbled away under the surface for a while. In 1950 MGM finally filmed *Kim*. A flurry of lacklustre empire pictures followed including a reworking of *Gunga Din* without its old title character: *Soldiers Three* (1951).[52] In 1967 Walt Disney delivered his animated *Jungle Book*, which in its music and vocal characterizations said more about domestic American stereotypes than Kipling's India.[53] Yet the shadow of Kipling was still discernable in America's own empire. In the later stages of World War Two, American officers in Teheran nicknamed their mess servant Gunga Din.[54] Teddy Roosevelt's grandson, Kermit Roosevelt – the head of CIA operations in the Middle East who choreographed the overthrow of Mussadiq in Iran in 1953 – retained the Kiplingesque family nickname Kim. The incident now looks like the original sin of the American presence in the Middle East.[55] But literary tastes were elsewhere. With a Bond novel on his bedside table and a confidence unmeasured by the experience of European empire, John F. Kennedy committed his troops to war in Vietnam.[56]

The experience of Vietnam left its mark on both Westerns and empire films. In both genres the protagonists became alienated victims who found vindication in homoerotic buddy relationships and death in Mexico (*The Wild Bunch*) or Bolivia (*Butch Cassidy and the Sundance Kid*).[57] As will be seen below, John Huston's film of *The Man Who Would Be King* built directly on these themes, remaining faithful to Kipling's short story with a few nods to *Gunga Din*. British India remained a perennial presence in movies whether in worthy British-made end-of-empire epics, or such lively American escapism like Disney's 1994 Kipling adaptation: *Tales from the Jungle Book*. Old themes endure. *Gunga Din's* Thugs popped up in Steven Spielberg's *Indiana Jones and the Temple of Doom*.[58] Serious debate about the empire is elsewhere. The United States may never have acknowledged the inner-warnings of Kipling, but the same messages were learned the hard way in Vietnam and again in Iraq.

Notes

[1] Herrick Library: George Stevens Papers, file 2628, *Gunga Din* clips, *Box Office Digest* 1940 annual estimated grosses: # 1 *Jesse James* $3,250,000; # 2 *Gunga Din*, $3,100,000; # 3, *Mr Smith Goes to Washington*, $2,700,000; # 4, *The Rains Came*, $2,600,000; # 9, *The Wizard of Oz*, $2,300,000. Some sources question the film's initial earnings and have it only making back costs during re-release, see Rudy Behlmer, *Behind the Scenes* (Hollywood: Samuel French, 1990), p.101.

[2] Herrick Library, George Stevens Papers, file # 2613, *Gunga Din* costs. The total costs were $1,909,669.28 against a budget of $1,305,437.19. The overrun of $600,000 came from overspending on a number of elements including extras, stars and music.

[3] Jeffrey Richards, 'Boys Own Empire: Feature Films and Imperialism in the 1930s', in John M. Mackenzie (ed.), *Imperialism and Popular Culture* (Manchester: Manchester University Press, 1986), p.144. For a narrative of production see George E. Turner, 'The Making of Gunga Din', *American Cinematographer*, September 1982, pp.895–9, 958–64.

[4] Sayre graduated from Exeter College, Oxford in August 1922 with a BA in English. Contrary to Philip French, 'Kipling and the Movies', in John Gross (ed.), *Rudyard Kipling: The Man His Work and His World* (London: Weidenfeld & Nicolson, 1972), p.166, he was not a Rhodes Scholar. He co-wrote the screen play for *Annie Oakley* (RKO, dir. George Stevens, 1935), and later served as *New Yorker* war correspondent in Persia: Joel Sayre, *Persian Gulf Command* (New York: Random House, 1945).

[5] The development of the screenplay for *Gunga Din* is well documented in Behlmer, *Behind the Scenes*, pp.88–90. Hecht and MacArthur were co-authors of the hit play

The Front Page. For versions of the script see Herrick Library: George Stevens Papers, files 2608–11.

6   Rudyard Kipling, *Rudyard Kipling's Verse: The Definitive Edition* (London: Hodder and Stoughton, 1977), pp.184–5, 577–8. For a summary of Kipling's sojourn in the USA. see Norman Page, *A Kipling Companion* (London: Macmillan, 1984), pp.17–20.

7   *Kipling's Verse*, pp.323–4.

8   I am grateful to Kermit Roosevelt III and Corinne Roosevelt for confirming this connection.

9   Dillon Wallace, *The Lure of the Labrador Wild* (New York: F. Revell, 1905) as cited in Alan Williams, 'Explorers Wild: The Hubbards in Labrador', in C. E. Gittings (ed.), *Imperialism and Gender: Constructions of Masculinity* (Hebden Bridge: Dangaroo Press, 1996), p.77.

10   Carmine A. Prioli (ed.), *The Poems of General George S. Patton Jr.: Lines of Fire* (Lewiston NY: Edwin Mellen Press, 1991), p.vi. Patton quoted Kipling in his memoirs: George S. Patton, *War as I Knew It* (Boston: Houghton Mifflin, 1947), p.337.

11   Finley Peter Dunne, *Mr. Dooley on in the Hearts of His Countrymen* (Boston: Small, Maynard, 1899), pp.13–17.

12   For a selection of usage and parodies of the poem see Nell Irvin Painter, *Standing at Armageddon: The United States, 1877–1919* (New York: W. W. Norton, 1987), pp.141–69.

13   For an account of the development of American ideology during this period see Michael Hunt, *Ideology and US Foreign Policy* (New Haven: Yale University Press, 1987).

14   Roderick Nash, *The Uncertain Generation: American Thought, 1917–1930* (Chicago: Elephant Paperbacks/Dee, 1990), pp.140–1; Edward Buscombe (ed.), *The BFI Companion to the Western* (London: Deutsch/BFI, 1988). On the Western in the 1920s see pp.33–5, on the relative decline of the Western in the 1930s see pp.41–3. For production figures see pp.427–8. In 1933 Westerns constituted only 13 per cent of all films made in the USA as against 28 per cent in 1926. This was the lowest ebb for the genre until the 1960s. 'A' Westerns were an even smaller section of these films, representing only 1 film in every 80 produced between 1930 and 1939. In 1934, the year in which both Paramount's *Lives of a Bengal Lancer* and Fox's *Clive of India* were made, not one Hollywood studio released an 'A' Western.

15   In order to persuade Gary Cooper to appear in *Lives of a Bengal Lancer* (Paramount, dir. Henry Hathaway, 1935); the director urged him 'to think of it as a Western set in India'. Richards, 'Boys Own Empire', p.145.

16   Interview: Douglas Fairbanks Jr.

17   On revenues at MGM see H. Mark Glancy, 'MGM Film Grosses, 1924–1948: The Eddie Mannix Ledger', *Historical Journal of Film, Radio and Television*, 12: 2 (1992), pp.127–44. On Warner Brothers' bid to maintain export revenue in wartime see Nicholas J. Cull, *Selling War: British Propaganda and American 'Neutrality' in World War Two* (New York: Oxford University Press, 1995), pp.51–2.

18   *The Lost Patrol* (RKO, dir. John Ford, 1934); *Beau Geste* (Paramount, dir. William Wellman, 1939); see also *Beau Ideal* (RKO, dir. Herbert Brenon, 1931); *Beau Geste* (Paramount, dir. Herbert Brenon, 1926) and *Beau Hunks* (Hal Roach, dir. James W. Horne, 1931), starring Laurel and Hardy.

19   *The Black Watch* (released in the UK as *King of the Khyber Rifles*, and based on the novel by Talbot Mundy of this title) (Fox, dir. John Ford, 1929); *Lives of a Bengal Lancer*

(Paramount, dir. Henry Hathaway, 1935); *Clive of India* (Twentieth-Century Fox, dir. Richard Boleslawski, 1934); *The Charge of the Light Brigade* (Warner Bros., dir. Michael Curtiz, 1936); *Four Men and a Prayer* (Twentieth Century-Fox, dir. John Ford, 1938) and *Storm over Bengal* (Republic, dir. Sidney Salkow, 1938).

20 *Bonnie Scotland* (MGM/Hal Roach, dir. James Horne, 1935), in which Laurel and Hardy join a Scottish regiment in India. *Wee Willie Winkie* (Twentieth-Century Fox, dir. John Ford, 1937). For an extended discussion of this film see J. A. Palace, *The Non-Western Films of John Ford* (Secaucus NJ: Citadel Press, 1979), pp.250–2.

21 The original story provided little more than the name of the title character (originally a boy) and the general scenario for the film: Rudyard Kipling, *Wee Willie Winkie and Other Stories* (Allahabad: A. H. Wheeler, 1888).

22 These projects were accomplished in 1937 and 1941 respectively: *Captains Courageous* (MGM, dir. Victor Fleming, 1937); *Elephant Boy* (London, dirs Robert Flaherty and Zoltan Korda); *The Light That Failed* (Paramount, dir. William Wellman, 1939) and *The Jungle Book* (London, dirs Zoltan Korda and André de Toth, 1941). MGM first announced its plan to film *Kim* in 1938, the film did not appear until 1950. *The Light That Failed* had been filmed three times in the silent era, as had a version of Kipling's poem 'The Vampire' which appeared as *A Fool There Was* in 1915 and 1922. For a survey of Kipling in film see French. 'Kipling and the Movies', pp.162–9.

23 French, 'Kipling at the Movies', p.162, also Jeffrey Richards, *The Age of the Dream Palace: Cinema and Society in Britain, 1930–1939* (London: Routledge, 1984), p.49. The failure of Gaumont British to complete *Soldiers Three* is documented in Jeffrey Richards, '"Soldiers Three": The "Lost" Gaumont British Imperial Epic', *Historical Journal of Film, Radio and Television*, 15: 1 (1995), pp.137–41. Kipling was also quoted in movies. Lines from 'Recessional' accompany the death of Queen Victoria in *Sixty Glorious Years* and it is a love of Kipling which persuades a young soldier to join up in *The Lost Patrol* (RKO, dir. John Ford, 1934), cited in Jeffrey Richards, *Visions of Yesterday* (London: Routledge, 1973), pp.148, 174.

24 In 1935 R. J. Minney submitted a screenplay for a film entitled *Gunga Din* which incorporated the character from the Kipling poem but nothing else. The film was never produced and RKO apparently developed its own version of *Gunga Din* quite independently. Richards, *The Age of the Dream Palace*, p.140.

25 The advisers were Sir Robert Erskine Holland, Capt. Clive Morgan and one Sergeant-Major William Briers. At times the film is absurdly specific. The site of the opening Thug attack is identified by a title as 'Village of Tantrapur, 15 miles to the north' of the British camp. There were also a number of Indian advisers on the film. Stevens considered the most useful to be one Gurdial (Paul) Singh, who advised on customs, costumes, translated dialogue and acted too. On completing the film Stevens wrote to Fox suggesting they hire Singh as adviser on their own Indian film *The Rains Came*. Herrick: George Stevens papers, file # 2616 – *Gunga Din* production correspondence, Stevens to Harry Joe Brown (producer of *The Rains Came*), 13 April 1939.

26 The three first appeared in short stories written for the *Civil and Military Gazette* from 1887. Their stories were included in *Plain Tales from the Hills* (Allahabad: A. H. Wheeler, 1888) and a second volume devoted to the *Soldiers Three* (Allahabad: A. H. Wheeler, 1888). Related stories appeared in *Life's Handicap* (London: Macmillan, 1891), *Many Inventions* (London: Macmillan, 1893) and a final story written for the *Saturday Evening Post* in December 1899 which did not appear until *Actions and Reactions* (London: Macmillan, 1909). For bibliography see Kipling, *Soldiers Three and In Black*

and White (Penguin Twentieth Century Classics edn, Harmondsworth: Penguin, 1993), p.208.

27 Hence the three are introduced in *Plain Tales from the Hills* in a story called 'The Three Musketeers'. It might also be noted that the Sergeants are placed in the Royal Engineers and are responsible for such things as repairing telegraph wires. Kipling's soldiers are identified as 'privates of the line' first in 'The Black Tyrone' (in the case of Mulvaney) and then in 'The Ould Regiment'.

28 Mark Paffard has suggested this echoes Shakespeare's four regional soldiers in *Henry V*; see Mark Paffard, *Kipling's Indian Fiction* (London: Macmillan, 1989), p.61.

29 Hence Indian troops as shown using the command *panee lao* (bring water). There are other borrowings from the poem. Enraged that Din has stolen his elephant, McChesney calls him a 'Lazarushian beggar' – but the insult is specifically Christian rather than Anglo–Indian, Lazarus being the archetypal leper.

30 Zoreh T. Sullivan, *Narratives of Empire: The Fictions of Rudyard Kipling* (Cambridge: Cambridge University Press, 1993), p.15. Mulvaney's sorrow is explored in 'The Courting of Dinah Shadd' collected in *Life's Handicap* which also includes 'On the Greenhow Hill' in which Learoyd loses the love of his life to consumption. Ortheris is driven to the brink of insanity by an awareness of the futility of his position in 'The Madness of Private Otheris' in *Plain Tales from the Hills*.

31 In a similar spirit *Beau Geste* (1939) (which deals with brothers) opens with the invented Arabic proverb: 'The love between a man and woman waxes and wanes like the moon, but the love of brother for brother is constant like the stars and endures like the word of the Prophet.'

32 The marriage in 'The Man Who Would Be King' – first published in *The Phantom Rickshaw* (Allahabad: A. H. Wheeler, 1888) – is doubly taboo as it is to a 'native' woman, but the 'contrack' prohibits all women 'white or black'.

33 Herrick Library: George Stevens Papers, file # 2616, *Gunga Din* production correspondence, Breen to McDonough (RKO), 11 August 1938.

34 Earlier drafts of the script had Ballantine leaving the army and marrying Emmy, and McChesney then producing his enlistment papers, as signed earlier in the film and arranging for him to be arrested for desertion on his honeymoon.

35 His role is in keeping with that which Toni Morrison has identified as typically given to African–American characters in American literature; see Toni Morrison, 'Unspeakable Things Unspoken', *Michigan Quarterly Review*, 28: 1 (Winter 1989), pp.1–34.

36 'Drums of the Fore and Aft' was first anthologized in *Wee Willie Winkie and Other Stories*.

37 Unlike Dravot, who actually wishes to become a noble, Cutter merely longs to be 'rich as Dooks'. It is a lesser 'crime' and it earns a lesser punishment. Oddly, while Kipling's Otheris also speaks of 'Dooks' in the opening of 'The Madness of Private Otheris' (*Plain Tales from the Hills*) it is to point out that he is not one.

38 *Kipling's Verse*, pp.400–1, 479–81. These sentiments may also be identified in the battle scene of *The Light That Failed*. Cited in Paffard, *Kipling's Indian Fiction*, pp.56–7.

39 *Kipling's Verse*, pp.406–9: there is no line in the film equivalent to "An' for all 'is dirty 'ide,/he was white, clear white, inside,/when he went to tend the wounded under fire!" An analogous (patronizing) message of acceptance is contained in the closing tableau of the film as McChesney sheds a tear for Gunga Din.

40   *Kipling's Verse*, pp.398–9.

41   Ibid., pp.406–9.

42   Here, as in the short story 'Naboth' (*Life's Handicap*), Kipling's narrator's unwitting use of a biblical allusion turns in the mind of the reader to offer a critique of the imperial project. For a discussion of Naboth see Sullivan, *Narratives of Empire*, p.12. The use of Kipling's poem raised concerns with the Production Code. On 27 October 1939 Breen wrote to J. R. McDonough:

> We take this opportunity of advising you that it is our fear that political censor boards may delete from the quotation from the poem GUNG DIN on page 187 the use of the words 'damned' and 'hell', and the use of the line 'By the living God that made you'. Since such deletion may disastrously effect the quality of this scene, you may wish to take some counsel as to the possibility of changing this scene, so as to avoid the use of this material.

43   Behlmer, *Behind the Scenes*, pp.100–1. It was in this form that the film began its illustrious career in re-release.

44   Richards, *The Age of the Dream Palace*, p.137.

45   Interview: Fairbanks; Ben Hecht, *Charlie: The Improbable Life and Times of Charles Macarthur* (New York: Harper, 1957), p.210; Cull, *Selling War*, pp.62, 74, 77; John Balderston, the British-born screen writer of *Lives of a Bengal Lancer* also campaigned for Britain as part of the interventionist movement.

46   On Hollywood and Britain 1940–1941 see Cull, *Selling War*, pp.139–40, 179–84.

47   Clayton R. Koppes and Gregory D. Black, *Hollywood Goes to War: How Politics, Profits and Propaganda Shapes World War Two Movies* (New York: Free Press), pp.224–5, also Richards, *Visions of Yesterday*, p.5.

48   *Stagecoach* (Walter Wanger, dir. John Ford, 1939); *Destry Rides Again* (Universal, dir. George Marshall, 1939).

49   On John Ford's empire films and his opinion of the subject see Richards, *Visions of Yesterday*, p.3.

50   *Shane* (Paramount, dir. George Stevens, 1953).

51   Richards, 'Boys Own Empire', p.157; *Sergeants Three* (UA/Essex-Claude, dir. John Sturges, 1961).

52   *Kim* (MGM, dir. Victor Saville, 1950); *Soldiers Three* (MGM, dir. Tay Garnett, 1951) similar films included *Rogues March* (MGM, dir. Allan Davis, 1953); *King of the Khyber Rifles* (Twentieth-Century Fox, dir. Henry King, 1954).

53   *Jungle Book* (Disney, dir. Wolfgang Reitherman, 1967).

54   The servant embraced the name. He wrote an allegorical story to entertain the British and American officers for whom he worked, which was published as Ali Mirdrekvandi Gunga Din, *No Heaven for Gunga Din* (London: Gollancz, 1965).

55   On 'Kim' Roosevelt and the overthrow of Mussadiq see James A. Bill, *The Eagle and the Lion: The Tragedy of American–Iranian Relations* (New Haven: Yale University Press, 1988), pp.86–97.

56   On James Bond and Kennedy see David Burner, *John F. Kennedy and a New Generation* (Glenview IL: Scott, Foresman, 1988), p.63.

57   *The Wild Bunch* (Warner, dir. Sam Peckinpah, 1969); *Butch Cassidy and the Sundance Kid* (Twentieth Century-Fox, dir. George Roy Hill, 1969).

58   *Indiana Jones and the Temple of Doom* (Paramount/Lucasfilm, dir. Steven Spielberg, 1984).

4
THE BRITISH EMPIRE AT WAR
Burma Victory (1945)

It is sometimes overlooked that when the British government declared war on Germany on 3 September 1939, it also committed India and the colonies to war as it had in 1914. The four major self-governing dominions, however, all declared war of their own volition: Australia and New Zealand the same day, South Africa on 6 September and Canada on 10 September. Eire was the only dominion to remain neutral. A significant proportion of British manpower was provided by the empire: approximately a third of the 60 divisions fielded by 1942 were from India and the dominions.[1] It was only to be expected, therefore, that the participation of the British Empire in the war effort would be recognized in official propaganda and publicity campaigns. Short films such as *From the Four Corners* (1941) were commissioned to explain the role of the dominions in the war and there were many newsreels focusing on mobilization throughout the empire. British propagandists focused on promoting an idea of the empire as a progressive organization. A policy document of October 1940, for example, sought to project 'the British Commonwealth of Nations' as a democratic alternative to National Socialism:

> The Nazis are proclaiming loud and long that they are creating 'a new world order'. In fact, they are merely resurrecting the old vicious idea of a slave Empire in which the subjugated races are held down by force and exploited for the benefit of the *herrenvolk* – 'the master folk'. It is not the Nazis and the Gestapo who have the goods to deliver, so to speak, for the post-war world, but the British Commonwealth. This is true because the Empire has been gradually transformed from being a political organisation owing obedience to central authority in London to an association of free and equal partners. It is in itself a League of Nations.[2]

This policy can be seen as an attempt to counter the German propaganda machine, which was quick to exploit Britain's imperial record in films like *Ohm Krüger* (1941) and *Carl Peters* (1941), which – however inaccurate in their representation of British policy in Africa – were highly effective anti-imperialist propaganda.[3]

The fact was, however, that the empire represented a significant problem for British propagandists. On the one hand the involvement of the colonies and dominions was valuable propaganda for domestic consumption in that it reassured the British people that the country was not 'alone' – an assurance that was especially timely in the summer of 1940 following the fall of France when Britain faced the prospect of a German invasion. On the other hand, however, the participation of imperial troops created expectations about the future of the colonies that were left largely unresolved. In 1940 Winston Churchill, who in the 1930s had fiercely opposed the Government of India Act (a measure now largely overtaken by events), was persuaded to offer dominion status for India after the war in recognition of its significant contribution to the defence of the 'motherland'.

In November 1942, as part of his 'end of the beginning' speech to mark the Battle of El Alamein – important politically as well as militarily because it was Britain's first major victory against the German armies – Churchill famously declared: 'I have not become the King's First Minister to preside over the liquidation of the British Empire.'[4] Yet in truth the process that would eventually lead to the dissolution of the empire had already been set in train. To a large extent the process was an inevitable outcome of the war. The pressures were economic, political and military. In the first place the mobilization for total war placed a huge burden on the British economy. Britain was dependent upon buying arms and munitions from the United States, but by the end of 1940 its dollar reserves were so depleted that Churchill had to go cap in hand to US President Franklin D. Roosevelt. Britain had already relinquished its naval bases in the West Indies and Newfoundland in return for 50 old destroyers needed to combat the menace of German U-boats. In addition, Churchill had to agree to sell off British assets worth £4,000 million including £500 million of gold reserves. The institution of the Lend-Lease Agreement in March 1941 was exacted at a high price: America would provide equipment for any country 'whose defense the president deems vital to the defense of the United States' but this created the conditions in which US exports could force out British exports from world markets after the war. The depletion of Britain's assets and its negative balance of exports made its future survival as a global power uncertain to say the least. Some felt that Britain had pawned its empire in order to buy American aid.[5]

Economic problems were compounded by political pressures. Since becoming Prime Minister in 1940 Churchill had placed an almost blind faith in the entry of the United States into the war. There was, however, very strong isolationist sentiment in America: Americans were determined that they would not be dragged into another war to prop up the ailing British Empire. The Atlantic Charter, a joint declaration by Churchill and Roosevelt in August 1941, was partly an attempt to address these concerns. From the British point of view the aim was to commit the United States to an international organization after the war – to this extent the Charter has sometimes been seen as the founding document of the United Nations. For the Americans it was a means of guarding against the expansion of British imperial ambitions. Article 3 declared that the signatories 'respect the right of all peoples to choose the form of government under which they will live'.[6] This clearly had significant implications for the 600 million subjects of the Crown living in British colonies and mandated territories.

Finally there was the military threat to the empire. In the 1930s the Imperial General Staff had advised that Britain could not wage war simultaneously against Germany, Italy and Japan – this had been one of the calculations that informed the policy of appeasement. At the end of 1941, however, this was precisely the situation in which Britain found itself. The strategic priority of defending the British Isles – there were still invasion scares as late as May 1942 – meant that the Far East was left under-protected. This strategic imbalance was further affected by Japan's surprise attack on the US Pacific Fleet at Pearl Harbor on 7 December 1941 which left Japan, albeit temporarily, as the dominant power in the theatre. When Japan occupied Hong Kong (December 1941), Singapore and Malaya (February 1942) and Burma (May 1942) the sun might be said to have literally as well as metaphorically set on the British Empire. Some nationalists, particularly in Malaya and Burma, welcomed their 'liberation' from British rule. The Japanese advance in Burma, moreover, threatened India and made acute the need to secure support for the war effort there. In March 1942 Sir Stafford Cripps was sent as a special envoy to India with a promise that the British government would grant independence to India after the war. This was insufficient for the Indian National Congress, however, which demanded immediate independence and instituted a campaign of civil disobedience that resulted in the imprisonment of its important leaders including Nehru and Gandhi.

This was the political context in which the production of *Burma Victory* needs to be understood. *Burma Victory* has usually been seen as the third in a trilogy of 'Victory' films – the others were *Desert Victory* (1943) and *Tunisian Victory* (1944) – produced by the British Army Film and Photographic Unit

(AFPU) compiled from actuality footage shot at the front by service camera-men.[7] While there are certainly many continuities with the other 'Victory' films, principally the involvement in all three of director Roy Boulting, however, the origins and production of *Burma Victory* were more histor-ically specific than has sometimes been allowed. It provides a fascinating case study not only of the production of an official film record of an aspect of the empire's war but also of the sometimes tense relationship between the British and their American allies over the campaign in South East Asia. It also reveals the extent to which the representation of the Allied war effort for public consumption was fiercely contested by the various parties and agencies concerned.

Burma Victory was the pet project of none other than Admiral Lord Mountbatten, the British naval commander who had served with distinc-tion in the Mediterranean (he was the model for Noël Coward's perform-ance as Captain Kinross in the film *In Which We Serve* in 1942) before being promoted to Chief of Combined Operations (1942–3) and thence to the posi-tion of Supreme Allied Commander South East Asia in 1943.[8] Mountbatten planned the counter-offensive in Burma which, after a false start in 1943, succeeded in the spring of 1944 in driving back the Japanese. Mountbatten had to balance strategic objectives and political considerations. His American deputy, General Joseph Stilwell (nicknamed 'Vinegar Joe'), was a known Anglophobe, suspicious of British motives and concerned not to be a pawn in the reacquisition of their empire. The Americans even referred to Mountbatten's South East Asia Command (SEAC) by the nickname 'Save England's Asian Colonies'.[9] From the British point of view the primary strategic objective was to recover lost territory by pushing southeast into Burma, which would then provide a base for the re-conquest of the Malay peninsula. The Americans, however, wanted to drive north to relieve the Chinese. These strategic and political differences would be mapped onto the production of *Burma Victory*.

Mountbatten's aim in commissioning the Burma campaign film was his concern that the war in the Far East received less publicity than the Allied campaigns in North Africa and Europe. Not for no reason was the British Fourteenth Army known as the 'forgotten army'. There had already been major feature-length campaign films of El Alamein (*Desert Victory*) and 'Operation Torch' (*Tunisian Victory*). *Desert Victory* had been compiled by Major David Macdonald and Captain Roy Boulting from actuality film shot by the AFPU. Macdonald and Boulting were both commercial film-makers recruited to the services. It was regarded as a propaganda triumph and had received wide distribution in America. Churchill personally sent prints to both Roosevelt and Stalin. The latter replied rather mischievously: 'The film depicts magnificently how Britain is fighting, and stigmatises those scoundrels (there are such people also in our country) who are asserting that Britain is not fighting at all but is merely an onlooker'.[10] The AFPU completed a follow-up to *Desert Victory*, entitled *Africa Freed*, but it was shelved in order to make way for a joint Anglo–American campaign documentary which became *Tunisian Victory*, compiled by the AFPU's Major Hugh Stewart and Colonel Frank Capra of the US Army Signal Corps. (Capra was one of those Hollywood directors who, like William Wyler, John Ford and John Huston, joined up to make films for the US services.) *Tunisian Victory* was a troubled production, however, beset by differences between the allies over the emphasis given to their respective roles in the campaign. Various delays meant that it was not released until the spring of 1944, nearly a year after the defeat of the Axis powers in North Africa, by which time its value as propaganda had passed.[11]

Mountbatten, however, was determined to proceed with an official film of the Burma campaign. He had already intervened to head off a film that Sir Alexander Korda proposed to make in Hollywood about the Chindits. The Chindits (or, to give them their formal name, the Long Range Penetration Group) had carried out several special operations in Burma in 1943 and 1944 under the command of the charismatic Brigadier Orde Wingate. Air Marshal Sir Philip Joubert, Mountbatten's deputy for publicity and civilian affairs, felt that such a film 'would offend informed Military opinion and would be distasteful to Chindits themselves'.[12] Korda was told that it 'is impossible to give official sanction to the making of this film until more details are known' and the project was dropped.[13] It may have been that Mountbatten and his staff objected to the film because they had already decided to proceed with a film of their own about the Chindit operations. However, the scope of the project soon became more ambitious. In July 1944 Mountbatten told the US Chief of Staff, General George C. Marshall, that he had approved a 'plan for [a] film on Burma activities on much larger scope than originally planned, giving opportunity to show all activities [of] British and American air and ground forces, instead of centralising on one operation'. 'Such a limited objective', he now felt, 'might have caused disappointment and possible resentment from troops taking part in conjoint or supplementary operations in the Theater'.[14] At a meeting on 21 July Mountbatten explained his decision to his staff officers:

> The Supreme Allied Commander outlined for the Commanders-in-Chief the background of this question by pointing out that sev-

eral agencies had produced motion pictures of operations in this theatre, and he now considered that in order to give an impartial picture of South East Asia Command operations it would be desirable to combine these into a documentary film of all the principal activities. It was proposed to produce the film under the auspices of the US Office of War Information and the Ministry of Information, and he was anxious that it be put into production as quickly as possible. The Commanders-in-Chief expressed their agreement with the project.[15]

Even at this early stage, however, there were suggestions of dissent. The minutes record that Stilwell 'did not have any particular enthusiasm about the making of the film, but if it were undertaken he wished assurance that he would have an opportunity to approve the final version before its release'. No reason was given, though bearing in mind Stilwell's antipathy for the British it is not difficult to guess what the nature of his objections might have been.

It was when news of the film reached the Ministry of Information (MOI) in London, however, that problems really began. The MOI was the department responsible for official propaganda, including film. It advised commercial producers on the sort of subjects it wanted to see treated in films and directly commissioned shorts and documentaries on all aspects of the war effort at home and abroad. In 1940 it had taken over control of the GPO Film Unit, subsequently renamed the Crown Film Unit, for the production of its more prestigious 'long' documentaries including *Target for Tonight* (1941), *Coastal Command* (1942), *Fires Were Started* (1943) and *Western Approaches* (1944). The MOI did not have the same control over the AFPU, which came under the direction of the War Office, but it was responsible for the distribution of its films. It soon became clear that the MOI had reservations about the Burma campaign film. It was evidently piqued that Mountbatten had commissioned the film without consulting the MOI and reminded SEAC tersely 'that distribution of any Government film for Public showing must be through [the] MOI'.[16] 'Never any intention of producing film except through you', Joubert reassured the MOI, but added that the 'peculiar difficulties of this theatre have necessitated prolonged negotiations with the interested parties before [a] firm decision could be taken'. He then asked the MOI to 'set the usual machinery in motion'.[17]

What SEAC had failed to realize, however, was that there was no 'usual machinery' for joint Anglo–American productions. The arrangements for first *Tunisian Victory* and then for the film that would become *The True Glory*

(1945) had been *ad hoc* and unsatisfactory. Brendan Bracken, the Minister of Information, tried to explain the problems involved:

> You do not know what trouble you have launched on in projecting a film on the whole Burma campaign with British and American ends. We have had some experience of this with [the] Tunisian campaign and now the Normandy operations and there is no doubt that an overall campaign film which is to suit British and American tastes is slow to produce and that the effectiveness of the film suffers in the process. I should urge you strongly there-fore whatever the actual decision about this that you keep to the previous plan of a British film covering the Wingate operations ... Please reassure me.[18]

SEAC stuck to its guns, however, insisting that a film focusing on Wingate 'would not give a true picture of the Burma campaign' and maintain-ing its line that there was an 'urgent need to give wide publicity to close co-operation between British and US air, land and sea forces in this theatre'.[19] An impasse had been reached.

It was not only the British who had reservations about the film. The Americans, for their part, were concerned that the film might become part of a British propaganda campaign to reassert colonial rule in South East Asia. John Paton Davies at the US State Department opposed the film for this reason: 'There would therefore seem to be a good deal to be said against continuing the attempt to produce a cinematic document purport-ing to show an identity of American and British interests and objectives in Southeast Asia.'[20] Davies was worried that the Americans would be seen as party to the restoration of the British Empire. His concerns were shared by Secretary of State Cordell Hull: 'With specific reference to the proposed motion picture, the political implications of a production under joint aus-pices would seem to be undesirable, no matter how carefully the script might be edited'.[21]

There were now so many parties with a stake in the Burma film – SEAC, the MOI and War Office on the British side, the OWI and State Department on the American – that there is little wonder its production became bogged down in a mire of inter-departmental and service rivalries. Frank Capra, who had been brought in to supervise the compilation, was becoming increasingly frustrated at having to negotiate the conflicting demands. At Mountbatten's own request David Macdonald was flown out to work on the film. In the meantime Mountbatten's ambitions for the film were expanding. He now felt that two films rather than one would be desirable to do full justice to the subject. Early in 1945 he suggested to Capra 'due to certain continuance of Burma Campaign for many months that your picture should end at the first major crossing of the Chindwin River and construction of Kalewa Bridge without attempting to include further victories which would hold up its completion and release'.[22]

It was not until March 1945 that a rough cut of the film was ready. Unsurprisingly, it satisfied none of the parties concerned. The MOI found it 'completely unacceptable because it has been based on the idea that the Burma campaign was waged to bring aid to China'.[23] The Americans responded that their public would not be interested in a feature-length film of a campaign in which the US Army had not played the major role. Marshall suggested reducing the film to a two-reeler. Mountbatten was not happy with the suggestion: 'I trust the proposal ... will not have the effect of glorifying General Stilwell and the Ledo Road at the expense of the larger British share in the liberation of Burma.'[24] The strategic differences and personal tensions within SEAC were coming to a head. In a terse cable to the War Office Mountbatten declared: 'I do not think however that we should overlook the fact that American object in Burma is not – repeat not – the same as ours ... Any film likely to pass critics eyes in the War Department and State Department is bound to reflect US outlook.'[25]

It was now apparent that a joint Anglo–American film would be unable to reflect both British and American objectives in South East Asia. This was a grave disappointment for Mountbatten, who had genuinely believed in the project as a means of furthering the cause of Anglo–American partnership. It was now decided that the allies would go their separate ways. Capra would produce a two-reel film, *The Stilwell Road*, showing the American side of the campaign, while Macdonald and Roy Boulting would produce a feature-length documentary entitled *Burma Victory*. This did not please the MOI, however, mindful of the problems it had experienced in securing distribution for other British official films in the United States. Brendan Bracken predicted gloomily that 'the only certain result will be that the Americans will get in first with nationwide distribution of a short film unsatisfactory from our point of view and that we shall follow some time later with a film, satisfactory from our point of view, but getting little distribution in America'.[26] In the event, however, *The Stilwell Road* was not released theatrically, while *Burma Victory* was distributed by Warner Bros. (The main US distributors had agreed a rota for handling British official films, about which they were less than wholeheartedly enthusiastic. Twentieth Century-Fox had distributed *Desert Victory* and MGM had released *Tunisian Victory*.)

Burma Victory was not completed until after the surrender of Japan: the atomic bombs dropped on Hiroshima and Nagasaki on 6 and 9 August 1945 brought the war to an abrupt end. The film was released in November 1945 and was a critical success, though it did not match the popular success of *Desert Victory* or *The True Glory*, which preceded it by three months. The *Daily Mail* thought it 'a magnificent close to the series of great British documentary war films'. William Whitebait in the *New Statesman* felt that '*Burma Victory* can take its place with *Desert Victory* and *The True Glory* among war documentaries, and I am not sure that it isn't a better film than either. It realises the jungle, for example, as *Desert Victory* – fine and dramatic though that film was – never realised the desert.' Campbell Dixon of the *Daily Telegraph* declared that it exhibited a 'dignity, honesty and generosity of spirit that puts the makers of some other so-called factual war films to shame'.[27]

The reception of *Burma Victory* needs to be understood in the context of the furore caused in Britain by the Hollywood film *Objective: Burma!* (1945), which provoked such controversy that it was withdrawn by its distributor (Warner Bros.) and not re-issued in Britain until 1952.[28] Directed by Raoul Walsh, *Objective: Burma!* was a combat film about an American patrol sent to destroy a radio station behind Japanese lines and then having to fight its way out of the jungle. It was the object of a sustained hate campaign from the British press which vilified it for suggesting that the war in Burma was won by Errol Flynn and a platoon of Yanks and for not acknowledging the role of the Fourteenth Army. In hindsight this reaction seems grossly unfair. For one thing, *Objective: Burma!* was not the entirely fictitious farrago that its detractors claimed. American special operations units were active in Burma – the film is loosely based on the 5307th Provisional Regiment led by Brigadier-General Frank Merrill (popular known as 'Merrill's Marauders') – and far from suggesting that the US Army won the war in Burma the film focuses on a single patrol with limited tactical objectives. And, for another thing, *Objective: Burma!* is very far from being the sort of flag-waving propaganda film that some critics have painted. It is, rather, an example of the mature combat film that had emerged in Hollywood by the end of the war. It provides a realistic representation of the physical hardships of jungle warfare – the platoon is decimated by a combination of Japanese attacks and disease – and acknowledges the human costs of war in that many of the men die. The film ends with Flynn's Captain Nelson holding up the dog tags of those killed during the mission and remarking: 'Here's what it cost'.[29]

Burma Victory, nevertheless, was promoted as the '*real* Burma film'. The opening of the film, indeed, sets up a contrast between documentary and fiction, as a short studio-shot sequence shows a couple of British soldiers sheltering in their tent from a tropical monsoon. One is cleaning his rifle; the other is reading a magazine. He reads aloud: 'Burma – there is romance in the very word, recalling a vision of white pagodas on the Irrawaddy gazing out across the peaceful countryside, a land of light-hearted people, lovers of flowers and bright colours, and women, dainty and self-possessed, ascending the pagoda steps, the morning sunshine beating down through paper parasols on the delicate beauty of their gay silks.' At this point he snorts in disgust and tosses the magazine out of the tent where it lands in the mud. Immediately the film disavows any notion that this was an 'easy' war in some exotic eastern paradise. Throughout the film, indeed, there is an emphasis on the extreme physical hardships faced by the troops. The terrain is inhospitable, the weather conditions inclement in the extreme and there are constant references to tropical diseases – malaria, dysentery and typhus are 'enemies more deadly than the Jap'.

Burma Victory is a record of the war in Burma from the British retreat in 1942 to the Japanese surrender, though it focuses mostly on the Allied offensive of 1944–5. It adopts the same story-telling techniques as the other 'Victory' films, particularly *Tunisian Victory*, such as explanatory maps and the device of multiple narrators: we see some events from the point of view of extracts from the diary of a British officer. Most of the film is compiled 'from material taken by British, Indian and American combat cameramen of SEAC', though there are some reconstructed sequences: Mountbatten discussing strategy with his chiefs of staff, unseen Japanese voices calling out in English at night in an attempt to trap the British troops, and General Slim planning the crossing of the Irrawaddy. The film chronicles the Japanese occupation of Burma in 1942; the creation of SEAC and appointment of the 'innovative and unorthodox' Mountbatten; the defence of Imphal and Kohima against heavy Japanese attacks in April–May 1944; Stilwell's advance to the north and building of the Ledo Road to connect with the Chinese; the Wingate operations to disrupt Japanese communications; Merrill's bold move to seize the strategically important airstrip at Myitkyina; Slim's advance south through the monsoon season in the late summer and autumn of 1944; the crossing of the Irrawaddy; and the hard-fought battles for Mandalay and Rangoon. The film ends on an emotive note as, following news of the Japanese surrender, the barrels of the field artillery are lowered and the guns go silent. Mountbatten's victory address to the men of SEAC is read over several shots of graves marked with crude wooden crosses bearing the legend 'A soldier of the XIV Army'. This elegiac ending differentiates *Burma Victory* from the triumphalism of

Desert Victory or *The True Glory* and locates it instead within a culture of remembrance.

That said, however, the politics of *Burma Victory* are fascinating both for what they include and what they exclude. Unlike *Tunisian Victory*, for example, there is no discussion of what ordinary soldiers believe they are fighting for – the sentimental talk of bringing 'the smiles back to the kids' faces all over the world' that intruded at the end of *Tunisian Victory*. This is understandable, however, given the political context of *Burma Victory*: indeed the film is careful to avoid any reference to the post-war world that would have raised the problematic question of what was to become of Burma after the war. Instead the film focuses on the collaborative nature of the campaign. The central theme of the film is teamwork and collaboration between the Allies and the different services on land, sea and air. Most films leave traces of the travails of their production: *Burma Victory*, however, presents a picture of a united and harmonious command with no suggestion of the strategic and political divisions that had existed. To this extent it fulfilled Mountbatten's primary objective. At the height of the difficulties with the production, he had written to Marshall: 'I can assure you that we are a very happy and united Command. The Anglo–American film being made by Colonel Capra of the Burma campaign will I am sure bring this out.'[30]

Burma Victory is also concerned to represent the campaign not just as an Allied effort but also as an imperial effort. It is at pains to show all the different nationalities involved, including British, Australians, Indians and East Africans. When Mountbatten addresses the troops, for example, he is surrounded by a racially diverse group which includes Sikhs and Gurkhas alongside British and Australians. The commentary emphasizes the heterogeneous make-up of the Commonwealth forces: 'In twelve months the men of the Fourteenth Army – British, Indian and African – had made a fighting advance of over a thousand miles across the worst country in the world.' Obviously mindful of the deteriorating situation in India, the film explicitly acknowledges the Indian contribution to the campaign. Thus SEAC's 'main strength was drawn from the great volunteer armies raised throughout India' and there are mentions for acts of heroism by the Gurkha Rifles (recruited from Nepal) and Victoria Cross winner Jermadahl Pakash Singh – the only individual mentioned by name in the film other than generals. The Fourteenth Army, indeed, like the British armies in the Middle East, should properly be described as an Anglo–Indian army.[31]

At the same time, however, there are significant omissions from the film's record of events. There is no mention of either the Burma Defence

5. Lord Louis Mountbatten addresses the troops of the Fourteenth Army in a staged scene from *Burma Victory* (1945).

Army or the Indian National Army – nationalist forces raised by the Japanese to fight against the British 'colonialists', though in the event they proved highly ineffective and made no significant military contribution. The Indian National Army was led by Subhas Chandra Bose, a Bengali nationalist who had lived for a time in Nazi Germany before returning to South East Asia where he raised an army from Indian prisoners of war in Malaya and Burma. Such indications of anti-British feeling are entirely absent from *Burma Victory*. The film avoids the touchy question of Burmese nationalism by presenting Burma as a piece of land to be fought over (hence the recourse to maps and diagrams) rather than through its people. Indeed, the Burmese themselves are conspicuously absent, except for one sequence that shows British troops welcomed into a village, including an obviously staged shot of an uncomfortable-looking General Slim with a 'peace garland' of flowers around his neck. The film suggests that the British were welcomed back: 'The villagers delighted to see us. Many had given us valuable information about the enemy before we got in. Tomorrow they're laying on a sort of festival which they call a *piu* – the first since we left Burma.' To be fair, however, the Japanese occupation had been notable for its brutality rather than offering the 'liberation' from colonialism that some had expected. The efforts of the Japanese to create their 'Greater East Asia Co-Prosperity Sphere' brought no material benefits for the people of the occupied territories. Although Japan offered Burma independence in August 1943, it was nominal rather than actual.

Yet in the longer term the main effect of the Japanese occupation was to accelerate the drive towards independence. As it turned out American fears that the British objective in Burma was to reassert their colonial authority were misplaced. In fact the British showed no desire to hang on to Burma after the war. In 1946 the Burmese nationalist leader Aung Sang, who had been installed at the head of a puppet government by the Japanese before joining the British and Indians in 1945, was invited to London where the Labour government of Clement Attlee agreed to independence for Burma. Aung Sang was assassinated shortly after returning to Rangoon and the negotiations were continued by U Nu, who became Burma's first prime minister following independence on 4 January 1948. By this time India had also gained its independence. This was ushered through by the last Viceroy of India, none other than Lord Mountbatten, appointed specifically by the Attlee government to oversee a speedy transition to independence. On 15 August 1947 British rule on the subcontinent ended and colonial India was partitioned into two new states: India and Pakistan. The liquidation of the British Empire had begun in earnest.

Notes

1   Peter Calvocoressi, Guy Wint and John Pritchard, *The Penguin History of the Second World War* (London: Penguin, 1999), p.349.
2   The National Archives, Kew, London, formerly the Public Records Office (hereafter TNA PRO), INF 1/849: 'Empire Publicity Campaign', Policy Committee Paper, 1 October 1940.
3   David Welch, *Propaganda and the German Cinema 1933–1945* (Oxford: Clarendon Press, 1983), pp.257–80.
4   Quoted in John Charmley, *Churchill: The End of Glory* (London: Hodder & Stoughton, 1993), p.431.
5   This argument is advanced by Correlli Barnett in *The Collapse of British Power* (London: Macmillan, 1972) and *The Audit of War: The Illusion and Reality of Britain as a Great Nation* (London: Macmillan, 1986). For a counter-argument see Paul Kennedy, *The Realities Behind Diplomacy: Background Influences on British External Policy 1865–1980* (London: Fontana, 1985).
6   Quoted in A. J. P. Taylor, *English History 1914–1945* (Oxford: Oxford University Press, 1965), p.535.
7   James Chapman, *The British at War: Cinema, State and Propaganda, 1939–1945* (London: I.B.Tauris, 1998), pp.144–54. See also I. C. Jarvie, 'The Burma Campaign

on Film: *Objective Burma* (1945), *The Stilwell Road* (1945) and *Burma Victory* (1945)', *Historical Journal of Film, Radio and Television*, 8: 1 (1988), pp.55–73; and Michael Paris, 'Filming the People's War: *The Dawn Guard, Desert Victory, Tunisian Victory* and *Burma Victory*', in Alan Burton, Tim O'Sullivan and Paul Wells (eds), *The Family Way: The Boulting Brothers and British Film Culture* (Trowbridge: Flicks Books, 2000), pp.97–108.

8   Mountbatten had a keen interest in the film industry. He would later become president of the Royal Naval Film Corporation, the Kinematograph Renters' Society and the Society of Film and Television Arts. Mountbatten's son-in-law was the producer John Brabourne, whose films include *Murder on the Orient Express* and *A Passage to India*. See Adrian Smith, 'Mountbatten Goes to the Movies: Promoting the Heroic Myth through Cinema', *Historical Journal of Film, Radio and Television*, 26: 3 (2006), pp.395–416.

9   Andrew Roberts, *A History of the English-Speaking Peoples since 1900* (London: Weidenfeld & Nicolson, 2006), p.302. See also Christopher Thorne, *Allies of a Kind: The USA, Britain and the War against Japan* (London: Hamish Hamilton, 1978).

10 TNA PRO PREM 4 12/1: Stalin to Churchill, 29 March 1943.

11 See Anthony Aldgate, 'Creative Tensions: *Desert Victory*, the Army Film Unit and Anglo–American Rivalry, 1943–5', in Philip M. Taylor (ed.), *Britain and the Cinema in the Second World War* (London: Macmillan, 1988), pp.144–67; Aldgate, 'Mr Capra Goes to War: Frank Capra, the British Army Film Unit and Anglo–American Travails in the Production of *Tunisian Victory*', *Historical Journal of Film, Radio and Television*, 11: 1 (1991), pp.21–39; and Clive Coultass, '*Tunisian Victory* – A Film Too Late?', *Imperial War Museum Review*, 1 (1986), pp.64–73.

12 TNA PRO WO 203/5165: Joubert to Mountbatten, 18 April 1944.

13 Ibid., Joubert to Korda, 2 June 1944.

14 Ibid., Mountbatten to Marshall, 14 July 1944.

15 Ibid., 'Film of the Burma Campaign', extract from minutes of SAC's 135th meeting, 21 July 1944.

16 Ibid., Telegram from MOI to SEAC, 22 July 1944.

17 Ibid., Joubert to Bracken, 24 July 1944.

18 Ibid., Bracken to Joubert, 27 July 1944.

19 Ibid., Joubert to Bracken, 31 July 1944.

20 National Archives, Washington DC, RG 59/740.0011, Microfilm 982 Roll 246: 'South East Asia Motion Picture', 19 September 1944. My thanks to Ian Jarvie for this reference.

21 Ibid., Cordell Hull to Henry Stimson (Secretary of State for War), 17 October 1944.

22 TNA PRO WO 203/5165: Mountbatten to US War Department, 21 January 1945.

23 TNA PRO FO 371/37750: George Archibald to Radcliffe, 24 March 1945.

24 TNA PRO WO 203/5165: Mountbatten to Bracken, 27 March 1945.

25 TNA PRO CAB 122/1163: Mountbatten to War Office, 25 April 1945.

26 TNA PRO WO 203/5165: Bracken to F. M. Wilson (Joint Staff Mission, Washington DC), 7 May 1945.

27 BFI Library microfiche on *Burma Victory*: *Daily Mail*, 26 October 1945; *New Statesman*, 3 November 1945; *Daily Telegraph*, 25 October 1945.

28 I. C. Jarvie, 'Fanning the Flames: Anti-American Reaction to *Operation* [sic] *Burma* (1945)', *Historical Journal of Film, Radio and Television*, 1: 2 (1981), pp.17–137.

29 See Jeanine Basinger, *The World War II Combat Film: Anatomy of a Genre* (Middletown CT: Wesleyan University Press, rev. edn, 2003), pp.120–38.

30 TNA PRO WO 203/5165: Mountbatten to Marshall, 28 January 1945.

31 For an account of the role of imperial troops in the British armies, see Ashley Jackson, *The British Empire and the Second World War* (London: Hambledon Continuum, 2006).

5

FACING THE STAMPEDE OF DECOLONIZATION

Elephant Walk (1954)

It was a familiar story. A young woman marries a handsome stranger and travels to his home. She finds that home sinister, haunted by a dark past with locked doors that may not be opened. Her husband seems like a different person in this environment and his familiars resent her entry into their world. She takes her stand. Will love triumph or will his world subsume her? Variants of this archetypal scenario have graced human literature for centuries from Bluebeard and Scheherazade to Charlotte Bonté's *Jane Eyre* and Daphne DuMaurier's *Rebecca*, and became part of movie culture thanks to the successful screen adaptations of the latter novel in 1940 and the former in 1944. In 1954, Hollywood – ever open to fusions between genres – cemented a match between these gothic marriage melodramas and the imperial adventure in the form of the Paramount film *Elephant Walk*. Elizabeth Taylor played the ingénue out of place and Peter Finch her husband, but the empire was more than just the setting for this film. In *Elephant Walk* the role of the genre's sinister secret – the mass murdering husband, mad woman in the attic or faithless first wife – was played by the institution of imperialism. *Elephant Walk* flirted with a vein of criticism of the imperial project. It pays especial attention to the role of women in empire and uses a woman's point of view as the sounding board for its critique. More than this, the process of making the film reveals the stirrings of an American awareness of a different empire – an empire not of tea plantations but of ideological influence – and the celluloid heart of Hollywood itself.

The Plot

The movie opens with a diary entry in which a narrator – Ceylon tea planter John Wiley (Peter Finch) – speaks of the 'evil' that has haunted his home since his father killed the mate of a bull elephant and defiantly built his bungalow – Elephant Walk – across the trail the beasts used to get to water. He speaks of the perpetual vigilance necessary to keep the elephants at bay and his regret that he forgot the danger when he met his wife. The scene shifts to post-war England and a bookshop in Shillingworth-on-Thames where Wiley is meeting his secret fiancée Ruth (Elizabeth Taylor) to discuss the final plans for their marriage and journey to his home in Ceylon. They fly to the island via Paris, a plot device which explained the breathtaking array of clothes worn by Taylor in the rest of the movie (designed by Edith Head). On landing in Ceylon they drive to his plantation in his father's Rolls Royce. Ruth is entranced by the beauty of the island but their journey is interrupted by an encounter with the rogue bull elephant on the road. Ruth sees a darkness in her husband as he confronts the beast and scares it off. It bodes ill for their future.

Ruth is initially overwhelmed by the magnificence of Elephant Walk but life on the plantation proves lonely, with no other European woman in the district. Things are made worse by weekly visits of a contingent of male guests from the neighbouring plantations. Her husband entertains these guests lavishly and with excessive diversions such as drunken games of bicycle polo on the veranda. They are all obsessed with celebrating the memory of his father – 'the guv'nor' – and keeping his traditions alive. The head servant, Appuhamy (Abraham Sofaer), is similarly obsessed, praying each morning at the father's grave on the back lawn, and confiding his suspicion of the new mistress of the house. Ruth grows to hate the guv'nor and resent the traditions maintained in his name. She is appalled to learn that he forced his own wife to return to Ceylon from convalescence in England, and that this led to her death in childbirth. She fixates on his locked study, kept as a shrine to his memory.

Ruth's only friend is the American overseer on the plantation – Dick Carver (Dana Andrews) – who is sceptical of the cult of the guv'nor and is planning to leave Ceylon. When her husband John breaks a leg in a drunken escapade, Ruth prevails on Dick to stay and help run the plantation until he is fit again. Ruth and Dick are drawn towards an affair, but Ruth holds back. Ruth is placated when John promises her a surprise and she is initially charmed when a troupe of native dancers arrives to perform at the plantation. To her horror she realizes that this is a celebration of the guv'nor's birthday. She slips away from the party and finds that the door to the forbidden study is open. The room inside is dominated by a vast and intimidating portrait of the guv'nor. When John collapses drunk, Ruth throws his regulars out of the bungalow. He rebukes her the following morning. He accuses her of secretly hating his father; she leaves the house and asks Dick to help her escape. Their escape is interrupted by an outbreak of cholera. But the outbreak gives Ruth's life at Elephant Walk a purpose. She rallies to help fight the disease and wins the admiration of Appuhamy. Crazed by a coincidental drought the elephants stampede towards the bungalow where Ruth is sleeping. Cholera has removed the beaters who usually keep the herd at bay and the elephants break into the compound. They crush Appuhamy against his old master's grave and smash into the bungalow, starting a fire and driving Ruth upstairs. John arrives in the nick of time to rescue her. They escape through the forbidden

6. Stampede: Appuhamy (Abraham Sofaer) tries to turn back the elephants, while Ruth (Elizabeth Taylor) looks on in *Elephant Walk* (1954).

study where they see the portrait of the guv'nor burn in the fire. As the house burns Dick accepts that he has lost his chance with Ruth, and John and Ruth are reconciled. As the Monsoon rains fall at last, Ruth says that she is sorry that the house has burned. John replies: 'I'm not. Let them have their elephant walk, Ruth. We'll build a new place; a home somewhere else.'

Reading *Elephant Walk*

In its final form *Elephant Walk* included several major strands that commented on European imperialism. The most interesting element of the story was the elephants themselves. The idea of a bungalow built arrogantly across their migratory path, the perpetual effort to keep them in check, and the final confrontation in which the imperial edifice of the previous generation is swept away, seemed like a thinly veiled metaphor for the rising tide of Third World nationalism and on-rush of decolonization. The characters in the movie make no direct reference to the establishment of an independent Ceylon in 1948, and the forces of law enforcing the quarantine are white, suggesting a colonial setting. Against this John Wiley at one point curses government regulations which prevent him from shooting 'their precious beasts' in a way that suggests it is not quite 'his' government any more.[1] The imperialists are unflatteringly depicted: the guv'nor is a veritable Cecil Rhodes by appearance and by deed; each revelation of his doings is accompanied by the most unsettling chords in the score by Franz Waxman. His acolytes seem to be sponging, drunken relics, and his son is a weak prisoner of his own history.

The American character, Dick, offers a different approach to the developing world. He eschews liquor and has no interest in the native women. He has brought a modern approach including new technology to tea production, and even dresses in modern clothes. He seems to represent the America of the Marshall Plan and President Truman's 'Point Four aid'. He is content to work hard in the developing world and then leave. He seems like the wave of the future.

But there is a level of complication. The elephants may be in revolt, but the Ceylonese are not. The old retainer Appuhamy is as devoted to the guv'nor and his ways as any of the Europeans and the staff of the plantation are shown to clearly respect John Wiley. The conflict is chiefly in the mind of Ruth, and is based around her outsider's perspective – the prejudice doubtless shared by most of the audience with its implicit rejection of the old ways, repulsion at the excesses of plantation life when compared to the austerity of post-war Britain, and attraction towards the values of the American what ever the Ceylonese think. There is a conflict over her gender role. She wants to have an active part in managing the house but is blocked by Appuhamy. Her designated function is symbolized by the classical dress she wears at the guv'nor's birthday celebration and the heavy gold chain with an elephant motif that the guv'nor created for successive mistresses of Elephant Walk – a blend of goddess and slave girl in the decaying successor to Rome.

But *Elephant Walk* has a twist. As the film draws to a conclusion Ruth learns that she has been mistaken. When she rebukes John over the drunkenness of his friends he extols their hard work: 'These drunks as you call them work harder than dogs all the week. They go for months without taking a drink and you object to them coming here and having the little relaxation they can get.' She scoffs at this, but is impressed when two of these friends offer to help during the cholera epidemic. The American suddenly seems less worthy and even cynical in contrast, observing: 'What's the use of killing yourself tying to save some poor natives who are going to die anyway.' She defends her husband from Dick's criticism when he shoots a native who tries to break the quarantine in the leg. She finds purpose in fighting the epidemic. We see her driving a car and speaking to the natives in their own language. Her final reconciliation with John over the ashes of Elephant Walk suggests not that European empires are wrong and should be swept away by the stampede of decolonization, but rather that need to be better understood by outsiders, that the excesses of the past cannot be maintained, and that a new way of living with the developing world needs to be found which allows for the co-existence of the stampeding elephants and the European-owned tea plantation.

The First Steps of *Elephant Walk*

The process by which *Elephant Walk* came to the screen adds another layer of significance to the film. Like so many Hollywood movies, *Elephant Walk* sprang from a studio's desire to appeal to a profitable demographic group – in this case women – with the draw of a bankable star in fabulous gowns and the power of both the Technicolor process and a movie shot in a spectacular location. In the early 1950s Hollywood burst the bonds of Southern California and began a cycle of expensive location pictures. The practice also allowed the studios to access funds that had accumulated overseas which were frozen in foreign currencies and seemed likely to raise foreign interest in the films too. Biblical epics were a major genre for such treatment, but empire movies also flourished. European empires provided the perfect locations – exotic with the necessary infrastructure to make filming possible – and a wealth of stories to tell. MGM led the way in 1950 with the authentic African locations of *King Solomon's Mines* and landed the third best grossing film of that year. Their adaptation of *Kim* (1951) with its Indian locations did respectable business in 1952 earning 12th place. John Huston followed and did better with *The African Queen* (1951) and Twentieth Century-Fox hit pay-dirt with the Egyptian and Kenyan locations in *The Snows of Kilimanjaro* (1952), providing the sixth and fourth best earners of 1952 respectively. MGM packed John Ford off to East Africa to make *Mogambo* (1953) with Clark Gable, Ava Gardner and Grace Kelly – a remake of a rubber plantation melodrama from 1932 called *Red Dust* and earned a respectable eighth place at the US box office.[2] By January 1953 with 5 fewer pictures in production in Hollywood than in 1952 and 16 scheduled to begin shooting overseas in the first quarter of the year alone, the trade unions were expressing concern.[3] *Elephant Walk* would be Paramount's entry into what seemed a lucrative field.

The source novel *Elephant Walk* had been published in 1949, written by Robert Standish (the pen name of British-born writer Digby George Gaherty). Walking in the footsteps of Somerset Maugham, Standish had a reputation for novels set in foreign climes, specializing in East Asia and the Caribbean. His book jackets alluded to an exotic life including experiences planting tea in Ceylon, working on a sheep station in Australia and living in Japan. His first hit – *The Three Bamboos* – a family saga set in Japan was eagerly read in the aftermath of Pearl Harbor as a window on the 'mind' of the enemy.[4] *Elephant Walk* had its own claim to topicality, being published in the immediate wake of Ceylonese independence in 1948. There were significant differences between the novel and eventual film. Standish set his story around the time of the Great War. His planter – George Carey – was already middle aged at the time of his wedding, and his foreman – Wilding – is not American but simply younger. As in the movie, a love triangle develops. In the novel, however, Wilding and Ruth consummate their affair on the eve of his departure for the Great War. She bears his child but, when she is told Wilding is missing in action, she passes the infant off as her husband's. Wilding returns from war a changed man. He roughly attempts to rekindle his affair with Ruth and also maintains a native concubine – Rayna – directed into his path by Appuhamy in an attempt to head off his relationship with Ruth. Ruth realizes that she no longer loves Wilding and is reconciled with her husband. The single rogue bull elephant attacks and demolishes the house, freeing them from the shadows of the past and allowing them a clear start.[5]

Hollywood was swift to recognize the potential of *Elephant Walk* to become a motion picture. Shortly after its publication, *Gunga Din* star Douglas Fairbanks Jr secured the rights for some $35,000. His motives remain obscure, but at the time he was deeply committed to a personal crusade to find material to promote understanding of Britain and its ways in the United States and also interested in producing motion pictures overseas to take advantage of frozen funds.[6] He opened negotiations with MGM to secure Deborah Kerr as his co-star,[7] and hired the screenwriter D. M. Marshman Jr (fresh from his Oscar for *Sunset Boulevard*) to provide the script. By February of 1952 Marshman had completed two drafts of the screenplay based closely on the novel, but with a full stampede rather than a single rogue elephant attack as the finale.[8] Fairbanks had already suspended plans to film until late 1952 blaming inclement weather in Ceylon.[9] In March 1952 he travelled to the island with his business partner Alexander MacDonald.[10] Ceylon was receptive to international film production,[11] and Fairbanks successfully secured local co-operation for the film, but shortly after the trip decided to focus on pressing television projects. He sold the rights, script and associated research material to Paramount for $80,000. At Paramount the project became the responsibility of Irving Asher, a producer who had bid against Fairbanks in the original sale of the film rights. Asher had a personal knowledge of Ceylon stemming from his war service as a Lieutenant Colonel in the US army attached to the staff of Lord Mountbatten.[12]

Paramount knew that the journey to the screen would not be easy. When the studio's head of domestic and foreign censorship, Luigi Luraschi, sent a synopsis of the novel to the administrator of the Hays Code – Joseph Breen – he received a chastening, predictable reply. Breen found the whole story 'unacceptable' as 'a treatment of adultery without any compensating moral values or without any recognition of the immorality of such a situation'. He also raised concerns over the 'unacceptable side issue – the procuring of native women for the white men involved in the story'.[13] Paramount's writer would have his work cut out.

Asher's choice of talent on *Elephant Walk* revealed his sense of the film as a blend of landscape and melodrama. He had experience of big budget location pictures – including an associate producer credit on Korda's *The Four Feathers* (1939) – and he hired a team with similar experience. He secured John Lee Mahin, writer of *Mogambo* and *Red Dust* and still under contract to MGM, to write the screenplay.[14] He selected a director with a track record of historical pictures – William Dieterle – to direct,[15] he also recruited Loyal Griggs – veteran of *Shane* (1953), and a clutch of other outdoor films, as cinematographer. He then chose art director J. McMillan Johnson who

had worked in Korda's *Jungle Book* (1942). He then set about finding a star
with the pull to capture the target audience. Asher's first choice – Elizabeth
Taylor – was out of the running as she was soon to have a baby.[16] Instead he
fixed on Vivien Leigh – who carried memories of *Gone with the Wind* (1939)
and an Oscar for *A Streetcar Named Desire* (1951) in her train – and hoped
that her husband, Laurence Olivier, might also join the project.[17]

John Lee Mahin completed his first draft of the screenplay in October
1952. He had already taken a series of decisions that shaped the film –
transposing the action to the modern era, reducing the adultery to a temptation and making the romantic challenger an American.[18] At the PCA,
Breen now had few concerns. His caution was limited to a scene in which
Appuhamy procures the native dancer Rayna to distract the American
from his master's wife and a general worry that 'the greatest possible care
in the selection and photographing of the costumes and dresses for your
women'.[19]

No sooner had the issues with the PCA been resolved than another
crisis broke. The State Department refused to allow Dieterle to travel raising concerns over his connection to radicals including former vice president Henry Wallace. A payment of $10,000 to a lawyer settled the matter.[20]
Thus liberated, Dieterle and Asher travelled to the UK in December to
secure the British crew necessary to make a Technicolor film within the
Commonwealth and cast their stars. In mid-December they succeeded in
securing Vivien Leigh for the film. She told the newspapers that she jumped
at the chance to play a normal, healthy girl: 'Oh the bliss not to having to
go mad, commit suicide or contemplate murder.'[21] It would prove an ironic
quip. Although, after much press speculation, Oliver was unavailable to
play the plantation owner, the actor suggested some substitutes including
Rex Harrison and Michael Rennie. Asher asked after the availability of
Trevor Howard.[22] He had reportedly already also considered Clark Gable,
Claude Rains, Ralph Richardson and Marlon Brando.[23] In the end the studio settled on Olivier's protégé Peter Finch as a substitute. Sources are
divided on exactly how Finch came to be cast. Irving Asher said that it
was Olivier's idea born of his admiration for Finch,[24] but biographers of
Olivier and Leigh routinely paint the decision as Leigh's idea and her sub-
terfuge to be alone with the handsome young actor, thousands of miles
away from her husband.[25] One motive no one seems to mention is that
with Finch, like Leigh, under contract to Laurence Olivier productions,
Sir Larry collected a nice cheque for their joint loan to Paramount. Leigh's
agreement came with a catch. Her schedule required that the location
shooting be completed by the spring. The studio knew it would be working against the clock.[26]

Asher still had his doubts about the screenplay and brought in three experienced writers in succession to work over John Lee Mahin's draft. Each brought their own perspective. The first to doctor the script was Ketti Frings, a talented writer who would later find fame as the author of the Broadway hit *Look Homeward Angel*. Her role was acknowledged in the credits registered with the Writers' Guild only. With the film already in production Paramount hired British playwright Lesley Storm – fresh from adapting Graham Greene's novel of life in African colonies *The Heart of the Matter* (1953).[27] Paramount flew her to Ceylon, telling the press that her role would be to inject British idiom into the script. She was not credited on the eventual film.[28] The final hand in the script was that of Liam O'Brien, brother of actor Edmond O'Brien and a jobbing screenwriter who declined credit, whose input into the screenplay coincided with some of the most significant changes.[29]

The Hidden Hand

As post-war America embraced its destiny of global leadership and looked for ways to engage the foreign publics on whom the success of such leadership depended, the motion picture industry became increasingly aware of its international obligations. Hollywood had always appreciated export revenue – generally only breaking into profit when a film was released overseas – but in the new world, the studios began to perceive their own value as an ideological beacon for the world. The new president of the Motion Picture Export Association (MPEA), Eric Johnston, was evangelical on the subject. America needed to not only display its values to the world but also take care not to offend the world with thoughtless stereotyping.[30] At the same time as Hollywood was moving into the business of diplomacy the US government was realizing the need to exploit the power of mass communication. In late 1947, as Capitol Hill debated legislation to maintain the wartime international information machine for Cold War work, the newly created Central Intelligence Agency launched a program of covert propaganda and cultural influence aimed at both enemies and friendly states.[31] The system was chaotic, but all this changed in 1953 with the election of President Dwight D. Eisenhower. His election pledges included a promise to reinvigorate American propaganda around the world. To accomplish this task Eisenhower appointed publisher and wartime propaganda veteran C. D. Jackson to be his special adviser for psychological warfare. Now declassified, C. D. Jackson's files contain the evidence: letters from a CIA contact in Hollywood regarding the manipulation of film production to fit foreign policy needs. One of the movies so manipulated was *Elephant Walk*.[32]

The letters from the CIA contact are unsigned and addressed merely to 'Dear Owen,' but, using evidence contained within them, film historian David Eldridge has been able to conclusively identify the author as Luigi Luraschi, Paramount's head of domestic and foreign censorship. In addition to fielding the concerns expressed by Breen, Luraschi worked within Paramount to inject an awareness of the needs of foreign audiences. He also served as a leading light of the International Committee of the Motion Picture Association encouraging his peers at the other studios to do the same. Luraschi was uniquely well qualified for such work. An Italian born in London and educated in Switzerland, he spoke five languages including Arabic. He may not have been actually drawing a salary from the CIA, but referred to the agency as 'our organization' and his surviving letters make it clear that he was seeking to do its work.

Luraschi first mentions *Elephant Walk* in a letter of 16 January 1953. He billed the film as 'pure love, adventure, melodrama'. He noted: 'Perhaps can get a couple of points across with the American character, Dana Andrews, but unfortunately the role isn't exactly what we would have liked to have said.' One late change to the script that helped lift the American character within the piece was the deletion of his entire affair with the dancing girl Rayna. While Dick Carver's halo is somewhat tarnished by his cynicism during the cholera outbreak this is nothing compared to his character's arc in Mahin's original screenplay which culminates in his death in the cholera outbreak in Rayna's arms, let alone the caddish behavior of the parallel character in the Standish novel.

Luraschi's next mention of *Elephant Walk* came on 6 February 1953 when he updated his contact with his efforts to reduce the incidence of drunken American characters in Paramount's output. Of *Elephant Walk* he noted: 'Keeping drunkenness to strict plot purposes only, and instead of it spreading over a whole group of British planters, am trying to reduce it and condense it to one or two others.' While the theme was still prominent in the film, the American remained sober, moreover, although drunk, the planters leave most politely when that is requested and are redeemed by their willingness to help during the cholera outbreak.

In the same letter Luraschi talks about his work in improving the representation of 'Orientals'. He writes:

> In *Elephant Walk* we have had a scene before Bhuddist [sic] shrines re written, to remove jocular feeling, and possible disrespect from dialogue of principals. Understand, Bhuddist organization in

Ceylon made same request of producer, so we are on the beam.
New dialogue has been approved by Bhuddists.

His concern was over a scene in Mahin's draft in which Ruth and Dick
ride out to visit one of Ceylon's most famous sights: the ancient capital
of Polonnaruwa. Dick shows Ruth a massive statue of Buddha reclining.
In the original version of the scene the American incorrectly introduced
it to Ruth as 'the dead Buddha of Polonnaruwa – and his mourning dis-
ciple, Ananda'. though this was later changed to 'sleeping Buddha of
Polonnaruwa'. The jocularity came immediately after this as he answers
Ruth's curiosity about 'the history behind this' with an elaborate mono-
logue concerning ancient invasions, dynastic politics and an inappropri-
ately eager child bride. When Ruth asks how he learned so much history
he confesses that he made it all up.[33] The effect was potentially both dis-
respectful to the location and reflected poorly on the American character.
In the final version of the scene – dated 4 April 1953 – the characters are
simply awed by the place:

DICK: This is a very sacred place to all Buddhists. That's the
       sleeping Buddha of Polonnaruwa – and his faithful disci-
       ple, Ananda.
RUTH: It's so beautiful – and still. I feel like we're trespassing.
DICK: They like company ... let's sit somewhere.[34]

Though Luraschi does not report it, the final script also lost a line which
exposed European mockery of Eastern belief. In early versions, when Mahin
had the planter named Gilly explain the local belief that the elephants are
really 'elephant people', he follows up by scoffing: 'That's the stupid super-
stition of your Asiatics for you.'[35]

   Then there was the issue of the representation of Asian characters. The
prevalence of servants in the story posed a problem for Luraschi and underlined the need for some sort of balance. He assured his CIA colleague that

Have made sure that the character Dr. Pereira (good character)
will be cast with actor impersonating full-blooded Ceylonese.
Very dignified doctor, who takes care of our sick male lead, and
is spearhead against cholera epidemic. Have also asked, during
epidemic, he send for a couple of Ceylonese interns and nurses to
help; this is to balance Ceylonese against coolie labor. Educated
Ceylonese will handle themselves on equal level with when dealing with Europeans.

Pereira was indeed portrayed as obviously 'other' by one of Hollywood's pan-ethnic character actors, Abner Biberman, in heavy tan make-up, who ironically had also played the archetypal evil Indian: the leading Thug warrior, Chota, in *Gunga Din* (1939). The Mahin/Frings version of the screenplay described him as 'a cultured, humorous Sinhalese of 50 or so in a Palm Beach suit.[36] He proved an admirable character, cool under pressure, knowledgeable in Western medicine, and the only character other than the bull

7. Doctoring the Picture: Elizabeth Taylor (Ruth) with Abner Biberman in the 'positive' native role as Dr Pereira, inserted into the Script *Elephant Walk* (1954) at the request of CIA agent Luigi Luraschi.

elephant to have confronted the guv'nor in his lifetime, but the problem of the other Ceylonese characters remained.

Though the PCA had cleared the script, the potentially negative character of Rayna – the seductress hired by Appuhamy to distract Dick who was set to promise 'I won't make you angry like the master's lady did' – remained until she was cut either because of Luraschi's wish to minimize negative elements in the portrayal of the American and Ceylonese characters or to simplify the final section of the movie in the difficult circumstances of the change of female star. For whatever reason, the final film included only sustained visual introduction of Rayna (played by the Hawaiian actress Mylee Haulani) which goes nowhere beyond Dick remarking to John that she was not his 'type'.[37] As for the other characters, the plantation workers were shown to be docile and obedient, if in some cases given to panic in the face of the epidemic, but there is no humour at their expense to parallel the comic drilling of Gunga Din back in 1939 or the fun at the expense of the native characters present in a film as late as John Huston's *The Man Who Would Be King* (1975). A substantial burden of representing Ceylon fell on the shoulders of Abraham Sofaer as Appuhamy. He retained his dignity as a character and rose above his 'Mrs Danvers' role in the plot. In the final phase of the writing he acquired a speech in which he not only accepted Ruth but also expressed his admiration for Pereira and looked to a more Western future for Ceylon: 'Yes, mistress – a day will come when my people will no longer fear inoculation. They will listen to the master – and Dr. Pereira, as I did. They will learn. They are learning fast.'[38] At this point Luraschi's attention shifted elsewhere, while the story of making of *Elephant Walk* unfolded, as bizarrely as any fiction, on location in Ceylon.

Filming *Elephant Walk*

The cast arrived in Ceylon in the final days of January 1953 to the delight of the locals. *The Times of Ceylon* reported 'the biggest boom that the elephant hiring industry has known since Noah'.[39] But the production was troubled and immediately ran into difficulty with its star. Vivien Leigh was acting so strangely off camera that Dieterle began to routinely shoot scenes in such a way that she would be anonymous in long shots and more easily replaced at a later date. Some biographers writing in a manner worthy of authors of colonial melodrama speak of Leigh somehow reawakening dark, repressed memories of her own childhood in India. Most focus on the lurid facts of her torrid affair with Finch and swing into a mania that included hallucinations. The 72-hour flight back to Hollywood from Ceylon finally pushed her over the edge and shortly into the filming at Paramount she began to miss appointments on set. The crew made it up by filming material that did not require her presence but the problem did not ease and the picture shut down on 12 March. It soon became clear that she was suffering from a full-blown nervous breakdown, eventually expressed in her lapsing into monologues from her stage/screen role as Blanche DuBois in *A Streetcar Named Desire*. Paramount looked desperately for a substitute.[40] On 20 March press reported that Elizabeth Taylor – whose baby had now arrived – would be taking the role.[41] Filming resumed on 21 March. With some swift refitting of costumes, nine days of filming to duplicate the scenes already shot, and bold use of back-projection, the picture returned to schedule.[42] Long shots of Leigh were used for scenes at the airport and on the car journey to the plantation, but no one seemed to notice.[43]

For Irving Asher, Elizabeth Taylor truly saved the day. Years later he told her unauthorized biographer Kitty Kelly:

> Even after Vivien left I had problems. Peter Finch continued to carry on about his tremendous romance and love affair with her, which had been going on in Ceylon, and Dana Andrews was drinking so heavily that sometimes we couldn't shoot his scenes. Elizabeth was a dream to work with. She arrived on time, knew her lines, and was really quite patient and helpful with Dana. Sometimes he was in such bad shape that we had to shoot him from behind, and in their scenes together Elizabeth led him. She was thoroughly professional.[44]

The film still had some stings in the tail for Asher and his crew. They had real difficulty getting the elephants to trumpet during the final stampede.[45] To avoid 'trouble', the team used only female elephants for the scene, which required the gluing of prosthetic tusks to a gentle female named Emmy.[46] Abraham Sofaer broke seven ribs while lifted aloft by a mechanical trunk and Elizabeth Taylor nearly lost an eye to a metal splinter while posing for stills with her co-stars in a jeep in front of a wind fan.[47] The team breathed a sigh of relief when production finally wrapped on 20 May with the total budget still under $3,000,000 – albeit a princely sum for the era.[48]

Release and After

The film was held back for release until April 1954. Whatever the sensitivities that Luigi Luraschi had successfully injected into the script, the marketing campaign, within the USA at least, aimed for the Orientalist jugular. The poster screamed 'There's nothing bigger than *Elephant Walk*' with a banner image of elephants stampeding over fleeing dusky 'native hordes' clad only in dhotis and turbans. It promised: 'Romance! Action!' and 'The most dangerous scenes of destruction ever filmed!' Much publicity played on the idea of an elephant that never forgets: 'You'll never forget the scenes of stolen love... at the ancient temple of love! You'll never forget the exotic native dancing girls! You'll never forget the overwhelming spectacle as wild elephants run amuck!' One advertisement locked directly onto the idea of the elephants as a political allegory by promising the 'rebellion of the wild elephants'.[49]

Critics were not kind about the film. In *The New York Times* Bosley Crowther admired the Ceylonese backgrounds but felt the human story was a joke, and contrasted it with more believable drama of Paramount's low-budget contemporaneous South American pot-boiler *The Naked Jungle*, which he thought looked as if it had 'made on a California celery farm'.[50] The *Chicago Tribune* found the film 'colorful and lavishly done', but unfairly considered Elizabeth Taylor merely 'pretty if plump'.[51] *Variety* complained: 'the plot plods along as ponderously as the pachyderms'.[52] *Time* opined 'though hardly a work of art, [it] is an astonishing feat of manufacture', for the skilled substitution of Taylor so late in the process.[53] The Ceylon Association of America was outraged by the picture and wrote letters of protest to leaders on the island. Its secretary, Ivan Nicolle, told the *New York Herald Tribune* that he considered the film to be 'in extremely bad taste and horribly distorted' and that it 'does not promote the understanding which is essential to peace and goodwill among nations'.[54] The only compensation was that the film raised almost no objections from censors around the world. The MPEA reported only one deletion in a foreign market. The Danes cut the shot of Appuhamy lifted up in the elephant's trunk as simply too horrific.[55]

Audiences made up their own minds regardless, and *Elephant Walk* earned an estimated $6 million gross in its domestic release alone – paltry compared to the $16 million earned by the year's blockbuster – *White Christmas* – but more than covering the $2.8 million production costs. *Variety* listed *Elephant Walk* as the 27th best box office performer of 1954.[56] Undeterred, the studios continued to blend the melodrama and imperial subjects. Twentieth Century-Fox remade *The Rains Came* (1939) as *The Rains of Ranchipur* (1955) with authentic Pakistani locations but with an inauthentic Pakistani – Richard Burton in blackface – as the male lead. At MGM George Cukor directed *Bhowani Junction* (1956), again with elaborate scenes in Pakistan and Ava Gardner in top form as the mixed race protagonist. The films grossed around $5.2 million and $4.2 million respectively, earning the thirty-first and forty-third places among the best earners of 1956.[57] While *Bhowani Junction* ended the vogue for big budget imperial melodrama, Ceylon remained a valued location, starring as both itself and Burma in David Lean's *The Bridge on the River Kwai* (1957).

Luigi Luraschi continued to tune Paramount movies to international opinion in concert with his colleagues on the MPEA international committee. The relationship with Washington became formal following the establishment of the United States Information Agency (USIA), which as late as 1960 still spoke proudly of a special role reviewing Hollywood scripts for impact overseas. During the course of 1960 Luraschi left Parmount to work with Dino De Laurentiis in Italy. Coincidentally or not, by 1961 USIA's cozy relationship with Hollywood was a thing of the past. President Kennedy's new director of USIA, Edward R. Murrow, was left trying to influence Hollywood with broad speeches berating movie makers for showing the underside of American life. The studio bosses were unimpressed.[58]

Robert Standish continued to produce novels of doings in exotic places though he would never again be adapted for the screen. In 1962 he received a small compliment from the midst of America's own imperial adventure: a fable from his novel *The Three Bamboos* became the central metaphor of a 'breezy tract' entitled 'Bend with the Wind' created by the US embassy in Saigon to instruct Americans resident in Vietnam how to behave in various crises. Evidently an Englishman's novel about Japan was considered local knowledge – or local enough to help.[59] Standish died in 1981 at his home in Valbonne in France. His novels were long since forgotten. His passing was publicly marked only by a curt notice in *The Times*.[60]

In the 1980s the experience of women became a major window onto the experience of the latter days of empire with a string of worthy British and American literary adaptations including David Lean's *A Passage to India* (1984), Sydney Pollack's *Out of Africa* (1985) and the lavish Granada television adaptation of Paul Scott's Raj Quartet: *The Jewel in the Crown* (1984). The female perspective clearly brought a valuable dimension to the representation of empire, with its enduring masculine mythology. Perhaps *Elephant Walk* was headed vaguely in the right direction after all.

Notes

[1]   At an early stage of production the action was described by the artistic team as located in 1946; see, for example, Herrick library: Paramount Pictures production records, *Elephant Walk*, f3, Edith Head to Vivien Leigh, 20 December 1952; however p.34, of the 'yellow version' of the script, by John Lee Mahin 8 October 1952 mentions an event from 1946 as significantly distant. It is probable that in the end the studio simply fudged this issue.

2   The earnings are drawn from the annual estimates of domestic rental earnings compiled by *Variety* for their anniversary issue. The relevant issues are 3 January 1951, 2 January 1952, 7 January 1952, 13 January 1954. The domestic gross figure (combining rental earnings with the studio's share of the takings) is around double the rental figure. *King Solomon's Mines* (MGM, dirs Compton Bennett and Andrew Marton, 1950) earned c. $4.4 million rental, $8.8 million gross; *Kim* (MGM, dir. Victor Saville, 1950) earned c. $2.8 million rental, $5.6 gross; *Snows of Kilimanjaro* (Fox, dir. Henry King, 1952) earned c. $6.5 million rental, $13 million gross; *The African Queen* (Horizon/Romulus, dir. John Huston, 1951) earned c. $4 million rental, $8 million gross; and *Mogambo* (MGM, dir. John Ford, 1953) earned $5.2 million rental and $10.4 gross. All these movies would have been expected to roughly double these figures again through international exhibition. By comparison the decade's smash hit movies made abroad were *The Ten Commandments* (Paramount, dir. Cecil B. DeMille, 1957) – number one that year – which earned c. $18 million rental $26 million gross in its first year alone and *The Bridge on the River Kwai* (Columbia, dir. David Lean, 1957), which was number one in 1958 and earned roughly the same. *Variety* 8 January 1958 and 7 January 1959.

3   The currency motive and statistics are mentioned in Thomas M. Pryor, 'Hollywood Plans 30 Movies Abroad', *The New York Times*, 2 January 1953, p.11.

4   For background and reviews see John Cournos, 'The Recent Works of Fiction: A Striking Novel about Japan', *The New York Times*, 1 November 1942, p.BR6; Mary Johnson Tweedy, 'A House in Ceylon', *The New York Times*, 3 July 1949, p.BR5; 'Adventure in Ceylon Makes Dramatic Novel', *Los Angeles Times*, 3 July 1949, p.D8.

5   Robert Standish, *Elephant Walk* (New York: Macmillan, 1949).

6   Cull interview: Douglas Fairbanks Jr. Thomas Wood, 'Odd Saga of Elephant Walk', *New York Herald Tribune*, 31 May 1953, sec. 4, p.3.

7   Thomas M. Pryor, 'Decca Would Buy Universal Stock', *The New York Times*, 4 October 1951, p.38.

8   Herrick Library: Paramount Pictures script file, *Elephant Walk*, D. M. Marshman Jr Screenplay, February 1952.

9   Thomas M. Pryor, 'Metro Makes Bid to Moira Shearer', *The New York Times*, 27 December 1951, p.16.

10   Thomas M. Pryor, 'U-I Starring Role for Loretta Young', *The New York Times*, 17 March 1952, p.17.

11   The newly independent country welcomed West German crews for *Sterne über Colombo* [Stars over Colombo] (Gloria-film, dir. Viet Harlan, 1953) and British crews for *The Beachcomber* (London, dir. Muriel Box, 1954). It doubled for Burma in *The Purple Plain* (Two Cities, dir. Robert Parrish, 1954).

12   Herrick Library: Paramount Pictures production records, *Elephant Walk*, f2, John Mock Paramount Story editor to Sidney Justin, 2 June 1952. Thomas M. Pryor, 'Columbia Plans 39 Movies for TV', *The New York Times*, 10 June 1952, p.23; Hedda Hopper, 'Drama', *Los Angeles Times*, 10 June 1952, p.B6; Thomas Wood, 'Odd Saga of Elephant Walk', *New York Herald Tribune*, 31 May 1953, sec. 4, p.3.

13   Herrick Library: Production Code Administration records: *Elephant Walk* [Par. 1952], Breen to Luraschi, 28 May 1952.

14   Thomas M. Pryor, 'Rank Offers Role to Betty Hutton', *The New York Times*, 22 July 1952, p.22.

15   For a biography see Marta Mierendorff, *Willaim Dieterle: Der Plutarch von Hollywood* (Berlin: Henschel Verlag, 1993). Dieterle had cut his teeth in Germany in the 1920s and then excelled as one of Warner Brothers' stable of directors in the 1930s. He was

especially associated with biopics, working on *The Story of Louis Pasteur* (1936), *The Life of Emile Zola* (1937) and *Juarez* (1939) as well as *Doctor Ehrlich's Magic Bullet* (1940). His best-known film was probably *The Hunchback of Notre Dame* (1939) with Charles Laughton. By the early 1950s he was experiencing a degree of suspicion owing to his involvement in radically tinged project, *Blockade* (1938). *Elephant Walk* gave him a shot at the mainstream. For an announcement of his engagement for this film see Thomas M. Pryor, 'Kathryn Grayson Signed by Metro,' *The New York Times*, 27 October 1952, p.22.

[16]   Thomas Wood, 'Odd Saga of Elephant Walk', *New York Herald Tribune*, 31 May 1953, sec. 4, p.3.

[17]   Thomas M. Pryor, 'Paramount Awaits Reply of Oliviers', *The New York Times*, 11 December 1952, p.46.

[18]   Herrick library: Paramount scripts,

[19]   Herrick Library: Production Code Administration records: *Elephant Walk* [Par. 1952], Breen to Luraschi, 28 January 1953.

[20]   Marta Mierendorff, *Willaim Dieterle*, p.188.

[21]   'Choice Chore', *The New York Times*, 1 February 1953, p.X5.

[22]   Herrick library: Paramount Pictures production records, *Elephant Walk*, f3, memo by Frank Caffey, 15 December 1952 and undated cable from Asher, cirex 15 December 1952.

[23]   Elaine Dundy, *Finch, Bloody Finch: A Life of Peter Finch* (New Yok: Holt, Reinhart and Winston, 1980), p.178.

[24]   Trader Faulkner, *Peter Finch: A Biography* (New York: Taplinger, 1979), p.151. This version is supported by Anne Edwards, *Vivien Leigh: A Biography* (New York: Simon and Schuster, 1977), p.192.

[25]   Hugo Vickers, *Vivien Leigh* (Boston: Little Brown, 1988), p.211; Anthony Holden, *Laurence Olivier* (New York: Atheneum, 1988), p.274; Terry Coleman, *Olivier* (New York: Henry Holt, 2005), p.237. The now notorious biography by Spoto (who traded on claims of Oliver's homosexuality) even claimed that Leigh was seeking to head off an affair between Olivier and Finch, Donald Spoto, *Laurence Olivier: A Biography* (London: HarperCollins, 1992), p.242.

[26]   Thomas M. Pryor, 'Paramount to Cut 1953 Movie-Making', *The New York Times*, 7 January 1953, p.25; Herrick library: Paramount Pictures production records, *Elephant Walk*, f3, misc.

[27]   For Storm's background see her obituary, *The Times*, 20 October 1975, p.14.

[28]   Edwin Schallert, 'Nancy Davis Resuming as Star ...' *Los Angeles Times*, 9 February 1953, p.B9; Thomas M. Pryor, 'Paramount Halts New Kind of Love', *The New York Times*, 6 February 1953, p.16.

[29]   Herrick library: Paramount Pictures production records, *Elephant Walk*, f2, Memo by John Mock, Paramount story editor, 4 June 1953.

[30]   Hearings before a subcommittee of the Committee on Foreign Relations United States Senate, 83rd Congress, first session on overseas information programs of the USA, Washington: GPO, 1953, pp.231–98, esp. pp.235, 292. For a compendium of speeches, including material by Johnstone see Herrick, AMPTP files, box 1, 'American Films Abroad File'; Valentine Davies 'American Films: Ambassadors of Democracy'. Hollywood Reporter, 28 June 1950.

[31]   The story of the CIA's work is told in Hugh Wilford, *The Mighty Wurlitzer: How the CIA played America* (Cambridge, MA: Harvard University Press, 2008).

32   David N. Eldridge, '"Dear Owen": The CIA, Luigi Luraschi and Hollywood, 1953', *Historical Journal of Film, Radio and Television*, 20: 2 (June 2000), pp.149–98.
33   Herrick library, Paramount script collection, *Elephant Walk*, John Lee Mahin. 8 October 1952, yellow version, pp.80–1. The Buddha was sleeping in the version of 17 January 1953 credited to Mahin and Frings, but the joke history was still present (p.78).
34   Herrick library, Paramount script collection, *Elephant Walk*, Version of 26 February 1953 by Mahin, Frings and Storm, with O'Brien material added.
35   Herrick library, Paramount script collection, *Elephant Walk*, John Lee Mahin. 8 October 1952, yellow version, p.78 – the line was still in the version of 17 January 1953 by Mahin and Frings.
36   Herrick library, Paramount script collection, *Elephant Walk*, Mahin and Frings, 17 January 1953, p.67.
37   Herrick library, Paramount script collection, *Elephant Walk*, Mahin and Frings, 17 January 1953, p.71–2. The publicity stills in the Herrick core collection also over represent Mylee Haulani given the few moments she is actually seen the final film.
38   Herrick library, Paramount script collection, *Elephant Walk*, Version of 26 February 1953 by Mahin, Frings and Storm, with O'Brien material added. Scene dated 15 April 1953, p.138.
39   'Elephant Walk Filming Starts', *Times of Ceylon*, 31 January 1953, p.1.
40   Trader Faulkner, *Peter Finch: A Biography*, pp.153–4; Elaine Dundy, *Finch, Bloody Finch: A Life of Peter Finch*, pp.178–92; Terry Coleman, *Olivier* (New York: Henry Holt, 2005), pp.237–9.
41   Thomas M. Pryor, 'Skeleton Returns to Metro', *The New York Times*, 12 March 1953, p.24; Thomas M. Pryor, 'Ferrer to Appear in Film of Shrike', *The New York Times*, 13 March 1953, p.24; Thomas M. Pryor, '3-D Anxiety Costs Hollywood Jobs', *The New York Times*, 17 March 1953, p.26; Thomas M. Pryor, 'Miss Taylor Takes Vivien Leigh Role', *The New York Times*, 20 March 1953, p.27.
42   Paramount Pictures production records, *Elephant Walk*, f3, William G. Davidson to Frank Caffey, 26 May 1953. Thomas Wood, 'Odd Saga of Elephant Walk', *New York Herald Tribune*, 31 May 1953, sec. 4, p.3 reported that the 'loan' of Taylor required Paramount to pay MGM $150,000 outright and $3,500 per day.
43   Vickers, *Vivien Leigh*, p.212.
44   Kitty Kelly, *Elizabeth Taylor: The Last Star* (New York: Simon and Schuster, 1981), p.98. In defence of Dana Andrews, in passage through London to Ceylon he learned in the middle of an interview with the *Saturday Pictorial* that his brother Charles, to whom he was very close, had died of sudden heart failure. 'Bad News', *Saturday Pictorial*, 25, January 1953.
45   Thomas M. Pryor, 'Elephants Wreck a Paramount Set', *The New York Times*, 8 May 1953, p.28; Faulkner, *Peter Finch: A Biography*, p.155; Vickers, *Vivien Leigh*, p.214.
46   'Herd of Delicate Destroyers', *Life*, 10 December 1953.
47   Elizabeth Taylor, *Elizabeth Taylor: An Informal Memoir* (New York: Harper & Row, 1965), p.45 Herrick library, Paramount Pictures production records, Elephant Walk, f3, memo Irving Asher to Frank Caffey, 5 May 1953.
48   Herrick library, Paramount Pictures production records, *Elephant Walk*, f1, Production report for Frank Caffey, 15 June 1953, noting total cost of $2,871,000.
49   Paramount Press Book, 1954: Paramount Showmanship Manuel: *Elephant Walk*. The main advertisement in *The New York Times* 18 April 1954, p.X3 promised 'pagan revels

of native dancing girls', 'exotic wonders of the inner jungle in the legendary Temple of Love'.

50 Bosley Crowther, 'Elephant Walk Opens at Astor Theater', *The New York Times*, 22 April 1954, p.37; Bosley Crowther, 'Far Places in Films', *The New York Times*, 25 April 1954, p.X1.

51 Mae Tinée, 'Elephant Film Colorful and Lavishly Done', *Chicago Tribune*, 17 May 1954, p.B15.

52 'Elephant Walk', *Variety*, 29 March 1954.

53 'Elephant Walk', *Time*, 19 April 1954.

54 'Protest Ceylon Film', *New York Herald Tribune*, 23 April 1954.

55 Herrick library Production Code Administration records: *Elephant Walk* (Par., 1952), report 28 July 1954.

56 'Top Grosers of 1954', *Variety*, 5 January 1955, p.59.

57 'Top Grosers of 1956', *Variety*, 2 January 1957. Given that *Rains of Ranchipur* (Fox, dir. Jean Negulesco, 1955) was released in December, its true domestic gross was probably in excess of this figure.

58 'Murrow Furrows H'wood Brow – Criticizes 'Image' of U.S. Abroad Created by Films.' *Variety*, 6 November 1961, and 'H'wood asks Murrow provide consultant to mirror 'image.' *Variety*, 7 November 1961.

59 Homer Bigart, 'Safe Americans Warned in Saigon: Breezily Written Book Gives Instructions for Danger', *The New York Times*, 1 July 1962, p.22. The fable contrasted the fates of a family who survived a hurricane by lashing themselves to a supple bamboo against their neighbours who were lost because they tied themselves to rigid oaks which were simply blown away.

60 'R. Standish', *The Times*, 7 November 1981, p.8. The obituary notice reported that he also published books under the pen name of Stephen Lister. See also 'Robert Standish', *Variety*, 18 November 1981, p.94.

THE WATERSHED

Lawrence of Arabia (1962)

Lawrence of Arabia represents the apotheosis of the cinema of empire. David Lean and Sam Spiegel's film of the role of the enigmatic soldier-scholar T. E. Lawrence in the Arab Revolt against the Turks during the First World War won seven Academy Awards including Best Picture and Best Director – a double success for Spiegel and Lean following *The Bridge on the River Kwai* (1957) – and, along with contemporaneous films such as Stanley Kubrick's *Spartacus* (1960) and Anthony Mann's *El Cid* (1961), marked the high water mark of the epic. *Lawrence of Arabia* now regularly features in polls of the greatest British and American films – reflecting its status as an Anglo–American production – and has been acknowledged as a major formative influence by film-makers such as Steven Spielberg and Martin Scorsese.

Lawrence of Arabia was also one of the most troubled films in cinema history. It had a long gestation period and was nearly aborted during production as the logistical problems mounted and the budget escalated to over $13 million. It also gave rise to a bitter dispute over the authorship of the screenplay that persisted long after the deaths of those involved. Yet the controversy did nothing to damage the film's reputation, which was enhanced following its restoration and the release of a 'director's cut' in 1989 that restored some 20 minutes excised following its royal première in December 1962.

The controversies around the production of *Lawrence of Arabia* have been thoroughly documented elsewhere and need not be rehearsed again here.[1] Instead we focus on the film's representation of imperialism and colonial politics. *Lawrence of Arabia* was a watershed for the cinema of empire. Until *Lawrence* the dominant narrative was the projection of imperialism as a force for political and social stability. After *Lawrence*, however, there was a pronounced shift away from this narrative towards a more critical representation of the imperial project in films such as *Zulu*, *Khartoum* and *The Charge of the Light Brigade*. The trend thereafter would be for films debunking the heroic narrative of imperial expansion. *Lawrence of Arabia* itself reflects this shift. The film is in two parts: a heroic and triumphalist first half, seen through the eyes of Lawrence himself; and an anti-heroic second half, a study in imperial hubris, told from the perspective of the American journalist Jackson Bentley.

The Making of a Myth

T. E. (Thomas Edward) Lawrence (1888–1935) was an Oxford archæology graduate and Arabist who was an officer on General Murray's staff in Cairo during the First World War. In 1916 he was sent as a liaison officer to Jedda where he induced Emir Feisal to continue the revolt against the Turkish Ottoman Empire begun by his father Hussein. Lawrence led a series of raids on the Damascas–Medina Railway and captured the strategically import-ant port of Aqaba in July 1917. Throughout the winter of 1917–18 he har-assed the Turkish flank as General Allenby advanced to capture Jerusalem (December 1917) and Damascus (October 1918). The military significance of the Arab Revolt was minimal, but Lawrence's role in it had soon become the stuff of legend.[2]

It is not difficult to understand why Lawrence and his exploits appealed to the popular imagination. In the aftermath of a war characterized by the bloody attritional set pieces and deadlocked trench warfare of the Western Front the desert campaign seemed like a throwback to a more romantic ideal of warfare. It harked back to Britain's 'little wars of empire' in the nineteenth century. Lawrence became a particular hero of the boys' story papers in the 1920s and 1930s: he was 'the Silent Sentinel of the Sand' and 'the man who won a war on his own'.[3] Lawrence's habit of dressing in Arab robes and posing with a *khanjar* (a curved Arab dagger) further enhanced his public image as a mysterious, exotic, romantic figure.

It was through the emerging mass media that the myth of 'Lawrence of Arabia' took shape. In 1919–20 the American showman Lowell Thomas presented his illustrated lecture *With Allenby in Palestine and Lawrence in Arabia* to audiences in New York, London and throughout the British Empire. Thomas called Lawrence 'the Uncrowned King of Arabia' who 'brought the disunited nomadic tribes of Arabia into a unified cam-paign against their Turkish oppressors' and 'restored the Caliphate to the descendants of the Prophet'.[4] This is very much an Anglocentric narra-tive in which Lawrence provides the inspirational leadership the Arabs lack. A similar perspective, though without Thomas's gift for hyperbole, informs early biographies by admirers such as Robert Graves and Basil Liddell Hart.[5]

Yet Lawrence was a man of contradictions. He had an ambivalent attitude to the cult of personality that developed around him. In the 1920s he enlisted under assumed names in the Royal Air Force (as John Hume Ross) and the Tank Corps (as T. E. Shaw). He began writing his own account of the Arab Revolt, *Seven Pillars of Wisdom*, in 1919, but despite the demand for the book he would publish it only in a limited edition in 1926. *Seven Pillars of Wisdom* is as much a work of literature as history: Lawrence's narrative is unreliable as a repository of facts and some of the events he describes are pure fabrication. Some critics have seen in its prose style and self-conscious narration the influence of modernist literature, including Joseph Conrad's *Heart of Darkness* and T. S. Eliot's *The Waste Land*. An abridged version of *Seven Pillars of Wisdom*, entitled *Revolt in the Desert*, was published in 1927.[6]

Lawrence before Lean

There had been numerous attempts to make a film about Lawrence long before Lean and Spiegel came onto the stage in 1959. In his autobiography British producer Herbert Wilcox claimed that shortly after its publication Lawrence approached him with a view to making a film of *Seven Pillars of Wisdom*. Wilcox, however, felt that the book was 'not good cinema and in spots rather sordid ... I ventured the opinion that I could not see cinema audiences seeking entertainment being attracted to such a subject ... Lawrence told me that one day it would make an outstanding film. He failed to sway me – but how right he was'.[7] There is reason to doubt this story, however, as other sources all suggest that Lawrence did not wish to see a film made about himself. In 1927, for example, in response to an enquiry from Rex Ingram, director of *The Four Horsemen of the Apocalypse*, Lawrence wrote: 'They babble sometimes to me of making a film of *Revolt in the Desert*. I have no property in it so that I hope they will not ... I'd hate to see myself parodied on the pitiful basis of my record of what the fellows with me did'.[8] Lawrence's published letters reveal his antipathy towards the film industry. To Robert Graves, for example, he wrote: 'I loathe the notion of being celluloided. My rare visits to cinemas always deepen in me a sense of their superficial falsity – vulgarity, I would have said, only I like the vulgarity that means common man, and the badness of films seems to me like an edited and below-the-belt speciousness.'[9] In 1934, however, Lawrence reluctantly acquiesced and sold the film rights of *Revolt in the Desert* to Alexander Korda, apparently at the instigation of his literary agent

Raymond Savage. To his trustees Lawrence wrote: 'Savage is a nuisance with his film-greediness; but I suspect that Korda will not play. I am too recent to make a good subject – too much alive, in fact.'[10]

Korda's project to film a Lawrence biopic went through several stages. In May 1934 Korda announced that Leslie Howard would play Lawrence in a film to be directed by Lewis Milestone, who had directed the acclaimed *All Quiet on the Western Front*.[11] He entered into discussions with Basil Liddell Hart, the military historian and biographer of Lawrence, about using his biography to flesh out the script. The project was aborted, however, when Lawrence asked Korda not to proceed with the film while he was alive. Korda agreed to Lawrence's request. In January 1935 Lawrence told Charlotte Shaw (wife of his friend George Bernard Shaw) that 'it will not be done. You can imagine how much this gladdens me'.[12]

Lawrence's death in a motorcycle accident in May 1935 changed the situation.[13] A half-hour documentary entitled *Lawrence of Arabia*, compiled largely from still photographs from the Imperial War Museum, was rushed into production by a company called Ace Films, who claimed it as 'the authentic and official story of the exploits of Colonel T. E. Lawrence', though it does not appear to have been very widely distributed.[14] Lawrence's trustees granted Korda permission to proceed with his film of *Revolt in the Desert*. Lieutenant-Colonel W. F. Stirling, the Governor of Jaffa between 1920 and 1930, was engaged as technical adviser. Zoltan Korda would direct. Lawrence was now to be played by Walter Hudd, an actor who resembled Lawrence physically and had played the character of Private Meek, based on the post-war Lawrence, in George Bernard Shaw's play *Too True to Be Good* in 1932.

Korda commissioned two scripts of *Revolt of the Desert* in 1935. The first was by British journalist James Lansdale Hodson. Hodson set out to locate the Arab Revolt in the wider geopolitical context of the Great War, including lengthy voice-overs that explained the war situation and short sketches of events on the Western Front (including the French army mutiny of 1917 and the arrival of American soldiers) and in London and Berlin. Hodson added a note on the script: 'I am doubtful if the idea of sketches will bear repetition and also whether there can possibly be space in the picture for them.' Otherwise Hodson's treatment is significant in several respects. It focuses on Lawrence's role in promoting unity between the Arab tribes and acknowledges his tactical acumen in taking Aqaba. But it also examines the darker side of his character. Thus Lawrence executes Hamed the Moor, who has murdered Salem of the Ageyl, in order to prevent a blood feud between their tribes; he is captured by the Turks at Medina and savagely whipped – though he does not reveal his true identity; and he is ruthless in exacting revenge when the Turks massacre the village of Tafas ('No prison-ers!'). Hodson's script ends with the entry of the Arab army into Damascus and celebrations of its liberation – celebrations from which Lawrence him-self remains aloof.[15]

It will be clear that this was to be no hagiography or romantic paen to imperialism. Hodson's script is highly critical of British policy in the Middle East. Feisal's ambition is 'freedom, independence, a government which speaks our language and will let us live in peace'. He accepts that he needs British support to fight the Turks ('Without England's help we shall be as unwatered land') and feels betrayed when it is revealed, following the collapse of Russia, that the British, French and Russian governments had made a secret agreement for the partition of the Turkish Empire. A voice-over suggests that the agreement 'appeared to destroy hopes of Arabian independence and aroused grave doubts in Lawrence's mind of British sin-cerity in promising freedom to the Arabs'. Lawrence becomes disillusioned with what he regards as British perfidy: 'I'm sick of responsibility ... and I'm tired of this daily posturing in an alien dress and preaching in a foreign tongue. And now this hollow pretence that we are leading a national revolt for freedom. That Treaty was a shock to me. I feel a fraud.' And he has an angry confrontation with General Allenby in which he declares that if the Arabs are not offered a fair settlement at the end of the war 'it is conceivable I may find myself fighting *against* British forces'. Allenby replies: 'I'm afraid that you have become so wrapped up in your Arabs that you have lost sight of your real duty to England.'

Hodson's screenplay is a fascinating and multifaceted treatment, but too long and unwieldy. It was revised by John Monk Saunders, an American who had won an Academy Award for writing *The Dawn Patrol*, based on his own experiences as a pilot during the war. Saunders compressed Hodson's treatment, cutting the sketches of other fronts and the voice-over narration and omitting some of the supporting characters. He plays up the military significance of the Arab Revolt – one character remarks that it is in the Near East that 'the real issue will be decided' – and suggests that the capture of Damascus marked the real end of the war. But Saunders maintained Hodson's structure and most of the incidents, including Lawrence's exe-cution of Hamed, his capture and beating by the Turks, the confrontation with Allenby and the massacre at Tafas. Saunders also included a scene where Lawrence orders his men to machine-gun 200 Turkish prisoners. This dramatization of a deliberate atrocity carried out on Lawrence's orders does not appear in any other version.[16]

Korda announced *Revolt in the Desert* in his production programme for 1936.[17] In the event, however, the project stalled. Korda had planned to film on location in Palestine and Transjordan, but civil unrest throughout 1936 made this impossible. Palestine had become a British mandate in 1920 but was riven with tension between Arabs and Jews. This caused Korda to rethink his plans. Early in 1937 he commissioned another script from Miles Malleson, an actor and playwright who had been a conscientious objector during the war but also scripted historical and imperial epics such as *Rhodes of Africa* and *Victoria the Great*. Brian Desmond Hurst was slated to direct. Amongst the actors considered for Lawrence were John Clements, Clifford Evans, Robert Donat and Laurence Olivier.[18] Later in the year Korda, in one of his frequent periods of financial crisis, sold the script to New World Films, a tenant production company headed by Sir Edward Villiers based at Korda's Denham Studios. Harold Schuster was to direct and the great Hollywood cinematographer James Wong Howe would photograph the film.[19] Again the project went nowhere. Howe went on to photograph *Fire Over England*, whose American director, William K. Howard, was the next director attached to the Lawrence film, the rights to which had now reverted to Korda. Leslie Howard was now confirmed to play Lawrence and even appeared in Arab dress in an article for *Film Weekly*. Howard, who claimed he would co-produce the film, sought to distance it from the current cycle of Hollywood-made British Empire films: 'The picture must be free altogether of the Bengal Lancer aspect; it must have nothing Kiplingesque or senti-mental; above all, it must have no shrieking Arabs riding across the desert in the manner of cowboys.'[20]

The final screenplay, now entitled *Lawrence of Arabia*, is credited to Miles Malleson, Brian Desmond Hurst and Duncan Guthrie.[21] It maintains the basic narrative of the previous scripts but with some significant alterations. A prologue is added before the war as Lawrence, on an archæological dig in Persia, intervenes when two German engineers flog an Arab boy. In this version the capture of Aqaba takes place off screen and the capture and beat-ing of Lawrence by the Turks is omitted. The script tones down the criti-cism of British policy present in previous versions: there is less emphasis on Britain's 'betrayal' of Arab independence and the angry confrontation between Lawrence and Allenby has been dropped. A new sequence is added in Damascus as Lawrence tries to establish Arab administration ('My aim is to have Arab government before Allenby arrives') and a scene at the disease-ridden Turkish military hospital where Lawrence is confronted by an out-raged medical officer – a scene that would feature in the Lean–Spiegel film.

Korda sold the script of *Lawrence of Arabia* to Paramount Film Services, the British subsidiary of Paramount Pictures, which submitted it to the British Board of Film Censors on 17 October 1938. Chief script examiner

Colonel Hanna hedged his bets, concluding that 'it may not be prohibitive to exhibit a film of this nature at this time but I venture to say that it would be most impolitic'.[22] The 'impolitic' issue of *Lawrence of Arabia* was its negative representation of the Turks. The Turkish Embassy had seen an earlier version of the script – at the time this was common practice for films concerning the activities of 'friendly foreign governments' – and had complained to the Foreign Office that the Turks 'were represented as tyrants and oppressors of Arabs' and that 'it was most undesirable that a film which cast such aspersions on Turkish history and national character should be exhibited'.[23] The Foreign Office told BBFC president Lord Tyrrell that it was concerned the film 'would give offence to the Turks'.[24] There was a flurry of letters and telephone conversations between the BBFC and the Foreign Office. The BBFC did what was expected of it. An addendum to the scenario reports records that 'eventually it was decided that it would be advisable not to hold out any hope to the producers that the film, if produced, would be certificated'. The hidden hand of Whitehall had intervened to block the film's production.[25]

This was still not quite the end of the matter. Korda bought back the rights from Paramount and in the summer of 1939 reopened communications with the Foreign Office. He expressed his conviction 'that the making of a picture about Lawrence's life is today very greatly in the National Interest, as nothing could have such good propaganda effect as the example of his life'.[26] He suggested that he would change the film so that the Arab Revolt was less central to the narrative, including Lawrence's life at Oxford before the war and his role as a member of the British delegation at the Versailles Peace Conference. This was Korda's last attempt to make anything of the film. Upon the outbreak of the Second World War he turned his attention to other projects to promote the British cause, including the RAF tribute *The Lion Has Wings* (1939) and the made-in-Hollywood *Lady Hamilton* (1941). This was clearly not the time to be contemplating a film critical of British imperialism: Lawrence's story did not fit the ideological demands of wartime propaganda.[27]

Korda's rights to *Revolt in the Desert* expired in 1945. The film rights passed first to an Italian company, Ortus Films, who commissioned a script from Robin Maugham, nephew of Somerset Maugham. The project collapsed when Lawrence's younger brother and trustee, Professor A. W. Lawrence, demanded full script approval.[28] In 1951 a Jordanian producer, Michel Talhami, bought the rights to *Revolt* and took the project to Columbia Pictures. Harry Cohn, head of production at Columbia, was interested. He approached Michael Powell to direct it. Powell, who had just finished *The Tales of Hoffmann*, was interested but reluctantly passed on the opportunity:

'*Lawrence of Arabia* would have been an ideal subject for The Archers at that time in history ... It was very much my subject, and Lawrence was very much one of my heroes, but at the time I couldn't see it as a film.'[29] Cohn then approached David Lean, who had just completed *The Sound Barrier*. Lean was interested and spoke to Terence Rattigan, who had written *The Sound Barrier*, but again the project went no further.[30]

The next attempt to put Lawrence's story on the screen was by the Rank Organization in the late 1950s. Rattigan worked on a screenplay between 1955 and 1958. The film would be produced by Anatole de Grunwald, directed by Anthony Asquith and star Dirk Bogarde. However, Rank got cold feet and pulled out, citing 'the problems existing in the domestic market, taking particularly into consideration the unreasonable burden of the entertainment tax, which takes over 30 per cent of the box office receipt'.[31] Rattigan used his research to write a play, *Ross*, which was performed to critical and popular acclaim at the Theatre Royal, Haymarket, in 1960 with Alec Guinness in the title role.

Producing *Lawrence*

The aborting of the Rank film demonstrates that the British film industry by the late 1950s was no longer able to produce a film on the scale of *Lawrence of Arabia*. The decline of cinema attendances in Britain meant that the domestic market was too small to guarantee a profitable return on a film costing over £500,000. The production of *Lawrence of Arabia* in the early 1960s was made possible only by the changing political and cultural economies of the film industry. In particular it was American capital that was needed to bring the epic to the screen. This was provided through the agency of producer Sam Spiegel.

Spiegel – an Austrian Jewish émigré who used the name S. P. Eagle until 1954 – had been an independent producer in Hollywood since the early 1940s.[32] His films included *The African Queen* and *On the Waterfront*, the latter winning the first of his three Academy Awards for Best Picture in 1954. *The African Queen* had been an early example of a so-called 'runaway' production: films shot overseas to take advantage of cheaper labour costs and subsidies from governments seeking to promote investment in their domestic film industries. Spiegel and director David Lean were a hot ticket following *The Bridge on the River Kwai*, which had won seven Academy Awards and grossed over $20 million against a production cost of $3 million. Columbia, which had backed *Kwai*, was clearly hoping for another hit on the same scale with *Lawrence of Arabia*.

There were still considerable difficulties in the way of the film. Spiegel had to head off a rival production by Herbert Wilcox, who had bought the rights to Rattigan's *Ross* and wanted to make a film with Laurence Harvey.[33] Spiegel covered all bases by buying the rights to a range of Lawrence biographies as well as both *Seven Pillars of Wisdom* and *Revolt in the Desert*. He then had to contend with A. W. Lawrence, who had the right of script approval. Spiegel won over Lawrence by showing him *The Bridge on the River Kwai* and persuading him, somewhat disingenuously, that the film would simply be an account of the Arab Revolt rather than a psychological examination of his brother's character.[34]

The casting of the film was undertaken before a script was in place. Marlon Brando was the first choice for Lawrence, but decided instead to take the part of Fletcher Christian in Lewis Milestone's remake of *Mutiny on the Bounty*. Lean made an elaborate screen test of Albert Finney.[35] But Finney declined the role on the grounds that he disliked 'being a certain kind of big-screen image'.[36] Peter O'Toole was then tested and accepted the part.[37] As the relatively unknown lead would have to carry the film (he is rarely off screen throughout), Spiegel decided to cast well-known actors in supporting roles. Amongst those in the frame were Cary Grant to play General Allenby and Kirk Douglas as an American reporter based on Lowell Thomas.[38] In the event Allenby was played by Jack Hawkins, who had originally been lined up for the part of Colonel Newcombe. Newcombe was later replaced by a composite character, Colonel Brighton, played by Anthony Quayle. Edmond O'Brien was cast as the American reporter, but was replaced by Arthur Kennedy when O'Brien suffered a heart attack during filming. Other major parts included Alec Guinness as Prince Feisal, Anthony Quinn as Auda and Claude Rains as the diplomat Mr Dryden. The last major role to be cast was Sherif Ali: Omar Sharif replaced Maurice Ronet three weeks into the shoot.

Scripting *Lawrence*

The first choice screenwriter for *Lawrence of Arabia* was Michael Wilson, who had revised Carl Foreman's script of *The Bridge on the River Kwai*. Wilson, like Foreman, had been blacklisted in the early 1950s when he had 'taken the Fifth' by refusing to confirm or deny membership of the Communist Party before the House Un-American Activities Committee.[39] Wilson began with a set of notes entitled 'Lawrence of Arabia: Elements and Facets of the Theme' in which he sketched out his ideas. The film 'should develop as a slow revelation of the man behind the myth ... a gradual exposure of the failure that lay at the core of a triumph'. It is evident that Wilson's primary interest was in the politics of the Arab Revolt:

> Both Lawrence and the Arabs were fired by an idea – freedom. But for him the word *liberty* was the romantic abstraction of a schoolboy, and he never stopped to ask whether it meant the same thing to Feisal and the Bedouin tribes ... His naive vision of liberty failed to perceive the giant chess game being played off scene. No sooner was victory achieved than it was snatched from his grasp by chess players who invested that victory with a content he had not foreseen.[40]

Wilson was also interested in the making of the Lawrence myth, which he saw in historical context: 'In the general disillusionment and cynicism following World War I, the Western world needed an authentic hero to shore up the ideals for which the war had allegedly been fought ... [If] Lawrence had never existed, it would have been necessary to invent him.'[41]

These themes are evident in the three drafts Wilson wrote between December 1959 and February 1961.[42] His device for exploring the creation of the Lawrence myth was to write Lowell Thomas into the story. Thomas appears in the prologue describing how he first saw Lawrence in Jerusalem and presenting one of his lectures in London. He accompanies Lawrence throughout the second half of the screenplay, filming his entry into Jerusalem and Damascus. Wilson emphasizes Thomas's role as a propagandist looking to influence US public opinion – he has been commissioned by 'American industrialists [who] wanted Uncle Sam to throw his full weight into the war' – and portrays him as a cynical opportunist who sees Lawrence as 'money in the bank'. Lawrence takes an instinctive dislike to Thomas: 'I won't help you. I hope you go bankrupt ... You're the most candid scoundrel I've ever met.' 'Takes one to know one', Thomas replies.

As far as the politics are concerned, Wilson presents Lawrence as being caught in the middle between the forces of British imperialism on the one hand and the cause of Arab nationalism on the other. The Arab leaders are suspicious of British motives ('They said they did not want the Sudan, yet they took it'), while the British are presented as pragmatists who regard the Arab Revolt as a sideshow ('Your British allies are hard-pressed too, and the Arab Revolt must be viewed in terms of England's strategic position', Colonel Newcombe reminds Feisal). In this version Lawrence is aware of the Sykes-Picot Agreement 'to carve up the Middle East after the war' and is therefore complicit in the 'betrayal' of the Arabs.

Structurally, Wilson's treatment, which in each draft begins with Lawrence's death in 1935 followed by his memorial service at St Paul's Cathedral, and ends with him driving out of Damascus in 1918, is identifiable as the basis of the finished film. His second draft opens with a long prologue that contrasts different views of Lawrence by contemporaries ('He was the greatest man I ever knew'; 'Are you serious? I always thought him something of a fake') and includes a flash-forward to the 25th anniversary of Lawrence's death as American broadcaster Ed Murrow conducts interviews with Winston Churchill ('I deem Lawrence one of the greatest beings to live in our time') and biographer George Huntingdon ('After sifting all the available evidence, I have come to believe that the Lawrence legend was the greatest hoax of our time'). With its non-linear narrative and its use of 'vox pops' to present opposing opinions, Wilson's prologue is reminiscent of the opening sequences of *Citizen Kane*.

As well as providing the structure of the film, Wilson devised much of the detail. The famous 'mirage shot' where Lawrence first meets Sherif Ali is present in each draft (this was an image that Lean had wanted to include since his first trip to scout locations in Jordan) as is the scene in the British officers' club in Cairo where Lawrence orders drinks for himself and Farraj before the eyes of his startled fellow officers. It was Wilson who made the man whom Lawrence saves in the desert (Gasim) and the man he has to execute the same person. The other key scenes are Lawrence's capture and flogging by the Turks and the massacre of the retreating Turks ('There is a mad smile on Lawrence's lips and his eyes are crazed with blood lust'). It would be fair to say, however, that the second half of Wilson's screenplay is structurally weak: the themes and characterization become lost amidst a succession of all-too similar attacks on trains and desert skirmishes.[43]

This, certainly, was Lean's view after reading Wilson's second draft. Lean told him: 'Prologue is too long and at the moment not related to theme ... Too many train raids which do not contribute to Lawrence's character. We lose the theme, the drive, to unite the tribes ... Many faceted aspects of Lawrence's character not yet in screenplay ... Let us not avoid or censor out the homosexual aspects of Lawrence's relationships.'[44] It is evident that Lean was less interested in the politics and wanted a more psychologically complex characterization of Lawrence. For example, he seems to have seen the relationship between Lawrence and Sherif Ali as an unconsummated love affair similar to the one at the heart of *Brief Encounter*.

Lean and Spiegel now turned to British playwright Robert Bolt, feeling that the author of *A Man for All Seasons* was the ideal person to deal with complex historical characters and the wider philosophical issues in a way that was still accessible to the general audience. Bolt was initially hesitant but accepted the commission to write a 'screenplay with reference to a script by Michael Wilson based upon the life and exploits of Lawrence of Arabia'.[45] By this time (February 1961) Lean was already on location with the unit in Jordan. Bolt, a member of the intellectual left associated with the 'Angry Young Men', told *The New York Times* that 'I was brought up to disapprove of figures like T. E. Lawrence as being the colorful ornaments and stalking horses of imperialism'.[46] Bolt delivered the first part of his screenplay, dealing with events up to Aqaba and Lawrence's return to Cairo, in April. But it took until December to finish the second half – delayed in part by Bolt's arrest for his role in a CND demonstration in Trafalgar Square – by which time the unit had left Jordan and resumed shooting in Spain.[47]

Bolt's screenplay retained Wilson's basic structure, but compressed the incidents, especially in the second half, and amalgamated some of the supporting characters. Thus Colonel Brighton is a composite of several officers who served in Arabia, while Dryden stands for various British government officials. Lowell Thomas became the fictional Jackson Bentley and his part was reduced to a more detached observer. Bolt made Lawrence unaware of the Sykes-Picot Agreement, thereby shifting the burden of blame for the 'betrayal' of the Arabs away from him and onto the politicians. But Bolt was more interested in psychology than politics. It is his script that first suggests Lawrence's torture by the Turks at Deraa might have been something more than a mere flogging: 'The material of this incident is violence; there is a danger that it will be seen as nothing else, that is, that it will not make its point ... If it "goes over the top" so that the understanding of the audience is simply swamped we have failed.' Bolt also made Lawrence an active participant in the massacre of the Turks.[48]

Filming *Lawrence*

The shooting of the film was now at an advanced stage. *Lawrence of Arabia* was shot largely in continuity, partly by design so that O'Toole's performance could reflect Lawrence's mental disintegration, partly from necessity because only the first half of the screenplay was ready when the cameras rolled on 15 May 1961. Most of the first half of the film was shot in Jordan, where it received the personal support of the Anglophile King Hussein. The king took a shine to the unit's telephonist Toni Gardiner and married her shortly after filming started.[49] Anthony Nutting, an Arabist and former Foreign Office minister who had resigned following the Suez Crisis, was employed to liaise between the Jewish Spiegel and the Arab states.[50]

It was a difficult shoot. The unit had to struggle with extreme heat. Lean, however, was more concerned about the lack of a complete script and his deteriorating relationship with Spiegel. On one occasion he wrote to his producer: 'I am worried to death by the dreadful state of unpreparedness and inefficiency ... You even told me that it was good we had no finished script!'[51] In the meantime the cost of the film was spiralling alarmingly. *Lawrence*, unusually, was 'a film with no fixed budget'.[52] Spiegel had promised Columbia it would be made for $3 million, but it was evidently going to exceed that amount. Columbia – no doubt eyeing the escalating costs of other early 1960s epics such as Universal's *Spartacus* ($12 million) and MGM's *Mutiny on the Bounty* ($19 million) – was getting cold feet. In September the production in Jordan was closed down and the unit relocated to Spain.

Shooting resumed in Seville, standing in for Cairo and Damascus, on 18 December. The capture of Aqaba was filmed at Almeria on the Mediterranean coast in March 1962. In May the unit moved again, this time to Morocco, to complete the desert exteriors. Lean returned to London only in August, leaving Nicolas Roeg with the second unit to shoot the close-ups for the massacre at Tafas. The only scenes in the film shot in Britain were

8. On location for *Lawrence of Arabia*.

the memorial service and Lawrence's death. However, Spiegel's canny use of a British crew and a largely British cast ensured that the film qualified for subsidy from the Eady Levy.[53]

Shooting eventually wrapped on 21 September 1962. Lean and editor Anne Coates then worked around the clock to ensure the film was ready for the Royal Film Performance on 10 December 1962. The final show print ran for 222 minutes. Lean was never entirely happy with the pacing of the film and would cut it before its general release.

Reading *Lawrence*

As a biopic *Lawrence of Arabia* needs to be understood not only in relation to the 'real' Lawrence but also to the image of Lawrence as it stood at the time. It came on the heels of several biographies that had renewed interest in Lawrence in the 1950s, particularly Richard Aldington's *Lawrence of Arabia: A Biographical Enquiry* and Colin Wilson's *The Outsider*.[54] Aldington argued that Lawrence was a pathological liar who perpetuated his own biographical legend by planting misleading stories about himself in order to stoke up further interest. The film's Lawrence is shown to be entirely complicit in the construction of his own legend as he willingly poses for the camera and clearly enjoys the acclaim as his followers chant his name ('Aurens!'). He is also portrayed as a man who comes to believe in his own legend ('They can only kill me with a golden bullet') until his aura of invincibility is stripped away (literally and metaphorically) when he is captured by the Turks at Deraa. Colin Wilson saw Lawrence as part of a lineage of visionary outsiders who did not fit into conventional society, comparing him to Nietzsche, Dostoevsky and Van Gogh, amongst others. There are echoes of this throughout the film as Lawrence repeatedly asserts his sense of difference from those around him: 'I'm different'; 'I'm not ordinary'; 'Do you think that I'm just anyone?'

In his study of the 'anthropology' of *Lawrence of Arabia*, Steven C. Caton argues that Lean and Bolt employed devices of Brechtian theatre to 'construct a more reflexive spectator ... who would be induced to form his or her own critical interpretations of the hero'.[55] Brecht's technique of 'alienation' was a means of distancing the audience from the drama in order to make them reflect critically on what they had seen and experienced. This is evident on several levels in *Lawrence of Arabia*. First there is the performative aspect of Lawrence's character. At certain moments in the film – such as the scene where he dances in the desert in his pristine new robes, or where he strides along the carriages of the captured train – Lawrence is performing for a spectator within the film (himself, Bentley), reminding the audience in the cinema that they are watching a performative act.

Another distancing device is the presence of the journalist, Bentley, who acts as both a biographer and commentator within the film. Bentley first appears on the steps of St Paul's following the memorial service where, in response to a reporter's request for a quotation, he calls Lawrence 'a poet, a scholar and a mighty warrior', then, to his companion, adds: 'He was also the most shameless exhibitionist since Barnum and Bailey.' Later, as Bentley films the Arab army's entry into Damascus while perched on top of a bakery van, we might see this as an allusion to the film-making process. If, as film theorists like to claim, all films are really about cinema itself, then *Lawrence of Arabia* is even more so than most.

The cinematic qualities of *Lawrence of Arabia* are most evident in its cinematography – which is almost *de rigeur* to describe in superlatives such as 'magnificent', 'breathtaking' and 'spectacular'.[56] *Lawrence* was shot in Technicolor and Super-Panavision 70 – one of several widescreen processes (others included Todd-AO, Camera 65 and Cinerama) that were used

9. Making the Myth: Lawrence (Peter O'Toole) plays to the crowd in *Lawrence of Arabia* (1962).

for only a handful of films to differentiate them from the 35-millimetre Panavision format that had become the industry standard by the early 1960s. This provided greater depth of focus, sharpness of detail and richness of colour: it is particularly effective in capturing the vastness of the desert and the indescribable quality of the light.

The film is structured in two parts, that differ in style and tone, and where the visuals are fully integrated with the narrative. Part I of *Lawrence* is, to most intents and purposes, an adventure story. Lawrence is introduced as an eccentric individualist. He treats his mission to Arabia as an adventure ('This is going to be fun') and is excited at the prospect. The structure is that of an adventure narrative: Lawrence makes an epic journey and befriends an ally (Ali) with whom he will share many perils. He overcomes the obstacles placed in his way, winning the respect of the Arabs and enduring the physical hardships of the desert. He achieves his objective (the capture of Aqaba) through his inspirational leadership and tactical brilliance. At this point in the film Lawrence is an extrovert and a show-off. The prevailing tone of Part I is one of excitement and adventure, as explained in Lean's notes on the Aqaba sequence:

> The mood is one of pure success, the visual impression that of irresistible momentum ... In other words let the suffering and squallor [sic] of war be evaded at all intent and the glamour of it deliberately exaggerated, so that the audience is left stirred, excited, breathless with no time to reflect, only to enjoy, after the long slog across the desert and with Sinai to come.[57]

This mood is matched by the visual style throughout Part I. The first half of the film is full of visual splendour, with vast panoramic shots of wide desert spaces bathed in colour and light.

Part II is very different. The tone is darker, thematically and visually. Lawrence starts to become disillusioned: he has discovered what it feels like to kill ('There was something about it I didn't like ... I enjoyed it') and becomes morose and introspective. He twice tries to have himself relieved of service in Arabia and is twice persuaded to return by Allenby, who skilfully manipulates Lawrence's vanity and sense of responsibility to the Arabs. Throughout Part II there are fewer grand vistas and more scenes shot in darkness and shadow. The Deraa sequence takes place entirely at night and is lit in a very low key. If the taking of Aqaba in Part I was a thrilling spectacle of the 'glamour' of war, the bloody massacre of the Turks in Part II reveals the 'suffering and squalor' that had been consciously avoided earlier in the film. It is shot in a series of medium and close shots – a montage of indiscriminate killing, including one moment where Lawrence shoots a man who is raising his hands in surrender. The heroic mood of the first half is replaced by a feeling of disillusion and disenchantment.

What, then, of the film's representation of colonialism? Postcolonialist critics such as Ella Shohat have accused it of adopting an Anglocentric perspective: '*Lawrence of Arabia* provides an example of Western historical representation whereby the individual Romantic "genius" leads the Arab national revolt, presumed to be a passive entity awaiting T. E. Lawrence's inspiration ... The unveiling of the mysteries of an unknown space becomes a *rite de passage* allegorizing the Western achievement of virile heroic stature.'[58] The charge that *Lawrence* represents a Western historical perspective is uncontestable; but at the same time it would be entirely unrealistic to expect a large-scale Anglo–American film to do otherwise.[59] It is the fact of the film's Anglo–American parentage, however, that makes its politics all the more intriguing. Neither the British nor the Americans are presented in a particularly positive light. The British characters are, variously, pragmatic (Allenby), unscrupulous (Dryden) and dim-witted (Brighton). Lawrence, for his part, is idealistic but naive: he is manipulated both by Allenby (who sees the Arab Revolt as a useful diversion that will assist his campaign) and by Feisal (who needs Lawrence to lead his army). The sole American representative, Bentley, is a cynic who tries to convince Feisal of his sincerity: 'Your Highness, we Americans were once a colonial people. We naturally sympathize with any people anywhere who are struggling for their freedom.' Feisal immediately sees through this pretence and Bentley drops the act, admitting instead that all he really wants is a story: 'I'm looking for a hero.'

In *Lawrence of Arabia* imperialism is represented as an impersonal historical force: Dryden and Allenby are its agents. So too, to begin with, is Lawrence, though he later rejects it and associates himself with the cause of Arab independence: 'Arabia's for the Arabs, sir. That's what I've told them anyway. That's what they think. That's what they're fighting for. They've only one suspicion. That we'll let them drive the Turks out and then move in ourselves. I've told them that's false, that we have no ambitions in Arabia.' It turns out that Lawrence's promise is hollow: the British have no intention of leaving Arabia.

Lawrence is unusual for a mainstream film, certainly for a Hollywood movie, in its suggestion of the futility of individual agency. This distinguishes *Lawrence* from films such as *Spartacus* and *El Cid* where the actions of a heroic individual succeed in rousing their people to resist tyranny. *Lawrence*, however, ends in failure: its protagonist is powerless to deliver on his promises to the Arabs. Arab unity disintegrates once victory is

10. The Agents of Imperialism: Lawrence (Peter O'Toole), Dryden (Claude Rains), Allenby (Jack Hawkins) and Brighton (Anthony Quayle) in *Lawrence of Arabia* (1962).

achieved: the Arab National Council proclaimed in Damascus is riven with factional strife and proves unable to govern effectively. The British have only to wait for the failure of the Arab administration to establish their control. Ultimately, the film endorses the old colonialist discourse that colonized people are unable to govern themselves.

Reception and Afterlife

The critical response to *Lawrence* in Britain was generally positive. Some reviewers were rhapsodic. For David Robinson in the *Financial Times* it was 'a landmark in the history of the cinema ... monumental in scope and in achievement'.[60] Nate Wheeler in *Scene* concurred that it was 'the first truly satisfying film epic ... a great film'.[61] Patrick Gibbs of the *Daily Telegraph* called it 'an extraordinary film'.[62] The fullest eulogy came from Dilys Powell in *The Sunday Times*: 'I think it is the first time for the cinema to communicate ecstasy ... *Lawrence of Arabia* taken as a whole is a genuine, sometimes even a profound interpretation of character. And that alone, even without the great aesthetic beauties, would make the film unique in the cinema of historical reconstruction'.[63]

Other reviewers, however, were more equivocal. While there was universal praise for the beauty of the desert cinematography, some felt that visual spectacle had overwhelmed the narrative. Eric Rhode in the *Listener*, for example, felt that 'the desert is far too dominating a force, and it takes over the film. The oppressive brilliance of Freddie Young's photography dwarfs the characters and makes their struggle for power seem irrelevant'.[64] *The Times* found it 'a film for the eye rather than the mind'.[65] For John Coleman in the *New Statesman* 'none of it is good enough. Setting to one side the obligatory, contemptible music, the film never decisively makes its mind up what it's after – a breathtaking portrait of Lawrence or a series of sandy battles and torments'.[66] Penelope Gilliat in the *Observer* found it 'a thoughtful picture with an intensely serious central performance, but it doesn't hold together in great excitement'.[67] And Penelope Houston in the *Monthly Film Bulletin* described it as 'a film in which grandeur of conception is not up to grandeur of setting'.[68]

The American critics – at least those who found it into print, as there was a newspaper strike in New York when *Lawrence* opened there – were less impressed. Andrew Sarris in *Village Voice* thought it 'dull, overlong and coldly impersonal'.[69] Bosley Crowther in *The New York Times* thought it 'just a huge, thundering camel-opera that tends to run down rather badly as it rolls on into its third hour and gets involved with sullen disillusion and political deceit'.[70] Roger Sandall in *Film Quarterly* disparaged it as 'a galumphing camelodrama'.[71] Bad reviews did not affect the box office, however: *Lawrence* grossed $7.7 million in its initial roadshow engagements in the United States and went on to be the second most successful release of 1963 behind *How the West Was Won*.[72]

One critic whom the film certainly did not please was A. W. Lawrence. The professor had been shown – and approved – a draft of Michael Wilson's script, but when he saw Bolt's final shooting script he complained that it was 'very different from that shown to me in the first place'. He averred that 'episodes inspired by the book [*Seven Pillars of Wisdom*] have been fictionalised, and completely imaginary episodes have been inserted'.[73] He particularly objected to the scene where Lawrence participates in the killing of the Turks. Upon the film's release he declared that it 'is above all a spectacle in which skilful directing, visual splendour and music sugar-coat the script's bitter treatment of character and events. The film Lawrence has more than any one man's share of psychological aberrations ... I need only say that I should not have recognised my brother'.[74] The film was also damned by Basil Liddell Hart, who thought it a 'striking work of fiction, with little relation to fact'. He deplored the portrait of Lawrence 'as a sadistical pervert who becomes aware that he has a maniac blood-lust, and eventually gives full vent to it in the last stage of the advance to Damascus'.[75]

Bolt, whose first screenplay this had been, was stung by the accusations and penned a response that was to have appeared as a foreword to the published screenplay (which in the event did not appear). He defended his dramatization of the massacre, pointing out that he had based it on Lawrence's account in *Seven Pillars of Wisdom*. He concluded: 'I sincerely regret whatever distress it has caused. I do not claim for it any authority to set against the opinion of people who knew him ... I do claim that it is a reasonably faithful dramatization drawn from his own account. As faithful, that is, as drama can be to a document'.[76]

The mixed reception of *Lawrence of Arabia* reflects the historical context in which it was finally produced. In the early 1960s the film had relevance for both Britain and America. For the British, in the aftermath of Suez and decolonization, it was a reminder of a lost imperial past. Upon its release it became the focus of a 'Make Britain great again' campaign in the *Daily Express* in response to US Secretary of State Dean Ascheson's observation that 'Great Britain has lost as empire and has not yet found a role'.[77] For America, however, the film had a different meaning. *Lawrence of Arabia* was released at a time when American imperialism was on the march in the Middle East and Southeast Asia. Bentley's rhetoric of support for 'any people anywhere who are struggling for their freedom' anticipates American propaganda in support of its presence in Vietnam. It is surely no coincidence that the first re-issue of *Lawrence* in 1970 came at the height of opposition to the Vietnam War. By that time the narrative of imperial hubris bore more relevance for America than it did for Britain.

The critique of imperialism suggested by *Lawrence of Arabia* indicated an ideological shift in the cinema of empire. This was evident in films produced in the wake of *Lawrence*, particularly *Zulu* (1964) and *Khartoum* (1966).[78] Both films dramatize successful challenges to British imperialism by emergent nationalist forces who are presented as worthy opponents. In *Zulu* the suggestion that the Zulus are 'cowardly blacks' is comprehensively repudiated in the hard-fought battle at Rorke's Drift ('I think they've got more guts than we have, boyo' one of the defenders remarks). *Khartoum*, which starred Charlton Heston as General Gordon and a black-faced Laurence Olivier as the Mahdi, was a clear attempt to trade on the success of *Lawrence* by examining another imperial hero whose effort to bring improvement to the Sudanese is thwarted by perfidious British colonial policy.

Lawrence, then, marked a watershed for the cinema of empire. It also became a watershed for those involved in its production. Lean and Bolt collaborated on two more films – the epic romance *Doctor Zhivago* (1965), a huge popular success, and the 'intimate epic' *Ryan's Daughter* (1970), which was savaged by critics – and on several unrealized projects including a two-part film of *The Bounty* and an ambitious film of Joseph Conrad's *Nostromo*. Bolt, who was deeply upset by the controversy over the screenwriting credit for *Lawrence*, won an Academy Award for his screen adaptation of his own play, *A Man for All Seasons*, directed by Fred Zinnemann in 1966. He returned again to the theme of European colonialism in his screenplay for Roland Joffe's *The Mission* (1986). David Lean's last film, *A Passage to India* (1984), was another examination of the divisive legacy of colonialism.

In the meantime the reputation of *Lawrence of Arabia* has grown to the extent that it is now generally regarded as one of the great masterpieces of world cinema. In the mid-1980s archivist Robert A. Harris embarked upon an ambitious attempt to restore the film to its original form following the cuts made for its general release in 1963 and again for its re-issue in 1970. Lean collaborated on the restoration, re-recording dialogue with several of the actors including O'Toole, Guinness, Quinn and Kennedy.[79] The restored *Lawrence* was released, to ecstatic reviews, in 1989. In 1990 Lean became the first non-American to be presented with a Lifetime Achievement Award by the American Film Institute. And *Lawrence* stands as his supreme achievement: one of the greatest of all epics, a complex psychological portrait, and a bitter and disillusioned study of the legacy of imperialism.

Notes

1   *Lawrence of Arabia* is one of the most-researched productions in film history. Its shooting, cutting and restoration are all thoroughly documented in Adrian Turner's lavishly illustrated *The Making of David Lean's 'Lawrence of Arabia'* (London: Dragon's World, 1994). Turner had access to the Columbia Pictures Archives, a privilege granted to few researchers. The book is out of print, but Turner's research is summarized in Kevin Jackson's entry in the BFI's Film Classics series, *Lawrence of Arabia* (London: British Film Institute, 2007). Another full account of the production, based on interviews with Lean and his collaborators, can be found in Kevin Brownlow, *David Lean* (London: Richard Cohen, 1996), pp.402–91. The controversy over the screenplay credit is documented by Joel Hodson, 'Who Wrote *Lawrence of Arabia*?: Sam Spiegel and David Lean's Denial of Credit to a Blacklisted Screenwriter', *Cineaste*, 20: 4 (1994), pp.12–18.

2   There is an extensive biographical industry around Lawrence. See in particular Malcolm Brown, *Lawrence of Arabia: The Life, the Legend* (London: Thames & Hudson, 2005); Philip Knightley and Colin Simpson, *The Secret Lives of Lawrence of Arabia* (London: Panther, 1969); Jeremy Wilson, *Lawrence of Arabia: The Authorised Biography of T. E. Lawrence* (London: William Heinemann, 1989); and Michael Yardley, *Backing into the Limelight: A Biography of T. E. Lawrence* (London: Harrap, 1985).

3   Lawrence inspired a number of imitations in juvenile fiction, including Percy
     Westerman's 'The White Arab' (a serial story in *Chums* in 1932) and Alan Western's
     Desert Hawk (1937). See Michael Paris, *Warrior Nation: Images of War in British Popular
     Culture 1850–2000* (London: Reaktion, 2000), pp.171–3.

4   Lowell Thomas's ' "The Uncrowned King of Arabia": Colonel T. E. Lawrence, the
     Most Romantic Career of Modern Times' was published in *The Strand Magazine* in
     1920. Quoted in Graham Dawson, *Soldier Heroes: British Adventure, Empire and the
     Imagining of Masculinities* (London: Routledge, 1994), p.178.

5   Robert Graves, *Lawrence and the Arabs* (London: Jonathan Cape, 1928); Captain B. H.
     Liddell Hart, *T. E. Lawrence: In Arabia and After* (London: Jonathan Cape, 1934).

6   The first edition of *Seven Pillars of Wisdom*, known as the Oxford Version, was completed
     in 1922. A condensed version, known as the Subscribers' Text, was issued in December
     1926 on a subscription-only basis for 30 guineas. *Revolt in the Desert* was published in
     1927 by Jonathan Cape in London and Doran in New York. It sold 30,000 copies in Britain
     and 120,000 in the USA before Lawrence had it withdrawn. *Seven Pillars of Wisdom* was
     published publicly in 1935 by Jonathan Cape in London and by Doubleday in New York.
     It has been continually in print since. See Jeffrey Meyers, *The Wounded Spirit: A Study of
     Seven Pillars of Wisdom* (London: Martin Brian & O'Keefe, 1973).

7   Herbert Wilcox, *Twenty-Five Thousand Sunsets: The Autobiography of Herbert Wilcox*
     (New York: A. S. Barnes, 1969), p.204. The 'sordid' content was 'the homosexual
     advances of a Turkish chief'. This is one of the incidents it is now thought Lawrence
     may have invented.

8   Quoted in Brownlow, *David Lean*, p.405. See also Brownlow's preface to Liam O'Leary,
     Rex Ingram: Master of the Silent Cinema (Dublin: Academy Press, 1980).

9   Lawrence to Robert Graves, 4 February 1935, in T. E. Lawrence, *Letters* ed., Malcolm
     Brown (Oxford: Oxford University Press, 1988), p.520.

10   Lawrence to Robin Buxton, 7 June 1934, *Letters*, p.490.

11   *Kinematograph Weekly*, 24 May 1934, p.26.

12   Lawrence to Charlotte Shaw, *Letters*, p.515.

13   Korda would later claim that Lawrence 'was coming to see me to talk about a movie
     of *Seven Pillars of Wisdom*, and he was killed on the way in a motorbike accident'.
     Quoted in Michael Korda, *Charmed Lives: A Family Romance* (London: Allen Lane,
     1980), p.340. In fact Lawrence's accident was en route to send a telegram to his friend
     Henry Williamson.

14   *Kinematograph Weekly*, 30 May 1935, p.23; *Kinematograph Weekly*, 11 July 1935, p.31.

15   BFI Unpublished Script Collection S8755: *Lawrence of Arabia* by James Lansdale
     Hodson, dated 1935. The opening of the script includes a 'Foreword':
     > This is no faithful history. Those who marched with Lawrence to Damascus will
     > know that events are omitted, that few characters are identified by name or other-
     > wise. He himself has put them on record in his books. We cannot hope to do just-
     > ice to them. We in this film can only measure Lawrence against his background,
     > indicate his significance in the world war, tell after our own fashion of this young
     > Englishman who stands out beyond all others as the unique example of the unpro-
     > fessional soldier – the apotheosis of the civilian at war.

     The script also includes some interesting incidental asides, including the sugges-
     tion that Cedric Hardwicke 'would play the Allenby part well' and that William
     Walton should be commissioned to write the score.

16   BFI Unpublished Script Collection S8756: *Revolt in the Desert* by J. Monk Saunders,
     20 December 1935.

17   *Kinematograph Weekly*, 9 January 1936.

18   Kulik, *Alexander Korda*, p.190.

19   *World Film News*, 2: 3 (June 1937), p.10.

20   Leslie Howard, 'How I Shall Play Lawrence', *Film Weekly*, 20 November 1937, p.

21   BFI Unpublished Script Collection S8734: *Lawrence of Arabia*, from *Revolt in the Desert* by T. E. Lawrence. Scenario by Miles Malleson, Brian Desmond Hurst & Duncan Guthrie, 4 October 1938. This final version of the screenplay has been published in Andrew Kelly, Jeffrey Richards and James Pepper, *Filming T. E. Lawrence: Korda's Lost Epics* (London: I.B.Tauris, 1997), pp.31–129.

22   BBFC Scenario Reports 1938, no.76. Held by the Special Collections Unit of the British Film Institute. Hanna also cautioned about the number of violent incidents that would require deleting: hangings, floggings, bayonettings and the stripping of corpses on the battlefield.

23   The National Archives, Kew, London, formerly the Public Record Office (hereafter TNA PRO) FO 371/20839: Minute by J. R. Colville, 26 October 1937.

24   TNA PRO FO 371/21839: Minute by R. V. Bowker, 25 October 1938.

25   See Jeffrey Richards and Jeffrey Hulbert, 'Censorship in Action: The Case of *Lawrence of Arabia*', *Journal of Contemporary History*, 19: 1 (1984), pp.153–69.

26   TNA PRO FO 371/23194: Alexander Korda to Sir Robert Vansittart, 26 June 1939.

27   Lawrence had in fact already been used for propaganda purposes in Soviet and German cinema. The Soviet film *Visitor from Mecca* (1930) featured Lawrence as a bearded Islamic 'holy man' who opposes an attempt by a Russian engineer to build a tunnel linking Russia and somewhere called 'Gulistan'. The German film *Tumult in Damascus* (*Aufruhr in Damaskus*) (Terra, dir. Gustav Ucicky, 1939) was an equally fictional story in which a heroic German officer escapes the siege of Damascus – Lawrence appears as a supporting character. For a complete synopsis, see K. R. M. Short (ed.), *Catalogue of Forbidden German Feature and Short Film Productions Held in Zonal Archives of Film Section, Information Services Division, Central Commission for Germany (BE)*, original text by John F. Kelson (Trowbridge: Flicks Books, 1996), pp.86–7.

28   Turner, *The Making of David Lean's 'Lawrence of Arabia'*, p.30.

29   Michael Powell, *Million-Dollar Movie* (London: William Heinemann, 1992), p.202.

30   Brownlow, *David Lean*, p.296.

31   '£550,000 Rank Film Postponed', *The Times*, 20 March 1958.

32   On Spiegel, see Natasha Fraser-Cavassoni, *Sam Spiegel: The Biography of a Hollywood Legend* (London: Little, Brown, 2003); and Andrew Sinclair, *Sam Spiegel: The Man Behind the Pictures* (London: Weidenfeld & Nicolson, 1987).

33   'Lawrence Film Race Is On', *Daily Mail*, 17 October 1960; Wilcox, *Twenty-Five Thousand Sunsets*, p.205.

34   Turner, *The Making of David Lean's 'Lawrence of Arabia'*, p.37.

35   'Film of Lawrence of Arabia: Mr Albert Finney's Test for the Part', *The Times*, 19 October 1960.

36   Thomas Wiseman, 'Why Finney Said No', *Evening Standard*, 3 February 1961.

37   'O'Toole Will Play Lawrence of Arabia', Columbia Pictures press release, 20 November 1960, on the BFI microfiche for *Lawrence of Arabia*.

38   'Sam Spiegel Announces Casting and Production Plans for January 2 Shooting of "Lawrence of Arabia"', Columbia press release, 16 October 1960, BFI microfiche.

39   Neither Foreman nor Wilson received a writing credit for *The Bridge on the River Kwai*, which was credited to Pierre Boulle, author of the original novel. Boulle collected the

Academy Award for Best Adapted Screenplay without having written a single word. In 1992 Columbia re-issued *Kwai* on video with an amended credit for Foreman and Wilson. See Kevin Brownlow, 'The Making of David Lean's Film of *The Bridge on the River Kwai*', *Cineaste*, 22: 2 (1996), pp.10–16.

40   Michael Wilson, 'Lawrence of Arabia: Elements and Facets of the Theme', 20 September 1959. This document was published in *Cineaste*, 21: 4 (1995), pp.30–2.

41   Ibid.

42   According to Turner, *The Making of David Lean's 'Lawrence of Arabia'*, p.67, Wilson's first draft was delivered on 4 August 1960. The BFI Library holds copies of Wilson's 'revised second draft' of 27 September 1960 (S15680) and his third draft of 2 February 1961 (S15681) – though confusingly this is labelled '2nd Draft Script'. Both are entitled *Seven Pillars of Wisdom*. The 27 September script is 296 pages, the 2 February script 273 pages.

43   BFI Unpublished Script Collection S15680: *Seven Pillars of Wisdom*. Screenplay by Michael Wilson, second draft – revised 27 September 1960.

44   Quoted in Turner, *The Making of David Lean's 'Lawrence of Arabia'*, pp.71–3.

45   Ibid., p.82.

46   'Clues to the Legend of Lawrence', *The New York Times*, 25 February 1962, p.16.

47   Adrian Turner, *Robert Bolt: Scenes from Two Lives* (London: Hutchinson, 1998), pp.197–8.

48   BFI Unpublished Script Collection S1096 *Lawrence of Arabia*. Screenplay by Robert Bolt. This is undated, though the date in the BFI Library card index (27 September 1960) is clearly incorrect.

49   Brownlow, *David Lean*, p.432.

50   Anthony Nutting also wrote a biography of Lawrence: *Lawrence of Arabia: The Man and the Motive* (London: Hollis & Carter, 1961).

51   Quoted in Brownlow, *David Lean*, pp.454–5.

52   '"Lawrence of Arabia" A Man-Breaking Party in Grim Desert and Spain', *Variety*, 20 June 1962.

53   Jonathan Stubbs, The Eady Levy: Runaway Bribe? Hollywood Production and British Subsidy in the Early 1960s', Journal of British Cinema and Television, 6:1 (2009), pp. 1–20

54   Richard Aldington, *Lawrence of Arabia: A Biographical Enquiry* (London: HarperCollins, 1955); Colin Wilson, *The Outsider* (London: Victor Gollancz, 1956).

55   Steven C. Caton, *Lawrence of Arabia: A Film's Anthropology* (Berkeley: University of California Press, 1999), p.103.

56   See the entry on Frederick A. Young in Duncan Petrie (ed.), *The British Cinematographer* (London: British Film Institute, 1996), pp.158–63. Young's own account of the shooting is in the *Journal of the Society of Film and Television Arts*, 10 (Winter 1962–3), a special issue on *Lawrence of Arabia*, pp.19–21.

57   'The Taking of Aqaba'. This is a replacement page in the shooting script of *Lawrence of Arabia* (BFI Unpublished Script Collection S13025, no date).

58   Ella Shohat, 'Gender and Culture of Empire: Toward a Feminist Ethnography of Cinema', *Quarterly Review of Film and Video*, 13: 1–3 (1991), p.52.

59   As far as I am aware, there is no Arab-produced film about Lawrence and the Arab Revolt. However, there is a Turkish film, *Ingiliz Kemal against Lawrence* (dir. Lütfi Ö. Akad, 1952), which interprets the story as a heroic Turkish struggle against the British colonizers. See Laurence Raw, 'T. E. Lawrence, the Turks, and the Arab Revolt in the Cinema: Anglo–American and Turkish Representations', *Literature/Film Quarterly*, 33: 4 (2005), pp.252–9.

60   'Lawrence of Arabia', *Financial Times*, 11 December 1962.

61　'A Freudian Oasis', *Scene*, 27 December 1962.
62　'Two Styles Combined in "Lawrence of Arabia"', *Daily Telegraph*, 11 December 1962.
63　*The Sunday Times*, 16 December 1962.
64　'Arabia Deserta', *Listener*, 20 June 1963.
65　'Full-Length Portrait of Lawrence in the Desert', *The Times*, 11 December 1962.
66　'El Aurens', *New Statesman*, 14 December 1962.
67　'Blood, Sand and a Dozen Lawrences', *Observer*, 16 December 1962.
68　*Monthly Film Bulletin*, 30: 349 (February 1963), p.18.
69　*Village Voice*, 20 December 1962, p.16.
70　*The New York Times*, 17 December 1962, p.5.
71　*Film Quarterly*, 16: 3 (Spring 1963), pp.56–7.
72　*Financial Times*, 7 June 1963; *Variety*, 27 December 1963, p.1.
73　'Lawrence Film "Divergencies"', *Daily Telegraph*, 1 December 1962.
74　A. W. Lawrence, 'The Fiction and the Fact', *Observer*, 16 December 1962.
75　Letter from B. H. Liddell Hart, *The Times*, 19 December 1962.
76　Robert Bolt, 'Apologia'. Published in *Cineaste*, 21: 4 (1995), pp.33–4.
77　Wendy Webster, *Englishness and Empire 1939–1965* (Oxford: Oxford University Press, 2005), p.211.
78　*Zulu* (Paramount/Diamond Films, dir. Cy Endfield, 1964); *Khartoum* (United Artists/Julian Blaustein, dir. Basil Dearden, 1966).
79　See 'Restoring Lawrence: An Interview with Robert Harris', *Cineaste*, 17: 2 (1989), pp.22–3.

7
PURSUING RESPECT
The Naked Prey (1965)

There are some stories which are so inherently engaging that they are fated to be told and retold, worked and reworked, imagined and re-imagined across multiple media. One such story is an offshoot of the hunter-in-empire adventure originally published by American journalist Richard Connell in 1924: 'The Most Dangerous Game', sometimes known as 'The Hounds of Zaroff'. The story concerns a big game hunter who is shipwrecked on a mysterious Caribbean island only to be hunted by a deranged Russian aristocrat, General Zaroff. As H. G. Wells' *War of the Worlds* was the perfect nightmare for Edwardian British readers, revers-ing their habit of colonizing other places, so 'The Dangerous Game' reflected back on an America with a taste for blood sports. RKO filmed the story first as *The Most Dangerous Game* (1932) with Joel McCrea on the run from Leslie Banks, and then again with an anti-Nazi spin as *A Game of Death* (1945). United Artists delivered their version as *Run for the Sun* (1956) with Richard Widmark as the prey and Trevor Howard as a British Nazi villain against a Mexican setting. The story was also plundered to become the grindhouse teen-horror *Bloodlust!* (1961). But 1966 brought an astonishing re-imagining of the 'hunter hunted' theme as actor-director-producer Cornel Wilde created a variant of the story which pulled the lion skin rug from under a decade of technicolour tributes to the Great White Hunters. In Wilde's retelling the Caribbean Island became the vast plains of Southern Africa at the height of the age of empire, and the hunters were neither Russians nor Nazis but the African tribesmen themselves. Yet this was more than an exploitation of fears of the African other; the story developed into a parable of the savage lurking in every man and the need for understanding and respect across the lines of race and nation.

The Script

Despite its debt to Richard Connell the immediate inspiration for *The Naked Prey* was a real incident, not in the Caribbean or Africa but in the American West. In 1809 a mountain man named John Colter – who had been part of the Lewis and Clark expedition – clashed with the Blackfeet Indians on the plains. While the Blackfeet killed a comrade outright, they allowed Colter a sporting chance, set him loose naked with a bow-shot's start and pursued him across the thorny wilderness. Colter killed his closest pursuer, outran the rest and escaped by hiding inside a beaver dam and then lived to tell the tale.[1] Elements of the story featured in Sam Fuller's 1957 Western *Run of the Arrow,* which moved the action to the post–Civil War era, but there was evidently even more mileage in John Colter's run. In 1963 two writers – Clint Johnston (whose previous works included the novel and screenplay *Young Daniel Boone*) and Don Peters – began touting a screenplay based on the incident around Hollywood with the title *The Day of the Savage.* It was a tough, pared down story, written with a striking directness. The script emphasized the visual and an uncompromising realism, which included requiring that the Indians speak 'in the *harsh guttural sounds of their own language'.* The writers underlined a symbolic dimension of the work by identifying the characters only by generic names: 'Man,' '2nd Man,' 'The Old One' and so forth.

The Day of the Savage followed the bones of the Colter story, though the action moved to the 1820s. Two hunters encounter Indians on the open plains. When 2nd Man accidentally kills one, both men are subjected to brutal retribution. The 2nd Man is tortured to death by being staked to the ground to be set upon by a tethered rattlesnake, but admiring Man, the Indians offer him 'the race of death'. They set him loose as naked as the Production Code would allow and give him a chance to outrun their braves. His escape becomes a gruelling cross-country pursuit of many days. During his run Man employs multiple strategies to outwit his pursuers, including using fire as a weapon. He resorts to eating raw snake for sustenance. Just when the Indians are about to catch him, Man reaches a frontier fort and finds his woman – thought lost – is there. The script ends with the Indians looking with admiration on the one that got away and Man triumphant: 'There is glory in his eyes. He has met the SAVAGE ... mastered and won his way back to ... WOMAN'.[2]

The screenplay came to the attention of actor/director Cornel Wilde. Wilde – then approaching 50 – had a 20-year career in motion pictures behind him. Born in New York in 1915 into a Hungarian/Czech family and educated in Europe, he had a talent for languages and an athletic frame. An Olympic-level fencer, he traded his place in the US team at the Berlin games to pursue a stage career (with a side line providing the foreign accents for the *March of Time*). His big break came in 1939 when he was recruited by Laurence Olivier to coach fencing for his Broadway production of *Romeo and Juliet* the following year. He would also play the role of Tybalt. With Olivier and Vivien Leigh both juggling film commitments, the production rehearsed in Hollywood and there Wilde won a contract at Warner Brothers. He was often cast in costume pictures. His most famous film role was as Chopin in *A Song to Remember*. His swordmanship and athleticism led to a string of swashbuckling roles, and his vaguely swarthy looks meant he was often employed playing Frenchmen, Arabs or even the title role in William Dieterle's *Omar Khayyam* (1957). In the mid-1950s he wisely moved to take greater control of his own career. Like Burt Lancaster before him, Wilde founded his own film production company, Theodora, producing and starring in a film noir called *The Big Combo* (1955). He also began directing. Initially he tackled standard adventure fare: heist gone wrong in *Storm Fear* (1956), car racing in *The Devil's Hairpin* (1957), oil fire fighting in *Maracaibo* (1958) and historical romance in *Lancelot and Guinevere* (1963), but he was looking to say more.[3]

As a youth Cornel Wilde had enjoyed the first RKO adaptation of *The Most Dangerous Game*, and now he was drawn back to the variation on the theme.[4] On 15 November 1963 the *Hollywood Reporter* reported that Wilde had purchased the *Day of the Savage* screenplay, now titled *The Naked Quarry*, which he described as 'the most exciting and unusual Western I've read in years'. Wilde planned to shoot in 70 mm in Arizona or Utah.[5] Just a few months later the same paper reported a major twist in the production. Wilde had decided to relocate the action from the American West to nineteenth-century Africa. Wilde wanted to further explore the African themes and locations touched by his work in *Beyond Mombasa* (1956), and his initial reworking of the screenplay specified a Kenyan setting. But it was also clear that an African location made economic sense. American locations were expensive compared to subsidized African alternatives; moreover, the *Hollywood Reporter* noted: 'the success of Joe Levine's *Zulu* in its London opening triggered interest in the Wilde project on the part of several distributors including a British major'.[6]

The South African government was well aware of the benefits that international film-makers could bring to their increasingly tarnished image. Like Franco's Spain and Tito's Yugoslavia, wooing the world's film-makers became a staple of their public diplomacy. Early beneficiaries included Howard Hawks who came to make *Hatari!* (1962) with John Wayne. In 1963 South Africa resolved to establish a National Film Board to facilitate this work and stimulate South Africa's own film production. The Board opened its doors under the chairmanship of Dr Francois J. de Villiers in April 1964. Wilde would be one of many film-makers to take advantage of its upgraded hospitality, which included generous tax breaks.[7]

By the spring of 1964 Clint Johnston and Don Peters completed their second draft of the screenplay, now set in Kenya and called *The African Adventure*, a title which flagged the film as a contribution to the Imperial Adventure genre.[8] The script developed the visceral violence of the original. The film would open with a brutal elephant hunt in which beaters would be horrifically killed. The writers suggested that two elephants might be slaughtered for effect.[9] Now, not only would 2nd Man be tortured to death with a snake, but also new characters from a wider safari party would be variously beaten to death, trussed like a chicken and stabbed, and most disturbingly of all, cased in mud and roasted over a slow fire in a scene which hinted at the ancient slander of cannibalism.[10]

The script evolved. Material added into the draft as a result of discussion with Wilde, and at some point actually written by Wilde,[11] included a prologue and a larger role for 'Woman'. Now the film opened inside a British fort. Woman pleads with her husband not to go on another safari; the Man explains that he cannot go back on his word and the two strip naked and make love. The party leaves the fort and encounters a group of Africans who request ritual gifts to allow the hunters to operate on their territory. The Man, as manager of the safari, moves to comply but 2nd Man as its financier forbids it and slights the Africans' leader, thereby establishing a motive for the Africans' later retribution.[12] Other innovations in the script included an erotic flashback in which Man remembers Woman in a dream.[13] Also, as the script moves to its climax the Man witnesses a raid by Arab slavers and their allies on a peaceful village.[14] The Man intervenes and rescues one African girl. The two travel together and develop a mutual understanding.[15] One final significant change came at the end of the script where, echoing the conclusion of *Zulu*, as the Man reaches the safety of the fort one of his surviving pursuers – the Old One – raises his spear 'in a sort of grudging salute' and the Man 'raises his hand weekly in return'.[16] The film was evolving beyond its origin in a story of simple survival into a parable of the hard road to respect and mutual understanding.

Wilde's enthusiasm for the project knew no bounds. He later recalled:

> This reliance upon visuals attracted me, of course. That and the fact that it had a realistic quality, and that I could find a theme in it to work toward all the time. The action was inherent, but so was what it had to say: that man must learn to understand his fellow

man, no matter how different he is, or all men will live like animals in the jungle.[17]

He was undeterred by the levels of violence in the screenplay, noting:

> I wanted to ... do a picture about Africa the way I believed it should be done. I didn't feel I should make compromises. Maybe six out of a thousand might have found it was too tough to take, but the other 994 people I think would get more out of the picture because it was done honestly, without compromise.[18]

Others felt compromise was necessary.

As the summer neared Wilde succeeded in bringing Paramount into the project,[19] but before they could announce the deal the studio needed to be sure that the script would be passed by the Production Code Administration. On 28 July 1964 Geoffrey M. Shurlock of the PCA informed Edward Schellhorn of Paramount Pictures: 'A film based on this script would be un-acceptable under the requirements of the Production Code because of an overemphasis of sadistic violence, brutality or gruesomeness.' Specific problems included the 'bold sex scene' in the prologue and dream, the mutilation of a bearer, 'toilet action,' and animal cruelty during the elephant hunt, and various scenes of 'dismembering', 'skull crushing', and animal slaughter. The depiction of torture attracted particular criticism. Shurlock noted: 'The torture scenes go into areas of sadism which we feel are completely unsuitable for screen entertainment.'[20] Schellhorn hastily scheduled a meeting bringing Cornel Wilde together with Shurlock and others at the PCA. Wilde made a string of concessions to secure the endorsement of the Code office including eliminating the dismemberment and 'toilet action'. He pledged to handle the torture scenes with care and stage acts of violence 'in such a manner as to avoid any excessive brutality of gruesomeness'. But Wilde stuck to his guns on one issue: native costume and especially that worn by the girl with whom the Man bonds. Shurlock noted:

> Mr. Wilde indicated a desire to have the girl in this sequence wearing an authentic native costume which would result in no covering from the waist up. We were assured that the girl is to be 11 or 12 years old rather than a fully mature or voluptuous young woman. In our opinion, such a costume will be acceptable with the important provisions that these scenes do not result in any undue exploitation of the girl's semi-nudity or include any suggestiveness with could be rendered offensive.[21]

Wilde's reassurance was enough to close the deal. On 7 August 1964 *The Daily Variety* reported that Paramount was backing Wilde to make a movie now called *The Naked Prey*.[22]

The Location

By the time Paramount announced the deal, Wilde was already en route to Africa. He arrived in South Africa on 8 August, casting the picture and setting up for the start of filming in September. He chose locations in and around the settlement of Sibasa, capital of the Venda people, in the Kruger National Park in the North of the Transvaal, close to the Limpopo River on the border with Rhodesia and Mozambique. The site had a rich variety of terrain and wildlife within relatively easy reach, though filming included travel to locations in the neighbouring countries. On 22 August he wrote to Jack Karp at Paramount:

> Our location sites are really breathtaking and wonderful in their various ways. Almost all of the casting has been completed with some really impressive types for the various roles. We have an absolutely adorable little African girl [Bella Randles] who will not give Jeff Shurlock any headaches! She is not quite ten and, although small, remarkably strong and intelligent. We will get an unexpected value from her because of her size and 'Shirley Temple' personality.[23]

Other casting successes included securing the services of two distinguished South African actors. A white Afrikaans actor named Gert Van Den Bergh as 2nd Man, who was familiar from his role as Lt Ardendorff in *Zulu*, and a young black actor called Ken Gampu to play the leader of the warriors. Already well known on the stage, he was soon to win fame in his own country as 'Africa's Gregory Peck' for his role in the courtroom drama *Dingaka* (1965).[24] Wilde also cast the reigning Miss South Africa – one Vedra Karamitas – to play the role of Woman, only to cut her role entirely in the first weeks of production.[25]

Preparations included a lot of attention to local detail. Studio publicity notes boasted that the dress, music and dance within the movie would draw on the traditions of the Venda and also the Nguni, Xhosa, Shangaan and Zulu. The Kenyan setting was written out forthwith. Wilde cautioned the studio publicity department 'not to release any synopses or scripts which refer to the Masai' as 'we are not referring to any specific tribe in either village, and we are definitely not using Masai or their costumes'.[26] On 10 September Paramount submitted a revised script fresh from Wilde in the field, which Shurlock duly cleared subject to the film-maker's care in staging the scenes of violence.[27] The film had begun shooting two days previously.[28]

Despite the help of its South African co-producer, Sven Persson, an experienced British production manager Basil Keys (associate producer of *Zulu*), and crew with local knowledge including the South African journalist, James Chapman who recorded the location sound, Cornel Wilde encountered no shortage of challenges filming on location. The chief location of Sibasa was remote and had been without rain for four years. The American trade papers saw access to the region as a special 'gesture of cooperation', from the South African government.[29] The crew worked closely with local Bantu commissioner, Gert Thomas Akron, but the real power-broker in Vendaland was the chief, Tshivase, whose personal village was used as the location for the torture scenes. Filming required the relocation of villagers and the Bantu Commission took the opportunity to raze their settlement and build a 'new and more modern village built in its place'. Local women cleared vegetation for a special road to allow the film crew to access an area remote enough to allow them to shoot the brush fire sequence safely.[30]

The exotic location of the shoot provided a steady stream of copy for the Hollywood papers, most of which delighted in revisiting traditional stereotypes of the colonial 'other'. The *New York Daily News* reported that colour-coded crew t-shirts from the set had replaced spears warped by lion killing as the number one status symbol in Vendaland.[31] Louella Parsons reported that following the filming of a tribal dance sequence Chief Tshivase had attempted to present Wilde with a 15-year-old bride as a gift. The polygamist was supposedly utterly puzzled when Wilde indicated that he already had one.[32]

Paramount's publicity department produced a range of stories to boost the exotic appeal of the film. They reported that the Venda were so excited by the presence of the crew that they had proclaimed 'the Time of the White Man's Magic Box', which they marked in songs and in special names chosen for children born during the auspicious visit. They added that 'witch doctors are prophesying great happenings for the tribe because the whole wide world will now know of it and its greatness'. They noted variously that Wilde had been obliged to hire all three wives of one villager, taught how to detect a vehicle an hour before its arrival through feeling vibrations in the ground, and how when his car became stuck in sand Wilde was able to pay local men to rescue him with cartons of cigarettes. The men fetched their wives to push the car and smoked the cigarettes while overseeing proceedings.[33]

The *Hollywood Citizen-News* was less restrained than the Paramount publicists in its portrait of the shoot, rehearsing clichés from the world of Tarzan:

> Recruiting of natives presented a tough and dangerous task in as much as many of the tribal groups still practice cannibalism while the bulk of the Venda warriors are constantly on the edge of savagery...Cornel discovered that in addition to being a writer director, producer and star of his picture he had to serve as psychologist and medicine man in treating the natives.[34]

Many snippets from the location suggested that the locals understood Western ways rather well. The *Citizen-News* concluded:

> The most effective cure-all Wilde revealed grimly was his pay deal with the Venda chief...enough to ensure the company's safety, and to create a boom in the Venda economy![35]

Some of these economic stories placed the joke on Wilde,[36] but most of the copy has a sour note. Wilde apparently told columnist Sheilah Graham that he paid the Tshivase only $500 which the chief used to purchase radios and cows in some accounts and vodka in others. Chief Tshivase in turn insisted that his subjects be paid only 60 cents per day to work as extras lest they expect a rise once the film crew had left town. The chief also reportedly pressed Wilde to supply a new Chevrolet to replace his recently wrecked Mercedes, but was disappointed.[37]

Wilde's gruelling shooting schedule took its toll. In mid-October, he fell ill with a fever of 98.5. The crew kept the film on schedule by filming pick-up shots and cutaways to the Man's feet, and took their rest day on a Thursday rather than a Sunday. Wilde responded to antibiotics and – with his acting roots firmly in 'the method' – was swift to turn the negative into a positive and stagger back into frame, and use his weakness and discomfort to add realism to his role.[38]

Paramount's publicity department reported only one incident of real trouble on the set: a bee attack which delayed shooting for a day.[39] The reality was more complicated. *Cinema* magazine reported that the

production manager was bitten by a cobra while filming the snake torture scene and

> Natives not attached to the village [in which filming took place] set
> grass fires and put water in the gas tanks of the company trucks.
> On another occasion, an attempt was made to blow up the Land
> Rover driven by cameraman Bill Thompson. Thompson fortunately
> noticed in time that his gas tank had been rigged for explosion.[40]

One Los Angeles newspaper reporting the same story added:

> The company was shooting about 300 miles from where all the
> whites were slaughtered in the Belgian Congo.[41]

The Congo was actually 700 miles away, but the tie-in to current events
doubtless helped to stoke interest in the project.[42] Oddly the sabotage incidents are not mentioned in the daily cables from the location to London
or Hollywood, or Wilde's other legion interviews about the film. It is possible that he repressed such incidents in deference to their South African
hosts or considered evidence of African hostility to the filming an embar-
rassment. On 2 November the production manager cabled the studios with
good news: 'happy to inform you principal photography completed Sibasa
Sunday, two days under schedule'.[43] Wilde promptly relocated to London
for two weeks of convalescence recovering from a tick fever that had col-
oured him black and blue.[44]

Though Wilde had the main action in the can, he also wanted to splice in
wildlife photography and especially scenes of animal combat as a symbolic
counter-point to the human action on the screen.[45] He returned to Africa in
early 1965 to capture more of the necessary footage. He paid the price. When
filming a fight between a python and a giant iguana, Wilde stepped in to
save the iguana and prolong the action. Unappreciative, the iguana sunk
its teeth into his leg and only let go when killed. The wound was such that
Wilde had to be flown to London for reconstructive surgery. He quipped to
friends at home in Hollywood that he was 'probably the only actor in town
who has had a shin lift'.[46] The previous week he had learned that one of the
hunters hired to help on the picture – Brian Glynn – had been murdered in
the Congo along with two native assistants while working as a mercenary.
Life and art were too close for comfort.[47]

In the end Wilde was content to make do with the animal combat footage
he had and to plug any gaps with stock footage. With the film complete he

had much to celebrate. He had created a remarkable location picture – with 1,300 camera angles including many extreme close-ups with an experimental Panavision Micro Panatar lens and some stunning widescreen compositions – for $73,000 under its million dollar budget.[48]

The Film

As finally produced, *The Naked Prey* went out of its way to underline its respect for the African experience and broke new ground in the imperial adventure genre. The warriors were front and center and their individual characters and relationships allowed to develop, despite all dialogue being rendered in their own Nguni language without translation in subtitles. This approach was underlined in the credits, which were accompanied by primitivist sketches of natives and hunters by local artist Andrew T. Motjuoadi, and by the musical score, which as an opening title proclaimed was entirely 'African music played by Africans on African instruments'.[49]

The symbolic names used in the screenplay were repeated in the opening credits: 'Cornel Wilde as The Man'. A voice-over narration set the scene for the action:

> A hundred years ago Africa was a vast, dark unknown. Only a few explorers, and missionaries, the ivory hunters and the infamous slavers risked their lives on its blood-soaked trails. Gleaming tusks were the prize and sweating slaves sold by their own kings and chiefs in the ceaseless tribal wars or seized by slavers.

The significance came in the final sentence as Wilde framed the problem of Africa's past in terms of a failure of humans to understand each other, and a mutual degeneration to the level of animals.

> The lion and the leopard hunted savagely among the huge herds of game, and man lacking the will to understand other men became like the beasts and their way of life was his.

The point is made visually by a camera pan across from a lion through blank screen into landscape pan to colonial fort where a safari is setting out.

The final film played up the nastiness of 2nd Man (Gert Van Den Bergh), whose arrogance in refusing gifts to the Bold One (Ken Gampu) and his tribe precipitates the disaster. The portrayal is a remarkable critique of the worst attitudes of the Afrikaners, made especially bold by the South African regime's record of support for the film. One can only assume that any government sight of the screenplay happened without the knowledge that the character would be played by an Afrikaner. 2nd Man nonchalantly reveals plans to go into the slave trade and suggests that the Man (Wilde) might join him. The Man declines. The elephant hunt is bloody and includes stock footage of two real elephant deaths. In its aftermath bearers are seen climbing out from inside an elephant carcass as though it were a fleshy tent. They drag great armfuls of organs to roast over the camp fire. The attack of the now hostile local tribe is swift and brutal. The scenes at the native village have the air of a macabre festival with a rotund chief (Morrison Gampu) presiding. The villagers laugh as if watching a circus while bearers from the safari and then the whites are put to death. The safari's overseer (Patrick Mynhardt), bound like a chicken, is told that he will be allowed to live if he can hop a short distance before being caught by the women of the tribe. He cannot. Overwhelmed by the women his death blows are shown from a high angle as a circle of hands rising and falling like a perverse, pulsating dance. The bearer's death – encased in clay with mouth, nose and ear tubes and roasted alive – is as troubling on screen as it was in the script. The Man is given his 'lion's chance' to escape, and warriors worthy of the pursuit are selected.[50] There is a moment in which a young warrior – Young One (Horace Gilman) – notices that the Man is wearing a wedding ring (now the only remaining trace of the Woman character) and moves to take it using his *panga* (machete) if necessary. The Bold One (Ken Gampu) blocks him and sets the Man running.[51]

The chase begins with an upset. The Young One, who is running ahead, throws his spear but misses. The Man impales him on his own weapon, takes his shoes, *panga*, flint and water, and runs on. The viewer expects that the next pursuer (Eric Mcanyana) will simply leap over the body and continue the chase. He does not. His burst of speed is motivated by a desire to get to the man the script reveals to be his brother. He cradles the body with palpable anguish. This is the moment in which Cornel Wilde as director establishes that for all the brutality of the village scene, there are human beings on both sides of this story. As the pursuit unfolds the action compliments both the pursuers and the pursued. The Africans track skillfully but the Man is cunning and ruthless. He maneuvers behind the Gaunt One (Jose Sithole) in a stand of Euphorbia bushes and stabs him at his back. The death is marked that evening by a funeral in the pursuers' camp.

11. Torture: Natives roast a captured bearer in *The Naked Prey* (1965).

12. Pursuit: The Man (Cornel Wilde) runs for his life in *The Naked Prey* (1965).

13. Grief: The pursuers, led by Ken Gampu (Back Right), reveal their humanity as they mourn one of their number in *The Naked Prey* (1965).

On the second day the Man kills two more pursuers, besting Big Warrior (John Marcus) only by throwing sand into his eyes. The Man uses a captured bow and arrow to start a bush fire and block his pursuers' passage through a steep valley. Exhultant, the Man leaps wildly and taunts his pursuers: 'you devils'. The pursuers press on, now driven by obsession. When one – Broken Nose (Sandy Nkomo) – attempts to turn back he is killed by the Bold One.[52] Another (Fusi Zazayokwe) is reluctantly left behind following a snake bite.[53] The Man is close to collapse with hunger, but manages to kill and eat a snake. He stumbles on a village where a festival is in progress. He is able to steal food under the cover of dark.

The Man is woken by the sound of a gun being cocked. The village is under attack from slave raiders. The raid is brutal. The Man meets a young girl (Bella Randles) and saves her by (rather implausibly) charging into the midst of the slavers to distract them. He kills their leader (a second role for Patrick Mynhardt, here in blackface) and escapes by diving into a river. The girl saves him from drowning and cooks him food. She cannot speak Swahili, Sesutho or Zulu and he cannot speak Venda, but she is able to teach him the Venda word for good: *zavoudi*. Walking together they teach each other songs. She sings a Venda work song. He sings 'Little Brown

Jug' (which dates the action to sometime after its composition in 1869).[54] He places a flower in her hair. She abruptly stops and refuses to leave her territory. He gives her his flint as a parting gift. The encounter has plainly lifted his spirits.

Suddenly he recognizes the territory. He is close to the fort, but an arrow thwacks into the ground beside him. His pursuers have caught up. Drums pound and voices yelp on sound track as the Man makes a desperate dash towards fort. His closest pursuer is the brother of the first warrior to die and, driven on by a need for revenge, he chases the Man into the clear ground in front of the fort. The Man collapses but is saved when 'the brother' is shot by a sentry. African soldiers and their European officer run forward to rescue the Man.[55] In a reversal of the scene as originally written, the Man turns and salutes the Bold One first, who lifts his spear to return the salute before turning to leave with the two other remaining warriors.[56] The final credits run with recap clips of the individual pursuers identifying each by name in the manner of credits in many contemporaneous ensemble films like *The Great Escape* (1963) or *The Dirty Dozen* (1967).

The Release

Perhaps seeking to establish his film's artistic credentials, Cornel Wilde opted to release *The Naked Prey* in Europe first. The film premiered at a gala opening night screening at the San Sebastian Film Festival in June 1965. Though not in competition, it received a standing ovation.[57] Initial reviews were mostly favourable. One British viewer could not resist a swipe at the concurrent civil rights situation in the United States: 'One is pleased to learn from the synopsis that it was to have taken place a hundred years ago; perhaps it would be wise for Cornel Wilde to state this on the credit titles if he plans for distribution in the Southern States.'[58] The film encountered some troubles with foreign censors. It was banned in Finland, and the PCA noted that the British release print of *The Naked Prey* lacked shots of one bearer's blood spurting after a beheading and the entire sequence in which the other bearer is encased in clay and roasted on a spit.[59]

The American release began in the spring of 1966. While the PCA had no objections to the final film, the National Catholic Office for Motion Pictures rated the film 'B' for violence. Wilde, a Catholic himself, 'had to wage a small campaign to get the change' to an 'A-III' rating as 'morally unobjectionable for adults'. His campaign included making some small cuts and collecting a file of supporting evidence including a letter from a Catholic missionary who considered *The Naked Prey* the 'best Africa film' he had 'ever seen'.[60] Wilde was also frustrated by Paramount's business plan for the film. They opened it simultaneously on 27 screens across Los Angeles, where the film excited comment from those who saw it but closed after a week. Paramount did much better in New York where it opened only at the New Embassy Theatre on Broadway and played to a packed house for 11 weeks.[61]

The American trade papers were intrigued by *The Naked Prey* if not always for the right reasons. *Box Office* reported: 'Definitely not for the squeamish, this film will appeal to the audiences who loved *Mondo Cane* and more of the documentaries that showed primitive customs and barbaric torturing.'[62] This element in the story was prominently featured in the American-release theatrical trailer for the film.[63] *Variety* thought it 'a very good prospect for exploitation selling, but the moving, often touching story is worth more fast playoff'.[64] James Powers in the *Hollywood Reporter* noted: 'There have been so many bad pictures about Africa, stereotyped, vacant, inaccurate, that it is doubly difficult to make a good one. *The Naked Prey* is one of the best.'[65] Critics considered the main drawback of the film to be the symbolic cutaways to animal combat. *Monthly Film Bulletin* complained of 'great chunks of indigestible symbolism' and that 'the patterning of man's predicament in the lives of the animals all around him is maddeningly trite'.[66] The criticism was unfair. Wilde used the animal cutaways as more than mere symbolic echoes of the human action. The Man is clearly shown to be repelled by the brutality of nature, which opens before him like an abyss into which he may tumble at any moment. The message of the film is not that man and nature are one, but that man has to be more than nature, it is a variation on the famous line spoken by Katharine Hepburn in *The African Queen* (1951): 'Nature, Mr Allnut, is what we are put in this world to rise above.'

The film's reception was not unaffected by the upheavals of American civil rights and challenges to previously acceptable representations of blackness. Certain black audiences were unwilling to wait around for the mutual respect to develop and took offence at the opening scenes of atrocity. The film critic of the *Los Angeles Times* reported that while she found 'nothing racially objectionable' herself, '[t]wo negro women demanded their money back at the theater I attended'.[67] Similarly the entrepreneur who booked the film for a run at the famous Apollo in Harlem misjudged audience taste. It closed amid audience protests on the first day and he had to substitute *Black Spurs*, a run-of-the-mill Western which only sounded as though it had African–American interest.[68] Detractors included the African–American theatre critic Lindsay Patterson. Writing in *The New York Times* in 1970 Patterson singled out *The Naked Prey* as one of the movies which enabled America to export its racial prejudice to the world: 'The Naked Prey offered an excellent study of whitey as supreme. How one unarmed white man could outwit for countless days, on their own terrain, the warriors of an African tribe remains steadfastly beyond my comprehension.'[69]

The answer to this was that the white audience of 1966 would have assumed the superiority of the Man anyway and at least the film showed his survival hinging on a great measure of chance. More significantly Wilde allowed his African characters to be depicted in something approaching their own terms, a remarkable accomplishment at the height of apartheid. The evils of white characters and excesses of slavery were also vividly drawn. More problematic, but unmentioned by critics, were the implications of the scenes in which the Man 'learned to love' Africa again. Although touching, his road back is through a relationship not with a fellow warrior but with a child. On leaving the girl he passes two boys herding cattle and pats both on the head. The Man is plainly comfortable in a paternalist role. This was not a solution that black Africa was prepared to accept.

A number of parties had much riding on their investment of time and money in *The Naked Prey*. Most were delighted with the result. Wilde's backers were happy,[70] and the actor/director was able to continue making highly personal, and equally visceral films. The writers Johnston and Peters were nominated for an Academy Award for their screenplay, but lost to Claude Lelouch's *Un homme et une femme (1966)*. Ken Gampu launched his distinguished career. The South African government, however, would be disappointed. Its hopes that *The Naked Prey* and other films that it assisted in 1964 and 1965 would help to remake its image proved short lived. World opinion was turning against the apartheid system. In June 1965 the governing council of the Actor's Equity Association for the United States banned members from working in South Africa. Cultural sanctions against apartheid had begun.[71]

Influence

Film-makers in the generation following Wilde including Martin Scorsese and John Milius have spoken of their admiration for *The Naked Prey*, while the Coen brothers who watched the film as children created their own version with a cast of neighbourhood children.[72] Critics have belatedly acknowledged *The Naked Prey* and Wilde's equally visceral follow-up war film *Beach Red* (1967) as neglected classics. Michael Atkinson called Wilde 'a cave painter of a filmmaker born straight out of the primeval ooze with the ideas and beliefs of a rogue hyena famished by drought'. He wrote of *The Naked Prey*: 'Here is the hemorrhaging heart under the darkest Africa safari romance, the thorn-spearfight-&-starvation bones beneath the chest-pounding adventure saga.'[73] *The Naked Prey* now seems like a film ahead of its time, trying the limits of the Production Code in what would be its last years. Ironically, had it actually been made as a Western it might have been more readily assimilated into the movie canon. It would have anticipated the style of *A Man Called Horse* (1970) and *Ulzana's Raid* (1972) by half a decade and been seen as a pioneering anti-Western. Other film-makers echoed its themes of man in nature and its minimalist structure – obvious comparisons include John Boorman's *Hell in the Pacific* (1968) – one comedy in 1970 paid the compliment of a scene spoofing its action.[74]

Cornel Wilde's hunt was certainly not to be the final spin on *The Most Dangerous Game*. Cultural icons subsequently subjected to variations on this theme include Captain Kirk, James Bond and Homer Simpson.[75] The 'hunted hunter' concept was at the heart of box office hits including *Deliverance* (1972) and *First Blood* (1982). Homages to *The Most Dangerous Game* became vehicles for Arnold Schwarzenegger (twice), Jean-Claude Van Damme, Ice-T and, in risible parody, John Leguizamo.[76] Such are far removed from Wilde's film, but in 2002 Paramount announced a plan to remake *The Naked Prey* translating the action to Nicaragua and pitting stranded West Pointers against a murderous drug gang.[77] This remake came to nothing, but Mel Gibson leant heavily on *The Naked Prey* for his blood-soaked tale of the pre-Columbian Maya: *Apocalypto* (2006).

What set Cornel Wilde's telling of the story apart from other spins on *The Most Dangerous Game* was the underlying element of hope. Wilde believed passionately that through the experience the participants could learn mutual understanding and respect. Shortly before his death from leukaemia in 1989, Wilde reviewed his career and noted: 'I am very concerned about the environment and psychological health of this beautiful planet. Throughout my work is the idea, over and over, that we must all learn to respect one another'.[78] He probably underestimated the extent to which his story could exist apart from the connotations of its images. The problem was that with rebellion in the Congo and race riots on the streets of the United States the images he used – black torture and slaughter of whites and the frenzied black pursuit of a white man – were so charged as to obscure his wider message. He was using gasoline to put out a fire in the mind of his audience.[79] But the attempt was noble and the metaphor apt. The parties to the real clashes of the colonial and postcolonial world had to overcome mutual slights every bit as visceral as the brutalities staged in *The Naked Prey*, and the world could not afford the luxury of everyone learning mutual respect through the ordeal of mortal combat.

Notes

[1]   For a typical telling see Addison Erwin Sheldon, *History and Stories of Nebraska* (Chicago and Lincoln: University of Nebraska Press, 1913), on-line at http://www. legendsofamerica.com/NB-JohnColter.html accessed on 3 June 2008. For full biography see Stallo Vinton, *John Colter: Discoverer of Yellowstone Park* (New York: Edward Eberstadt, 1926).

[2]   Herrick Library, Paramount script files, *The Naked Prey* file: Clint Johnston and Don Peters, *The Day of the Savage*, 9 November 1963.

[3]   There is presently no biography of Wilde. For a survey of this life see James Robert Parish and Don E. Stanke, *The Swashbucklers*. (New Rochelle NY: Arlington House, 1976), pp.498–554, despite their getting elements of the plot of *The Naked Prey* wrong. For a critical appraisal of his directorial work see Michael Atkinson, 'Naked Prey: The Cinema of Cornel Wilde,' *Film Comment*, November–December 1996, pp.70–5. For interviews see Gordon Gow, 'Survival!' *Films and Filming*, 17: 1, October 1970, pp.4–10 and John Coen, 'Producer/Director, Cornel Wilde', *Film Comment*, Spring 1970, pp.52–60.

[4]   Criterion DVD of *The Naked Prey*, commentary by Stephen Prince.

[5]   'Cornel Wilde Gets Western Screenplay', *Hollywood Reporter*, 15 November 1963.

[6]   'Cornel Wilde sets AFRICAN ADVENTURE', *Hollywood Reporter*, 30 January 1964.

[7]   On South African film policy see 'No Easy Answer for Film Set Up in South Africa', *Variety*, 29 April 1964; Evelyn Levison, 'South African Production Pace as Bigger Government Posture Helpful', *Variety*, 12 May 1965; ' "If We Exported More Films, Our Image Would Be Improved,' – South African', *Variety*, 12 October 1966. The files suggest that South Africa might not have ended with the deal they hoped for over *The Naked Prey*. The studio production files include a note that Paramount would need to adjust Wilde's deal with the South African government to make it clear that the South Africans could not expect share of worldwide earnings of film. See Herrick Library, Paramount Pictures production records: *The Naked Prey*, Frank 22 to Caffey, July 1964. The influx of foreign film-makers proved a mixed blessing. Wilde arrived in South Africa to find that colleagues from other studios had begun to 'poison the well' with badly behaved crews and unpaid bills. One camera store had seven law suits in progress against various defaulting foreign production companies (none of which were American). Michael Fessier, 'Deadbeat Producers Turn So. Africa Skeptical of Promoters – Cornel Wilde', *Variety*, 30 December 1964, p.4.

[8]   Herrick library, Paramount scripts, *The Naked Prey: African Adventure/Naked Prey*, 18 May 1964.

9   Ibid.: 'only one of two elephants need actually be shot, but photographed from many angles INTERCUT with continued shooting to give the impression of the decimation of a large herd' (p.4).

10   For a discussion of cannibalism as cultural libel see William Arens, *The Man-Eating Myth: Anthropology and Anthropophagy* (New York: Oxford University Press, 1979).

11   Herrick Library, Paramount Pictures production records: *The Naked Prey*, Memo to file by Allen Klein, 11 September 1964 notes that changes to script have been made by Wilde but he has stated that as these were 'in his capacity as producer and director' will not seek writing credit.

12   Herrick library, Paramount scripts, *The Naked Prey: African Adventure/Naked Prey*. These pages are inserted into the 18 May script and dated 25 March 1964. They also locate the action in 1840.

13   These pages are inserted into the 18 May script and dated 2 March 1964, p.66.

14   The script specifies Swahilis attacking Warushas.

15   These pages are inserted into the 18 May script and dated 25 March 1964, pp.87–91.

16   These pages are inserted into the 18 May script and dated 29 June 1964.

17   Gow, 'Survival!', p.10.

18   Coen, 'Producer/Director, Cornel Wilde', p.55.

19   The process in outlined in Rory Guy 'Africa goes Wilde', *Cinema*, 3: 1, December 1965, pp.44–5.

20   Herrick Library, PCA files, *The Naked Prey* [Par., 1964], Shurlock to Schellhorn, 28 July 1964.

21   Herrick Library, PCA files, *The Naked Prey* [Par., 1964], Shurlock to Schellhorn, 30 July 1964.

22   'Wilde to Stalk "Prey" for Par'. *Variety*, 7 August 1964.

23   Herrick Library, Paramount Pictures production records: *The Naked Prey*,

24   Herrick Library: Core collection, production file: *The Naked Prey*, Revised Paramount production notes and synopsis, 14 January 1966. For scholarly comment on Gampu see Jacqueline Maingard, *South African National Cinema* (London: Routledge, 2007), pp.132–3.

25   Herrick Library: Core collection, production file: *The Naked Prey*, Original Paramount production notes and synopsis, circa September 1964.

26   Herrick Library, Paramount Pictures production records: *The Naked Prey*, Wilde to Alvin Manuel at Paramount, 22 August 1964. He concluded: 'Be assured that everything is being carefully checked for authenticity.'

27   Herrick Library, PCA files, *The Naked Prey* [Par., 1964], Shurlock to Schellhorn, 15 September 1964. The script is preserved in the Herrick Library, Paramount script files, *The Naked Prey* file: script as sent 8 September 1964, it included polishing of the opening scenes with the natives including the torture scene.

28   Herrick Library, Paramount Pictures production records: *The Naked Prey*, R. H. Harrison (Paramount, London) to Caffey, 10 September 1964.

29   'Wilde gets Okay for area filming', *Hollywood Reporter*, 28 September 1964. New York Public Library for the Performing Arts (Lincoln Center), Paramount Merchandizing Manuel and Press Book for *The Naked Prey*, MFL + NC 1666, ZAN T-8, microfilm reel 217 (hereafter *Naked Prey* press book), Voice of Realism, James Chapman was the great-grandson of the nineteenth century African explorer of the same name (1831–72) but no relation to the co-author of this book.

30 'Wilde Gets Okay for Area Filming', *Hollywood Reporter*, 28 September 1964. See also production notes in Herrick Library: Core collection: production file, *The Naked Prey*.

31 'Colorful Experience', *New York Daily News*, 11 October 1964.

32 Louella Parsons, 'A Special "present" for Cornel Wilde', *L. A. Herald Examiner*, 26 September 1964. Paramount later claimed that in order to avoid causing offence Wilde offered one of the Zulu crew – a driver who stood in for him during the setups for the running scenes – as a substitute groom. The compromise avoided the sort of cultural offence which sparked the events within the story, and was reportedly agreeable to all parties including the bride. *Naked Prey* press book, 'Cornel Wilde Had to Find "Substitute" Husband'.

33 *Naked Prey* press book, 'Naked Prey Reveals an Africa as It Has Never Been Seen or Filmed Before!'

34 'Los Angeles', *Hollywood Citizen-News*, 17 December 1964. In a similar vein Wilde reported how one old lady extracted 5 shillings from the 'tall stranger from the far-off place' for knowledge of how to prevent snake bites. The secret was 'wear squeaky shoes', Abe Greenberg, 'Cornel Wilde on Squeaks 'n' Snakes,' *Hollywood Citizen-News*, 24 February 1966.

35 'Los Angeles', *Hollywood Citizen News*, 17 December 1964.

36 Stories at Wilde's expense include one in which he purchased a non-poisonous snake from a ten-year old for a shilling, and an hour later was obliged to buy several more snakes – poisonous – from his friends. The following morning the camp was besieged by children, some of whom had walked as far as 40 miles, bearing a menagerie of snakes, scorpions, a baby boa and a warthog. Wilde bought them all, donated them to Pretoria Zoo and proclaimed that he would be making no further purchases. [*Naked Prey* press book, 'Communication Goes Astray!'] Another report told how one old lady had extracted five shillings from the 'tall stranger from the far-off place' for knowledge of how to prevent snake bites. The secret was 'wear squeaky shoes'. [Abe Greenberg, 'Cornel Wilde on Squeaks 'n' Snakes', *Hollywood Citizen-News*, 24 February 1966, also in *Naked Prey* press book.

37 Sheilah Graham, 'Cornel Wilde's Wild Adventure', *Hollywood Citizen-News*, 12 June 1965; Michael Fessier, 'Deadbeat Producers Turn So. Africa Skeptical of Promoters – Cornel Wilde', Weekly *Variety*, 30 December 1964, p.4. The 60 cents pay rate was reported critically in 'Four bob a day,' *Films and Filming*, March 1965, p.10 with the aside 'Colonialism dies hard'.

38 Herrick Library, Paramount Pictures production records: *The Naked Prey*, Basil Keys to Harrison, 15 and 16 October 1964.

39 Herrick Library: Core collection: production file, *The Naked Prey*. Production notes.

40 Rory Guy 'Africa Goes Wilde', *Cinema*, 3: 1 (December 1965), pp.44–5.

41 *L. A. Herald Examiner*, 1 December 1964.

42 News of a massacre broke during the filming, and Wilde reported being disconcerted by radio reports. Wilde later recalled that the chief – owner of the other radio in the village – either didn't hear the report or was too tactful to mention the incident. Guy, 'Africa Goes Wilde,' pp.44–5.

43 Herrick Library, Paramount Pictures production records: *The Naked Prey*, Keys to Frank Caffey, 2 November 1964.

44 Guy, 'Africa Goes Wilde,' pp.44–5.

45 Paramount sent the PCA a copy of a letter from the director of the South African National Parks Board of Trustees to their South African co-producer, Sven Persson, certifying that the Kruger National Park was 'satisfied that your animal shots have been dealt with in a humane fashion and that no animal was killed specially for the purpose of your picture'. Herrick Library, PCA files, *The Naked Prey* [Par., 1964], Knobel to Persson, 4 January 1965. It seems that animals which would have been harmed in the normal run of things were harmed in the making of the picture as with the goat, bled out during the torture scene. The impala killing is a cleverly staged effect.

46 Dean Gautschy, 'Iguana Bite Lands Cornel Wilde in London Hospital for Surgery', *L. A. Herald Examiner*, 26 February 1965.

47 *L. A. Herald Examiner* 18 February 1965; Guy, 'Africa Goes Wilde', pp.44–5.

48 Syn Cassyn, 'Backstage', *Box Office*, 23 August 1965; Fessier, 'Deadbeat Producers...'

49 The soundtrack compiled with the help of 'musical adviser' Andrew Tracey was released by the Smithsonian on the Folkways label and retains ethnographic significance.

50 The translation in the 'release dialogue script' reveals that all the pursuers have killed at least ten lions: Herrick library, Paramount scripts, *The Naked Prey*, 28 September 1965.

51 The translation here is that the ring will go to whoever kills the man.

52 In his commentary track on the Criterion DVD of the film Stephen Prince makes the point that this action is typical of scenes depicting African on African interactions in movies at this time. He cites multiple representations of the Zulu chief Chetewayo (Cetshwayo kaMpande) including the summary killing of the Zulu warrior who tried to restrain the missionaries in the kraal scene in *Zulu*.

53 In action within the group Zazayokwe's character had earlier been rebuked for sneaking a drink of water. Bull Marked (Joe Dlamini) sucks poison from his leg, gives him a drink and pledges to come back for him.

54 This detail is consistent with the prologue which speaks merely of African a 'century ago', but is at odds with publicity for the film which located the action in the 1840s. British Film Institute micro-jackets: *The Naked Prey*, production notes.

55 According to the UK version of the studio production notes the Sergeant was also played by Patrick Mynhardt in his third role in the film. British Film Institute micro-jackets: *The Naked Prey*: production notes.

56 Commenting on this exchange of salutes Kenneth Cameron has noted: 'it suggested where movies where at that moment: the aging white star facing the upcoming black one. It was a portent of things to come in both movies and life.' Kenneth M. Cameron, *Africa On Film: Beyond Black and White* (New York: Continuum, 1994), p.126.

57 'Wilde Naked Prey Scores', *Hollywood Reporter*, 9 June 1965.

58 Richard Craven, 'Festival: San Sebastian', *Films and Filming*, 11: 11, August 1965, p.50. The most negative British review was in the Communist *Morning Star* where on 24 September 1966 Nina Hibben assailed the film for its violence and racism. She objected to the naming of Wilde's character as Man noting: 'The hundreds of Africans in the film...apparently didn't qualify for human status.'

59 Herrick Library, PCA files, *The Naked Prey* [Par., 1964], PCA memo, December 1963

60 *Variety*, 19 April 1966. A UPI story by Vernon Scott from 21 November filed in the Herrick library's clippings file for Cornel Wilde notes that Wilde was a catholic – distressed that Beach Red has been rated C by the board for violence. Wilde critical of 'medieval stands'.

61 Coen, 'Producer/Director, Cornel Wilde', p.55, p.56.

62 'The Naked Prey,' *Box Office*, 14 March 1966.

63 The trailer is included as an extra on the Criterion DVD (2008).

64 *Variety*, 11 March 1966.

65 James Powers, 'Cornel Wilde Pic Good Boxoffice Bet,' *Hollywood Reporter*, 11 March 1966.

66 *Monthly Film Bulletin* September 1966, pp.141–2.

67 'Margaret Harford, 'PREY Has Savagery with Point', *Los Angeles Times*, 1 April 1966.

68 'Villainous Africans Get Quick KO at Apollo, Harlem House', *Variety Weekly*, 22 February 1967.

69 Lindsay Patterson, 'In Movies, Whitey is Still King', *The New York Times*, 13 December 1970, p.131. The essay was anthologized with a fight still from *The Naked Prey* in the teaching text Richard A. Maynard, *Africa on Film: Myth and Reality* (Rochelle Park NJ: Hayden, 1974), pp.75–80 and cited in Bernard Rubin, 'International Film and Television Propaganda: Campaigns of Assistance', *Annals of the American Academy of Political and Social Science*, Vol. 398 (special issue on Propaganda in International Affairs), November 1971, pp.81–92.

70 Stuart M. Kaminsky, 'Interview: Cornel Wilde', *Film Reader*, 2, January 1977, pp.159–65. 'The investors have done very well indeed on their investment in *The Naked Prey*.'

71 'Equity Outlaws So. Africa; Members Can't Work There', *Variety*, 15 June 1965.

72 Martin Scorsese, 'The Scorsese Selection', *Access: DirecTV Magazine*, February 2008; Interview: John Milius, 31 July 2008; James Mottram, *The Coen Brothers: The Life of the Mind* (Dulles VA: Brassey's, 2000) p.14.

73 Atkinson, 'Naked Prey,' pp.70–5. For a recollection of impact of the original on a teenage viewer see Bruce Bennett, 'The Chase Scene That Scarred an Era', *New York Sun*, 15 January 2007, p.14. For a plea for critical reappraisal see Stuart Kaminsky, 'Getting back to basics with Cornel Wilde', *Take One*, 5: 4, October 1976, pp.22–4.

74 The bad-taste comedy *Where's Poppa?* (United Artists dir. Carl Reiner, 1970) includes a scene in which a gang of African–Americans ask George Segal if he has 'seen the movie' take his clothes and chase him across Central Park in the manner of *The Naked Prey*.

75 In *Star Trek*, 'The Squire of Gothos', season 1, ep. 17, orig. TX 12 January 1967; *Octopussy* (Eon/MGM/UA, dir. John Glen, 1983); *The Simpsons*, Tree House of Horror XVI, 'Survival of the Fattest', season 17, ep. 4, orig. TX 6 November 2006.

76 The films are *The Running Man* (Braveworld/HBO, dir. Paul Michael Glaser, 1987); *Predator* (Fox, dir. John McTiernan, 1987); *Hard Target* (Universal, dir. John Woo, 1993); *Surviving the Game* (New Line, dir. Ernest ZR. Dickerson, 1994) and *The Pest* (TriStar, dir. Paul Miller, 1997). *The Most Dangerous Game* has even been adapted into misogynist fantasy in *The Woman Hunt* (New World Pictures, dir. Eddie Romero, 1972), science fiction exploitation in *Slave Girls From Beyond Infinity* (Titan dir. Ken Dixon, 1987) and as one of the archetypal 'video nasties' of 1980s moral panic: *Turkey Shoot* (Filmco/Hemdale, dir. Brian Trenchard-Smith, 1982) released in the UK as *Blood Camp Thatcher*.

77 Dave McNary, 'Par Hunts Down "Prey" with Heffernan Script', *Variety* 19 September 2002.

78 Peter B. Flint, 'Cornel Wild, 74 Performer and Film Producer', *The New York Times,* 17 October 1989, p.B8.

79 For an endorsement of this and other films in this book by a White Supremacist see http://www.nationalistpartyusa.com/YML.htm (accessed 16 July 2008)

8
CAMPING UP THE EMPIRE

Follow That Camel (1967), *Carry On Up the Khyber* (1968)
and *Carry On Up the Jungle* (1970)

In 1936 a young English art-school graduate with a head full of tales of derring-do on the frontier, ran away from his job with Brighton City Council 'in search of adventure' and joined the Palestine police. In later years he recalled that 'despite being ambushed, shot-up, stabbed in a dark alley, fleeced by post card sellers', he 'stayed there for 18 months', whereupon 'pausing only to shake the sand out of things' he 'fled home'.[1] His name was Talbot Rothwell and he went on to write the bulk of Britain's most successful film comedy series of the 1960s – the *Carry On* films – including three parodies of the imperial adventure genre that had propelled him on his youthful adventure. These were *Follow That Camel* (1967), a spoof of *Beau Geste* and the desert movie; *Carry On Up the Khyber* (1968) which took aim at the British Raj film and *Carry On Up the Jungle* (1970) which drew on Tarzan and the safari movie. Hits at the box office, these films provided some of the most memorable images of all British popular film and served as a window on Britain's attitudes to empire as decolonization reached its final phase.

The *Carry On* films were part of the British tradition of camp comedy – from the French *se camper* – to posture or flaunt. In the world of camp manners and markers of identity (especially sexual identity) are exaggerated and repeated with a twist to comic effect. This subverts the existing order and creates a space for alternative ways of thinking and being. In terms of sexuality, camp allowed a challenge to the world of received sexuality, making its strictures apparent and creating a place in which gay performers could be more themselves than was usual. By tackling the empire film, the *Carry On* team applied the same approach to the markers of that genre and the views of the 'other', the 'self' and the national project which imperial popular culture had embodied. It is for the contemporary viewer to question the extent to which the films were challenging the foundations of the genre or somehow putting it to a new use.

The Birth of the *Carry On* Series

The *Carry On* cycle began in 1958 with the low-budget army comedy adapted from an R. F. Delderfield play *The Bull Boys* called *Carry On Sergeant*. Astonished by their own success, producer Peter Rogers, director Gerald Thomas and writer Norman Hudis followed up with a series of comedies using essentially the same cast of stock characters and actors tackling work-related situations: a hospital, a school, the police, an employment agency and a cruise liner.[2] The films showcased a cast of stock British types – the loveable cockney rogue played by Sid James; the pretentious, effeminate Kenneth Williams; the puny and bespectacled Charles Hawtrey; the strident and sexually assertive Joan Sims; the buffoon, Kenneth Connor or Peter Butterworth; the ingénue Jim Dale – who were always more recognizable as themselves than as the characters they purported to portray. In 1963, as success opened doors for Hudis in Hollywood, Talbot Rothwell – by this time an experienced comic writer – took his place.

Rothwell brought a change of direction to the series. The films switched from work-related material to genre parodies and adopted a more risqué humour which earned 'A' rather than 'U' certificates. The first film made in the new mould was a before-the-mast adventure called *Carry On Jack* (1963). Rogers and his team followed up with a Bondian spoof thriller: *Carry On Spying* (1964). They then had fun with the Roman Epic in *Carry On Cleo* (1964), the Western in *Carry On Cowboy* (1965) and Gothic horror in *Carry On Screaming* (1966). In 1966 the Rank Organization bought the series. Rogers temporarily abandoned the *Carry On* title for *Don't Lose Your Head* (1966), a parody of *The Scarlet Pimpernel* (1934), and the first of the imperial films *Follow That Camel* (1967). In 1968 he returned to the *Carry On* title and a work-related theme with *Carry On Doctor*. *Carry On Up the Khyber* (1968) followed. Flushed with continued success the series switched again to the contemporary settings of *Carry On Camping* and *Carry On Again Doctor* in 1969, before the final imperial spoof, *Carry On Up the Jungle* (1970).

The Films

The plots were not complex. In *Follow That Camel* in 1906 a foppish young English aristocrat named 'Bo' West is falsely accused of cheating at cricket and enlists in the French Foreign Legion with his faithful butler, Simpson. The two men accidentally discover that their lascivious American Sergeant, Nocker, has fraudulently invented his deeds of heroism and win themselves

an easy life, only to be pitched into a real mission when Bo's estranged fiancée Lady Jane is captured by the Riff chieftain, Sheikh Abdul Abulbul. The
legionnaires, led by Commandant Burger, attempt to rescue Jane and frus-
trate the Riff plan to capture the vital desert outpost Fort Zuassantneuf.
They eventually succeed and Bo wins the hand of Jane and returns to
England with his honour secure. Their first child looks suspiciously like
the Commandant, including his monocle.

In *Carry On Up the Khyber* British control of the Khyber Pass in 1895 is
threatened when an Afghan warlord, Bungdit Din, finds that a member
of the 3rd Foot and Mouth regiment is – contrary to their fearsome reputation – wearing underpants under his kilt. The British attempt to regain
their reputation by proving that this is an anomaly, but succeed only in
producing a photograph of the entire regiment in undergarments. Lady
Ruff-Diamond, the wife of the governor, tries to trade the photograph for
sexual favours with the malevolent local ruler, the Khasi of Kalabar, but is
captured in the process. Captain Keene succeeds in rescuing her with the
help of the Khasi's daughter, Princess Jelhi, but the photograph is dropped.

14. Camping Up the Frontier: Bungdit Din (Bernard Bresslaw) menaces Private
Widdle (Charles Hawtrey) in *Carry On Up the Khyber* (1968).

Encouraged by the evidence of British weakness the Khasi and the Afghans sweep through the Khyber Pass and assault the British mission. When the regiment forms a line and delivers proof that they are no longer wearing underpants the enemy flees the field.

Carry On Up the Jungle follows the fortunes of a Victorian expedition to the Congo led by ornithologist Professor Inigo Tinkle and a drunken hunter named Boosey. The party includes Lady Evelyn Bagley, who is trying to locate her son, lost 20 years previously as a baby. Her repressed maid June finds the son, Ug, and the pair begin a mutual journey of sexual discovery, but the rest of the party is captured by a hostile cannibal tribe: the Noshas. Before they can be eaten they are rescued by a mysterious tribe of pale-skinned women called the Lubbidubbies who carry them off to their valley intending to put the males to stud. Lady Bagley is astonished to find that the chief of this tribe is her long-lost husband Wally. She establishes herself as queen and sends only unattractive women to mate with the men in her party. As the tribe mount a coup, Boosey's faithful African bearer Upsidaisi arrives with a platoon of British soldiers, and Ug also mounts a rescue by stampeding elephants through the camp. The female tribe embrace the British soldiers as 'real men' and the safari party escapes back to England.

The three films were of varied quality. *Follow That Camel* suffered for the absence of Sid James, and turned into a vehicle for its American guest star Phil Silvers, who reprised his Sergeant Bilko character from the previous decade. Although the locations were nowhere more exotic than Camber Sands, Sussex, it was not hard for audiences to fancy themselves watching the Sahara. *Carry On Up the Khyber* was blessed with almost all the regular cast (Roy Castle substituted for Jim Dale) and a top notch script. The location scout managed to find a substitute for the Khyber Pass in Snowdonia (North Wales) and Pinewood's much-used Irish village set was redressed for an Indian setting. The effect mimicked the production values of mainstream Hollywood epics. *Carry On Up the Jungle* was not so fortunate. Kenneth Williams did not appear owing to other commitments and the script seemed tired. The Pinewood jungle set simply did not convince and gave no impression of the vast spaces of Africa or the movement across them implied in the screenplay. The cuts to stock footage were very obvious. Moreover, the film seemed to bog down in the four-way relationship of the three ageing, sex-starved British men and one ageing, sex-starved British lady in their party. Double entendres were increasingly single and the director even included a couple of long distance shots of a bare breast during a shower sequence as if to make up in visual titillation what was missing from the script. The signs of the decline of the series were apparent, but the film provides a window on its times nonetheless.

Camping the Genre

In creating the three films Talbot Rothwell ransacked the collective memory of imperial adventure fiction on screen and in print. *Follow That Camel* drew on multiple versions of P. C. Wren's *Beau Geste*, other evocations of the Foreign Legion and desert films in general. Rothwell's working title was *Carry On Bo*. Anita Harris's sultry dancer 'Corktip' is a nod to the character 'Cigarette' in the much filmed Foreign Legion story *Under Two Flags* (played by Claudette Colbert in the 1936 version). Bernard Bresslaw's sheikh in *Follow That Camel* draws on Anthony Quinn's performance in *Lawrence of Arabia*, and the shooting script included a scene in which the relief column encounter an Englishman in the desert who, the script noted, 'looks remarkably like O'Toole in full Lawrence kit', and continued:

> LAWRENCE: 'Excuse me, but am I going right for Arabia?'
> BURGER *(points back):* 'Straight on. As far as you can go.'
> LAWRENCE: 'Thanks awfully. Lovely weather!'
> *And goes on*
> *Burger looks after him, wondering. Then shakes his head.*
> BURGER: 'No, it couldn't have been.'[3]

The part was cast and one Peter Jesson contracted for the part, but the scene did not make it into the final cut of the film.[4]

    Carry On Up the Khyber cited numerous Kipling adaptations, including *Gunga Din* as the leader of the Afghans is called Bungdit Din. *Carry On Up the Jungle* alluded to John Huston's *The African Queen* in a rather obvious subtitle for the movie as well as in the character of the drunken hunter Boosey. The jungle boy elements in the plot – not least the swim in the water hole, scenes of June and the Jungle Boy Ug comparing their bodies and June teaching Ug English – are familiar from the *Tarzan* films, especially *Tarzan the Ape Man* (1932) and *Tarzan and His Mate* (1934). The working title was *Carry On Jungle Boy*, and but for the legal obstacles the movie would probably have been called *Carry On Tarzan*. The idea of a lost tribe of pale women chimed with the Rider Haggard story *She* in public minds following the production by Hammer Films in 1965.[5] The white man becoming a chief had parallels in Joseph Conrad's *Heart of Darkness*. Like *Camel*, *Jungle* was at one time supposed to include an encounter with a historical character with his own heritage in motion pictures: Henry Morton Stanley. Rothwell had him wonder out of the jungle in full tropical kit and hopefully greet Boosey with: 'Doctor Livingstone I presume?' He is disappointed by Boosey's reply: 'Never heard of him.' When Stanley departs with a plaintive 'Oh...if you should happen to run into him anywhere, tell him that Stanley's looking for him will you?', Boosey remarks: 'Stanley?! Blimey, you find 'em everywhere these days!' in a joke playing on the increasing visibility of homosexuality in the 1960s.[6]

It is curious that encounters with real historical figures – Stanley and Lawrence – should have been deleted from both movies. Their presence was quite consistent with the genre, which had a habit of embroidering around real events and personalities and benefited from the added kudos this brought. Often the transformation from script to final film required genre elements giving way for quicker laughs, but in this instance it is possible that the producers were uncomfortable mixing humour and real history. Though not playing with the imperial genre at that particular moment, Khyber at least kept a joke suggesting the presence of a real historical character. During the polo game Ruff-Diamond remarks 'Well played Philip' and adds 'that lad will go far if he makes the right marriage' – a quip which suggests that the player might be the future Prince Consort, Philip, Duke of Edinburgh.

The Carry Ons also made fun of the dialogue and visual clichés of the empire film. In Camel the aristocratic Bo West protests grandly: 'I must remember the family name.' His devoted butler Simpson replies with a helpful 'West'. When the Highlanders make their stand against the charging Burpar tribesmen in Khyber the command familiar from Zulu and numerous other empire films is heard: 'Fire at will', followed by the quip from the missionary Brother Belcher: 'Poor old Will, why do they always fire at him?' In Jungle Boosey hears native drums and turns to his bearer Upsidaisi and asks 'What are they saying?' only to be told: 'They're saying bum di di bum di di bum bum bum.' There is humour at the expense of the maudlin deaths in the imperial adventure genre. In Khyber, Brother Belcher describes British bodies lying on a battle field with spears stuck in them as looking like 'a lot of unwanted cocktail snacks', and Private Widdle's conversation with the dying Ginger spoofs the usual course of such scenes. 'Now give it to me straight. Am I gonna be alright?', Ginger asks. Widdle replies: 'Course not, Ginge mate...How could you be, with half a dozen dirty great holes in you? You've had it.' Ginger expires only after Wilde places a greatcoat over him. His last words are 'That's right...Bleedin' suffocate me!' In Camel the bullet-ridden Burger is given a drink of water and immediately springs multiple leaks like a punctured watering can.

Merely introducing the familiar *Carry On* gang into the genre was subversive. Part of the fun of the movie was to see their double evocation of their character – simultaneously Bernard Bresslaw and a Riff Sheik/Afghan Chief/African bearer or Joan Sims and a Moroccan bar owner/Governor's wife/Lady on Safari. Yet the *Carry On* imperial adventures, like the wider body of genre parodies, were ultimately content merely to render their targets visible by comic exaggeration and leave the core of the genre intact. The governor's residence is saved at the end of *Khyber*; honour is restored at the end of *Camel*; the family is reunited at the end of *Jungle*. Some empire films question the morality of the imperial project, questioning the impact of imperialism on its subjects or even – as in *Lawrence of Arabia* – on its perpetrators. There is no room for such questioning in the *Carry On* universe; rather the comic exaggeration is such that it might actually serve to re-inscribe elements of the genre that it emphasizes, not least the representation of the other and the self.

15. Camping Up the Legion: Burger (Kenneth Williams) expires, supported by Sgt Knocker (Phil Silvers) and Bo West (Jim Dale) in *Follow That Camel* (1967).

Camping Up the Other

The *Carry On* version of empire played on the notion that foreigners were different. These differences were rendered in three major ways: sex, violence and religion. While all the *Carry On* genre parodies played up the potential for sensational sexual situations, this was especially obvious in the *Carry On* version of empire. The costumes worn by the foreign women on the *Carry On* frontier emphasized cleavage and the plots dwelt on their sexual licence. *Camel* and *Khyber* have their harems and in *Jungle* an entire tribe of women seek to imprison the male protagonists for the sole purpose of harnessing their reproductive capabilities. The *Carry On* empire provided a place for repressed British male audiences to explore fantasies of sexual freedom, perhaps made more tangible when the male protagonists were character actors like Sid James or Jim Dale identified with authentic British types rather than distant Hollywood icons.

Foreigners in the *Carry On* empire were violent. British characters are threatened with 'having them both cut off' in Morocco, 'the death of a thousand cuts' in Afghanistan and being eaten in Africa. The films seem to be playing with the fears of reverse invasion and violation apparent in so many imperial adventures from *Gunga Din* to *Lawrence of Arabia*.

As in many examples of the imperial genre – including *Gunga Din* and *North West Frontier* – foreigners are shown to be fanatically religious. Despite the presence of a missionary the imperialist religious background is not explored while the religions of the natives are emphasized. The Riffs in *Camel* have a devotion to a prophet named Mustapha Leak and are required to prostrate themselves whenever his name is mentioned; a custom which allows the legionnaires to escape at one point. The gag is a tasteless play on Islamic prayer. A draft of the script included further banter at the expense of Islam cut from the final film:

> ABDUL (to new wife):   'Our union has already been blessed by The
>   Prophet.'
> JANE: 'I dare say, but your prophet looks like being
>   my loss.'[7]

The Burpers in *Khyber* have their fanatical devotion to Bungdit Din. *Khyber* was nearly much worse. Some religiously offensive jokes were cut from the script. The original draft had the 'comic' subtitle 'a Sikh-making saga' and a scene in which Captain Keene fantasizes about marriage to the Indian Princess Jelhi and discovers on their honeymoon night that she has extra arms like an Indian idol.[8] In *Jungle* both 'others' – the black Nosha tribe and pale all-female tribe – have elaborate religious rituals. There is a scene when Tinkle, not content to have successfully won a reprieve for his party through the familiar imperial adventure trope of impressing the natives with technology (in this case a pocket watch), overplays the part by promising blessings from heaven (a twist on the usual scene in which the European armed with knowledge of an impending eclipse threatens to call down judgement from heaven). In this case Tinkle's prayer unfortunately coincides with the arrival of a barrage of boulders launched by the juggle boy Ug and lands his party back on the cannibal menu.

The interplay between the rational West and fanatical East is a source for humour. *Camel* and *Khyber* both have word-play in which a ritual compliment from the 'other' is met with a response that conceals an obscenity from the Westerner:

KHASI:	May the benevolence of the god Shivoo bring blessings on your house.'
SIR SIDNEY:	'And on yours.'
KHASI:	'And may his wisdom bring success in all your undertakings.'
SIR SIDNEY:	'And in yours.'
KHASI:	'And may his radiance light up your life.'
SIR SIDNEY:	'And up yours.'

Camping Up the Self

The same process that developed an exaggerated image of the foreigner also exaggerated qualities of Britishness. From their earliest days the *Carry On* films were seen to have a special connection to British identity. The comedy evoked a cosy tradition of cheeky seaside post cards, music halls and Christmas pantomimes. In the three imperial *Carry On* films (and such others in the series as *Carry On Cleo, Don't Lose Your Head* and a later comedy which dealt with Britons on a package holiday called *Carry On Abroad*), Britishness is rendered explicit by being set against the behaviour of foreigners: the natives, in *Jungle* and *Khyber,* and in *Camel* both the Riff tribesmen and a host of other nationalities in the legion – most notably the American sergeant and Austrian Commandant.

British behaviour is written large in all three films. This typically involves an overemphasis on matters of honour. The plot of *Camel* turns on a young Englishman's shame at being wrongly accused of cheating in cricket. One character quips: 'His life wouldn't have been worth living here ... no cricket club would have had him.'[9] The most sustained discussion of British manners is in *Carry On Up the Khyber*. When cornered in an Afghan jail the young officer Captain Keene urges his fellow prisoners: 'Remember we are British ... keep a stiff upper lip.' The sceptical civilian missionary Belcher replies: 'I'm not going to wait around for mine to stiffen.' The dinner party at the climax of the film during which guests carry on eating and stoically refuse to acknowledge that the Residency is being demolished about their ears is not so much a satire of the 'stiff upper lip' as a celebration of it. It is implied by the formal dinner party in the jungle clearing in *Carry On Up the Jungle* and loudly asserted when Professor Tinkle protests against being eaten by cannibals crying: 'They can't possibly do this to us, after all we are British subjects!' Boosey replies: 'They've got no taste these people. They'll eat anything!' At its most basic level British behaviour drives outsiders to pronounce them insane. The final line of *Khyber* is 'Of course, they're all raving mad you know'.[10] In *Camel* the Riff sheikh observes: 'The mind of the infidel is like the action of the cleanser – clean round the bend', and 'the behaviour of the white infidels is like blood coming from a stone – a bleeding mystery'.

The three films comment on markers of British class identity but each in a different way. In *Camel* the relationship between the man and his servant is exaggerated to an absurd degree whereby West is incapable of bathing himself or dressing without the help of Simpson. *Khyber* inserts lower-class Cockney characters (called the Ruff Diamonds) into the aristocratic roles of the governor of the Northwest Frontier province and his wife, making their real-life exclusion from such roles visible, and perhaps drawing attention to the way in which imperial stories of upper-class coolness under-fire still helped underpin the social order in 1960s Britain. In *Jungle* the class comedy comes from the casting of Terry Scott as the jungle boy. The kind of role usually taken by an Olympic swimmer or bodybuilder is filled by a middle-aged and comically doughy British character actor, who at this stage of his career, was most closely identified with the part of the frustrated bachelor in the long-running sit com *Hugh and I* (1962–7), and would shortly be transformed into the archetypal married man in *Happily Ever After* (1974–8) and *Terry and June* (1979–87). If Edgar Rice Burroughs' original story argued that the jungle would make a lost European baby into a superman, *Carry On Up the Jungle* suggests that even the jungle cannot take the suburb out of the Englishman. Ug is unconvincing as a jungle boy, comically bumping into trees and breaking branches, but seems at home in the final moments of the film dressed in a business

16. Camping Up Tarzan: Ug the Jungle Boy (Terry Scott) and his mate (Jacki Piper) in *Carry On Up the Jungle* (1970).

suit and bowler hat returning from a hard day at the office to a suburban street. Only his bare feet and preference for living in a tree house mark him as different.

Carry On films became themselves part of British identity. They required and affirmed local knowledge and thereby created their own imagined community of humour. All three films relied on nationally specific slang. The oasis El Nooki in *Camel* puns on a London term for sex and Sheikh Abdul Abulbul is named for a character from a rugby song. A British army term for the lavatory, 'carsey', becomes the title of the Indian prince in *Khyber*, while London slang for the anus, 'jacksey', becomes a frontier town. The Yiddish 'Nosh' gives the name of cannibal tribe Nosha in *Jungle*. British nursery terms for urination – 'wee wee,' 'jimmy widdle' and 'tinkle' – appear in dialogue and as characters' names. Quick-fire puns abound, as in *Camel*, when Sergeant Nocker finds crates of laxative at the legion fort he muses: 'I guess they weren't regular soldiers.' And there is much general word-play – a part of Frankie Howerd's comic persona – in *Jungle* when he exclaims: 'I'm flabbergasted – my ghast has never been so flabbered.' You did not have to be British to laugh at these films, but it certainly helped.

Contemporary Comment

Many of the *Carry On* films included contemporary comment and some of this is to be found in the three imperial films. In *Camel* an address is given as 'number 10 on the street of many fools' and Sergeant Nocker adds: 'Ah, 10 Downing Street'. The final script included a joke about the pill but drafts had a running gag about Lady Jane being introduced to hashish by the Riff chief. Evidently the era was not quite liberal enough to permit levity on that subject.[11] In *Khyber* the beleaguered staff of the residency ask 'What will we do?' and are told by Sir Sidney: 'We are British, we won't do anything ... until it's too late.' Finally the social tensions over the presence of immigrants from the former empire to metropolitan Britain are noted. In *Khyber* as Bungdit Din fires a cannon at the British he remarks: 'That will teach them to ban turbans on the busses.' By *Jungle* there was perhaps a detectable concern over representation of the Africans. This does not push Rothwell to represent the Africans sympathetically or tastefully or to place them in the centre of the film, rather they are stereotypes marginalized in their own story. One can only wonder what the company of West Indian actors gathered to play the natives made of Bernard Bresslaw's turn as Upsidaisi. They were presumably glad to have the work in a business with still precious few opportunities for non-white performers.

Finally, given writer Talbot Rothwell's personal experience of empire, one might ask where, if ever, the real world of imperialism enters into the proceedings of *Carry On*. *Jungle* seems drawn wholly from the collective imagination, and *Camel* merely recycles fairly generic stereotypes of casbahs and belly dancers, with the insight at the end that cricket might provide a mechanism for postcolonial 'payback', but *Khyber* perhaps contains something more. By luck or perception, Rothwell's plot around the question of what exactly the Scottish regiment wear under their kilts plays into a real world issue of the body of the colonizer as a key element in colonial control. In his essay 'Shooting an Elephant', George Orwell makes a similar point as he describes how by suppressing fear and shooting a rogue elephant he held the 'natives' in thrall. Similarly, Franz Fanon's *Wretched of the Earth* stressed the way in which the body of the colonizer became an icon of imperial domination, which explained the extreme violence necessary for successful colonial rebellion.[12]

The *Carry On* series continued into the 1970s with contemporary themes, with occasional returns to domestic historical subjects but in a coarser style. Audiences drifted away, especially after the team attacked a bastion of working-class culture, the trade union movement, in *Carry On at Your Convenience* (1971). But even as the new films aimed ever lower, the classic *Carry On* films entrenched themselves deeper in the national consciousness in television reruns and clip-compilations. British comedy still explored the imperial heritage in sketches and a smattering of longer projects. Comedian Marty Feldman made *The Last Remake of Beau Geste* in Hollywood in 1977. Projects on television included *Roger of the Raj* (1979), a spoof imperial adventure story by Monty Python veterans Terry Jones and Michael Palin in the second season of their series *Ripping Yarns*, best remembered for a scene in which multiple dinner guests excuse themselves from a dinner in order to commit suicide over tiny social infractions. Despite their relentless camp, the three *Carry On* empire comedies neither opened the genre for further development, nor spoofed it so definitively that the same stories became impossible to tell with a straight face. Rather the films affectionately examined the characters, language and manners that went to make up British identity and the performance of that identity in the stories of empire and delivered an essentially affirming experience for their audience at the very point that the empire itself had clearly come to an end. All three films end with rousing acts of defiance. A comically bomb-damaged Bo West declares himself 'not out' at the end of *Camel*; the men give a collective two-fingered salute to Africa at the end of *Jungle*; and the flag is still flying at the end of *Khyber*. Like the legend on that flag fluttering over the ruined residence, the message of the three films was 'I'm Backing Britain'. However, by the alchemy of popular culture these films became part of the transformation of Britain from a community united by a shared experience of empire to a community united by a shared experience of *Carry On* films.

Notes

1   British Film Institute: Gerald Thomas Collection (hereafter BFI GT): Information
    Folder: *Don't Loose Your Head*, p.43.

2   Interview: Peter Rogers, 21 July 1998 (by telephone). The essential introduction to
    the *Carry On* series is Robert Ross, *The Carry On Companion* (London: Batsford, 1996).
    See also Sally Hibbin, *What a Carry On: The Official Story of the Carry On Film Series*
    (London: Hamlyn, 1988) and the author's own study of *Carry On Cleo* in ' "Infamy,
    Infamy, They've All Got It in for Me": *Carry On Cleo* and British Camp Comedies of
    Ancient Rome', in Sandra R. Joshel and Margaret Malamud (eds), *Imperial Projections:
    Ancient Rome in Modern Popular Culture* (Baltimore: Arethusa, 2001).

3   BFI GT/17/3: *Follow That Camel*, Box 1, Final script p.90, scene 137.

4   BFI GT/17/4: *Follow That Camel*, Box 1, contracts for *Follow That Camel*.

5   BFI GT/17/7: *Carry On Up the Jungle*, Box 1, script *Carry On Jungle Boy*. The ori-
    ginal screenplay opened with a voice of narration mocking the conventions of
    African adventures generally and then homed in on Tarzan. The sequence was
    designed as follows. After the credits the screen fades to black: Announcer:
    (VOICE-OVER) 'The time – 1873. The place – darkest Africa.' A second 'slightly
    hysterical scream' cuts in with a cry of 'lights!' and suddenly a panoramic
    view of jungle is revealed, The Announcer continues: 'Thank you. Deep in
    this last area of inpenetratable [*sic*] jungle, high amongst the branches of giant
    rhubarb tree, stands the magnificent figureof a powerfully built man proudly
    looking over his domain.' The figure of the jungle boy steps into the picture,
    gives his trademark call and then swings out of shot and – sounds of break-
    ing glass indicate – into camera equipment. The sequence continues with the
    second voice crying: 'Get out of it you stupid great ape!' before the announcer
    concludes: 'Meanwhile. A few miles to the north, through the dense steam-
    ing jungle of the interior comes a party of dense steaming nits.' Originally the
    Jungle Boy was to mistakenly take the name Jane, and Rothwell imagined only
    one European woman (thus adding an oedipal edge to the swimming scene).
    When the maid character was introduced she was originally named Jane. This
    morphed to June for the final script, probably to avoid copyright problems.

6   Ibid.

7   BFI GT/17/2: *Follow That Camel*, Box 1, 2nd script.

8   BFI Gerald Thomas papers, *Carry On Up the Khyber*, Box 1, final script.

9   BFI GT/17/1: *Follow That Camel: Carry On, Bo*; 1st script has the following dialogue
    omitted from the final film: Bo: 'They say the heat does funny things to white men.'
    Simpson: 'Really Sir?' Bo: 'Yes. Under its influence, perfect gentlemen have been
    known to embrace women they've only known for a bare six months!' Simpson (leer-
    ing despite himself): 'Embrace, sir? In what manner?' Bo (coldly): 'The position is
    immaterial.'

10 In the case of *Khyber* the outsider is the British missionary Belcher (Peter Butterworth)
    who doesn't share the ethics of the stiff upper lip.

11 BFI GT/17/2: *Follow That Camel*, 2nd script. Initially concerned on smoking hashish
    Lady Jane is reassured by her first drag, remarking 'oh yes I'm sure this could not be
    harmful' and later 'beats embroidery hollow'. The final screenplay substituted sher-
    bet for hashish.

12 Orwell's 1936 essay is widely anthologized, but can be found in George Orwell, *A Collection of Essays* (New York: Doubleday, 1946); Franz Fanon, *The Wretched of the Earth* (London: Grove Press, 1967). For a more recent examination of the body in British India see M. Sinha, *Colonial Masculinity: The 'Manly Englishman' and the 'Effeminate Bengali' in the Late Nineteenth Century* (Manchester: Manchester University Press, 1995).

THE IMPERIAL TRAP

The Man Who Would Be King (1975)

Like many of the great figures of Hollywood's Golden Age, John Huston was not averse to self-mythologizing, but one story he told fairly consistently concerned a bout of ill health in his early teens. Around 1920 he spent some months confined to a sanatorium with heart and kidney trouble, finding refuge in books. The stories he devoured at this time included several that took an almost obsessive hold on his imagination and became major projects during his eventual directorial career, including Herman Melville's *Moby Dick*, Stephen Crane's *The Red Badge of Courage* and a short story of imperial adventure by Rudyard Kipling entitled 'The Man Who Would Be King'.[1] Whether or not Huston actually read this story as a youth, there is no disputing its power for him as an adult. The project haunted him across more than 20 years from the early 1950s when he first began work on a treatment of the story to 1975 when he finally brought the film to the screen. The evolution of John Huston's *The Man Who Would Be King* illuminates both Huston's developing ideas and shifts in the world around him. It reaffirms the centrality of Kipling to the imperial adventure genre, and the influence of Hollywood's pre-war evocations of his world, especially George Stevens' *Gunga Din*. The starting point was – of course – Kipling's original tale.

First published in 1888, 'The Man Who Would Be King' was a work of Kipling's early career in India. The story concerns dealings between the narrator – a journalist – and two 'loafers' – disreputable Britons drifting round India swindling a living – named Daniel Dravot and Peachy Carnehan, who solicit his help on grounds that they are fellow Free Masons. The two men reveal a plan to travel to an uncharted territory beyond Afghanistan called Kafiristan, to establish themselves there as kings and pillage the country before returning wealthy men. They consult the narrator's books and ask him to sign a contract to establish the rules for their undertaking. The narrator thinks no more on the matter until – three years later – a battered Carnehan re-appears in the guise of a beggar. He explains that they successfully reached Kafiristan and were taken for gods by the population who seem to be some lost tribe of pale-skinned Europeans. The critical element is not their modern weapons, but the pair's discovery that the Kafiri religion is based on Free Masonry as imported by Alexander the Great more than two thousand years previously. Dravot is made king but after considerable success in government, he falls prey to pride. Dravot becomes convinced that he has a divinely ordained destiny, he decides to found a dynasty and prepares to marry so that he can sire a successor. When his chosen queen bites him during their wedding ceremony and draws blood, the Kafiris realize that he is not a god. They kill Dravot and torture Carnehan with crucifixtion, but then let Carnehan go. Carnehan returns to India, tells his story to the journalist and shows him the severed, crowned head of Dravot. He crawls away to die singing a snatch of the hymn: 'The Son of God goes forth to war, a kingly crown to gain'.[2]

The story echoed the real world achievement of an American adventurer named Josiah Harlan who in 1830s had ventured into uncharted parts of Afghanistan seeking a throne and earned himself the title of Prince of Ghor.[3] Kipling's tale had much literary merit, but its true significance was its critique of imperialism. Kipling was plainly comparing the British Empire to a get-rich-quick scheme hatched by a couple of ruffians, and predicting the doom that would flow from fancying it something more. It is this sweeping critique of the whole imperial project which prompted J. M. Barrie to famously dub the story 'the most audacious thing in fiction'.[4]

There was much in Kipling's story to appeal to the imagination of the adult film-maker John Huston. He had built his reputation with broadly drawn adventure pictures and was looking for a project which would consolidate this territory. He had radical politics and – steeped in his own Irish heritage – was no lover of the idea of empire. In 1952 he asked the young writer Peter Viertel who had worked on *The African Queen* (1951) if he could suggest a new project for Huston along the lines of *Treasure of the Sierra Madre* (1948). Viertel re-drew (or by his own account, drew) Huston's attention to Kipling's story. By mid-1954 Viertel had completed a treatment of 'The Man Who Would Be King'. It followed Kipling's outline fairly closely, fleshing-in events in Kafiristan and giving the narrator the character and identity of Kipling. One major departure from the original story was Viertel's making the principal characters Americans like Kipling's model, Harlan. More subtle departures included making the pair's use of Masonry a cynical mechanism to consolidate their reign in Kafiristan – an opiate of the masses – rather than the statement of universal human values of Kipling's original.[6] Huston was pleased with Viertel's progress, and while he had initially seen the film as a vehicle for his father – Walter

Huston – he now conceived of the film as perfect material for Humphrey Bogart (as Dravot) and Clark Gable (as Carnehan).[7] He began the long game of trying to draw the actors into the project and securing the necessary backing. On 25 August 1954 Huston cabled Gable:

> In January will be scouting India locations for Kipling picture stop am seizing opportunity and joining Maharajah Coochbehar tiger hunt on eighteenth stop this last of great hunts sixty elephants all the trimmings stop only be four guns one gun still open would you like me make res[ervation] for you stop and by the way Man Who Would be King should roll October Fifty-Five regards.

Bogart seemed shy of working in India and Gable had prior commitments, so Huston went on his tiger shoot – apparently oblivious to the irony of recreating the arch-imperialist lifestyle in the cause of an anti-imperial picture – scouted locations with Viertel, and resolved to make *Moby Dick* in 1955 instead.[8]

By the middle of 1955 Huston's producers at Allied Artists had begun to get cold feet over the project. July 1955 found Huston vainly reassuring one of them:

> The weather in India is thoroughly dependable, more dependable by far than the California weather, labor and studio space are the cheapest in the world. The only outstanding expense would be for travel. Originally I said that the picture could be made for something like two million and I will stand by that... I thought everybody agreed that the idea was to make pictures with unique backgrounds that in themselves enlist audiences' imaginations. If the others have forgotten, I haven't and still believe in this as a formula for pictures aiming at the jackpot... I don't think we should do Broadway successes or penthouse comedies... in other words the kind of material that is every bit as good on television.[9]

His parting swipe at the new medium of television suggested that Huston's interest in the imperial adventure material was routed merely in its potential for exotic wide screen spectacle, but a deeper interest was brewing.[10]

As the project bogged down, relations between Viertel and Huston soured. By the end of 1955 a new writer was collaborating on the film: the Scot, Æneas MacKenzie, well known for his work on costume pictures at Warner Brothers including *Juarez* (1939), *They Died with Their Boots On* (1941), and *Captain Horatio Hornblower* (1951) and MGM's *Ivanhoe* (1952). He had also written much of *The Ten Commandments* (1956). MacKenzie's arrival was testament to Huston's interest in developing the historical aspects of the film. Huston layed out his hopes for the film in a meeting with MacKenzie in Paris in November, stressing as MacKenzie put it, that his 'interest in this Kipling short story derives from a conviction that its characters and situations are fundamental ones' and 'disinclination to depart in any marked degree from the original material, or to make any major interpolations in the scripting of its screen play'. On the voyage home to the USA, MacKenzie worked up a number of early scenes taking the two protagonists as far as Kafiristan. His draft was full of witty period dialogue, which was destined to remain in final screenplay, including Carnehan's memorable rebuttal to a sour British official: ' "Detriments" you call us. "Detriments!" Well I remind you that it was detriments like us that made this bloody Empire and the Izzat of the Raj. Hats on'.[11]

Back in Hollywood Huston and MacKenzie developed their new approach further in two further conferences. MacKenzie related:

> During them he (Huston) advanced the theory that the events related in the story are fundamental ones because they represent a constant historical pattern in the evolution of empire; and that the characters within it are not governed by their own volition but by inevitable and irresistible pressures upon their instincts from the circumstances that surround them: Caesar, Cortes, Bonaparte, Danny Dravot, or any other of the breed – what is the difference between them? Only the names. The pattern of their actions is the same in the perspective of history ...
>
>   a. It begins with an adventurer in search of booty;
>   b. which, achieved, brings with it a distaste for security,
>   c. that breeds a desire for power ... or kingship.
>   d. But kingship breeds a dream of achievement that must endure beyond the dreamer's own life ...
>   e. through dynasty ...
>   f. to destruction?
>
> That is the constant pattern of the men who would be kings. But it is involved – though only involved – in the historical perspective by another element, which is the element of spirituality or divinity.[12]

Suddenly a new perspective on the material was clear. Huston was planning to tap directly into Kipling's original message. But what was the target of his parable? Britain's empire was clearly in decline. His concern was rather directed towards his own country.

The United States had ended World War Two with unprecedented power and was flexing its global muscles. The cause of containing communism saw American troops deployed in Europe and venturing out into the developing world in a string of advisory missions. Behind it all the USA had its growing nuclear arsenal. Huston also sought to develop *Moby Dick* (1956) as an allegory of America's temptation to over-stretch and obsessive and self-destructive pursuit of an enemy. He intended at one point to film the final confrontation between Ahab and the whale at Bikini Athol, location of America's post-war nuclear tests, to highlight contemporary significance and because he claimed that he had deduced Bikini to be the actual location imagined by Herman Melville.[13] But even as Huston's enthusiasm bubbled, the film hit a new snag. During the early months of 1956 Bogart's ill-health forced Huston to suspend plans to begin work on the film.[14] Huston later suggested that when Bogart died in January 1957 he had no stomach to make the film and had to be drawn back to the project by Gable during the filming of *The Misfits* (1961) together in the Nevada desert in 1960.[15] The archival record reveals little let up in Huston's plans for the film. As early as September 1957 he was sounding out Gable for a revival of the project now, in an echo of *Gunga Din*, playing opposite Cary Grant.[16] With Grant unwilling to commit, he also considered the pairing of Gable and Frank Sinatra.[17]

In the course of 1959 MacKenzie completed a full screen play for the film. It solved several of the narrative problems of Viertel's draft, especially the problem of explaining the interaction between the Western protagonists and the Kafiris. Kipling had his characters simply learn the native 'lingo' and had the subsequent action merely reported by Carnehan, an unworkable device for a substantial chunk of a motion picture. MacKenzie leapt over this problem by inventing a translator character, a lost bearer from an earlier British expedition. Other features of his script included an eye for historical detail. A passing allusion in Kipling's original text became a virtual footnote in the midst of the dialogue.

> DRAVOT: 'Did you ever hear tell of an English sailor who went ashore on an island called Sarawak and got to be king of the whole country.'
>
> KIPLING: 'Yes. That was Brooke – Sir James Brooke. The Queen knighted him for it.'
>
> DRAVOT: 'Well, we have decided there is only one place now where two men like us could do likewise. They call it Kafiristan.'[18]

Fired up with the project once again, Huston commissioned the art director Stephen Grimes to travel to Afghanistan with him in the winter 1959 and develop some designs for the film. The result was a magnificent series of sketches of Dravot and Carnehan in flowing native costume. But the progress was cruelly cut short in late 1960 by a second death: that of Clark Gable.[19]

17. Kipling Imagined: Location production sketches from 1959 by Stephen Grimes for John Huston's *The Man Who Would Be King*.

Despite Gable's death MacKenzie continued to work on the screenplay. He brought new twists of dialogue and plot into an increasingly complex whole. He wove in quotes from Kipling's verse. He gave Dravot the exotic oath: 'God's Holy Trousers!' He invented a simple plot device to both establish Carnehan's character and explain how he knew Kipling was a Mason and could be asked to help: Carnehan steal Kipling's watch and then spots a Masonic talisman on the fob. Kipling later gives this to Dravot for luck, and it is this talisman which, when seen by the Kafiri priests, establishes a link between the Englishmen and their Masonic-based religion.[20] The theme of empire was also strongly felt. MacKenzie had Dravot – at the height of his ambition – now explicitly dreaming of an empire for himself and now merely as an adjunct to the British Empire:

> There's Power, here, and glory, too. It's not a nation we could have, it's an Empire! There'll be a new colour on the maps ... We'll be in the history-books, you and me ... An Empire! That'll last long after you and I are gone. For I'll found a dynasty.[21]

Then, in 1962 Æneas MacKenzie also died leaving Huston in need of both stars and a writer.

Huston replaced MacKenzie with Anthony Veiller, a well-established screenwriter who had the distinction of having made an uncredited contribution *Gunga Din* in 1939 and worked on several of the US army's wartime *Why We Fight* films (especially *War Comes to America*, 1945). His projects with Huston included *The List of Adrian Messenger* (1963) and *Night of the Iguana* (1964). Huston was now an active partner in the writing process and the scripts produced between 1962 and 1965 were credited to both men.[22] These scripts had their own nuances. The MacKenzie versions had allowed the characters to sing snatches of Kipling ballads but the February 1964 version even has the protagonists allude to their acquaintance with a water bearer named Gunga Din.[23] The collaboration with Veiller was cut short by the writer's death from cancer in June 1965, but Huston soldiered on with what must now have seemed like a jinxed project. One significant change to the script during these years was a revised climax in which Dravot and Carnehan turn on each other, and their consequent fist fight reveals their mortality. Given that at the same time the imperial adventure of Vietnam was opening bitter divisions within American society, there was obvious contemporary parallel for a plot in which an imperial dream was destroyed by the fact that it divided the imperialists.[24]

During the Huston/Veiller period the project went through a number of changes of potential cast. Huston asked Richard Burton to play for

Carnehan and Marlon Brando Dravot for a production under the aus-
pices of Paramount. Burton's availability slowed the project. When Burton
insisted that he was only interested in playing Dravot, Huston hit on the
idea of getting Sean Connery as his Carnehan (the part eventually played
by Michael Caine). Connery could not be secured and Huston contem-
plated casting *Lawrence of Arabia* veteran, Peter O'Toole or Rod Taylor or
even Robert Mitchum. Still later, Huston toyed with a pairing of Burton and
Michael Caine. In 1967 Warner-Seven Arts announced plans to make the
film but with the key players still in doubt backing for the project eluded
him and the film slipped back into limbo.[25] For a season Huston backed off.
In 1968 the trade press announced that Martin Ritt, whose previous films
included *Hud* (1963), would both direct and produce the story for Warner-
Seven Arts. With other projects underway at the same time including *The
Molly Maguires* (1970) Ritt placed the film on a back burner.[26]

By the end of the 1960s the element of warning in *The Man Who Would
Be King* began to look like an exercise in closing the stable door after the
horse had bolted. America had dreamed its imperial dream, arrogantly
over-reached itself in Vietnam and paid the price. Yet the success of a late
Vietnam-era genre – the buddy movie – opened a new avenue into making *The Man Who Would Be King*. In 1970, flushed with the terrific success
of *Butch Cassidy and the Sundance Kid* (1969), producer John Foreman was
visiting Huston and contemplating similar projects. While browsing in
Huston's library he stumbled on the album of production designs created
by Steven Grimes in 1959 and was immediately intrigued and prevailed on
Huston to revive the project. Huston began the fourth set of revisions of
the screen play, this time in collaboration with his assistant Gladys Hill.[27]
Huston and Foreman made two films together first – *The Life and Times
of Judge Roy Bean* (1972) and *The Mackintosh Man* (1973) – both starring
Paul Newman. Huston suggested to Newman that he and Robert Redford
might repeat their *Butch Cassidy* pairing in *The Man Who Would Be King*,
sending various versions of the script to the actor to bolster his argument.
As Huston recalled in his memoirs, Newman had an abrupt but insightful
response: you need Englishmen; 'For Christ's sake John, get Connery and
Caine.' Connery and Caine agreed allowing the film to progress to the next
level.[28]

Huston and Gladys Hill began work on what would be the final version
of the script for *The Man Who Would Be King* in 1973. Hill completed a draft
by October but found some scepticism from the production company over
its viability. A diary entry in January 1974 records: 'To Foreman's for dinner. Tells me Allied Artists FIND SCRIPT TOO LONG, no one will understand
language, don't like narration or ending.' Revisions followed, but important

endorsement came in May with the first read-through with members of the cast. Michael Caine pronounced it: 'Great'.[29]

The new version of the script reflected its era including a fruitier turn of phrase – and terms like 'pissing' and 'bollocks' (used as a verb and noun respectively rather than oaths). When Dravot and Carnehan decline the 'hospitality' of women as a reward for their first victory in Kafiristan they are offered boys instead. Hill's attempts to respond to Allied Artists included an idea that Carnehan and Dravot might both be killed at the end of the film, falling from the rope bridge which symbolizes the material achievement of Dravot's reign. This double death idea – which would have precluded framing the film as a narrative told to Kipling – remained part of drafts for much of 1974 until Huston regained the courage of his convictions and restored his original design.[30] The scripts consistently played up the element of myth and the religious dimension in Dravot's ambition. Multiple drafts described the moment when Dravot, with apparent miraculous power, pulls an arrow from his shoulder and holds it aloft, thus: 'It was as if the arrow could have been Ahab's harpoon, or Excalibur, or a splinter from the true cross.'[31]

While the Kiplingesque language remained unchanged, casualties of the script editing included some of the discussion of Free Masonry. Cut portions included a fascinating snatch of dialogue from the scene with the district commissioner, which portrays the universality of masonry:

KIPLING: 'Once a Mason, always a Mason.'
DISTRICT COMMISSIONER: 'You don't say! Hmph! ... Had one here three weeks ago – a Bengali merchant – black as my boot. Demanded that we notify his mother; and when we tried to, damn-me if she hadn't been dead for thirty years.'
KIPLING (smiling):   'He didn't mean his natural mother, Sir, but his mother lodge.'[32]

In order to improve the military aspects of the story, Huston recruited a military advisor named Captain Dick Drew-Smythe, formerly of the forty-first King George V's Own Gurkha Rifles. Drew-Smythe created the necessary battle sequences and served on set to ensure verisimilitude in the sequences that required drilling or the use of weapons.[33]

Production problems included predictable pressure on the budget and the issue of location: Huston had hoped for Turkey, but a political dispute with the United States required relocation to Morocco in the course of 1974.

Selected sequences – principally the opening railway station scene – would be filmed in Pakistan, with mountain scenes to be completed in the French Alps and interiors at Pinewood in the UK. Then came the problem of casting the Kafiris. Huston had always intended to follow Kipling and depict them as essentially white, hence he cast Tessa Dahl (daughter of actress Patricia Neal and author Roald Dahl) in the part of Dravot's bride Roxanne. Unfortunately the available extras in Morocco simply did not support this idea of a lost tribe of Greeks. Huston's team experimented by handing out blonde wigs but the result was wholly unconvincing. Dispirited he wrote:

> These people are small, dark and ugly rather than handsome ... A Greek Goddess – like Tessa – towering in their midst would need (to be believed) to be supported by a legion of lesser goddesses strewn along our way – from the time we go into our very first village. The cost of such a legion is prohibitive – so this important story point must be abandoned.

By a happy coincidence Michael Caine's Indian-born wife Shakira was on hand to stand-in as a credible substitute. The Dahl family was un-amused.[34]

As the production gathered momentum Huston began to speak in interviews with the press about his plans for The Man Who Would Be King. His 20-year quest to make the film became a badge of the project's significance for him and, by implication, for the world at large. Although the moment had passed for a collective warning against imperialism, Huston still implied that the film had 'contemporary significance'. He pitched the film in terms of 'the disease of power that most of those who live in a rarified atmosphere are assailed with'. Though he refrained from making the point, the height of the Watergate crisis was an apposite moment for a film about the 'disease of power'.[35] Huston also emphasized the film as a warning against the delusion to think oneself divine. He was unimpressed by suggestions that this might somehow be a comment on the power of a film director.[36]

Huston was blessed by the result of his efforts. The final film was an obvious triumph. Connery and Caine lit up the screen with a rousing chemistry and the supporting players – Christopher Plummer as Kipling and Saeed Jaffrey as Billy Fish – excelled. Maurice Jarre delivered perhaps his most memorable score since Lawrence of Arabia. Edith Head – veteran of Elephant Walk (1954) and a host of Paramount classics – designed the costumes and a number of distinguished professionals – including editor Russell Lloyd and cinematographer Oswald Morris – rallied to work on the film. The final

18. Men of the Empire: Dravot (Sean Connery) and Carnehan (Michael Caine) light up while Kipling (Christopher Plummer) watches in John Huston's *The Man Who Would Be King* (1975).

script bristled with wit largely derived either directly from Kipling's story or extrapolated from his *Soldier's Three* stories. The film showed Kipling literally sweating over writing his contemporaneous poem 'The Ballad of Boh-da-Thone' of 1888. But the overall thrust of the film was not the same as Kipling's original short story: it came across as an energetic re-visitation and celebration of the empire genre rather than a subversion of it.

The opening of the film presented a vivid montage of Kipling's India – street entertainers, snake charmers and a man putting scorpions into his mouth – images to simultaneously fascinate and repel which, when seen against an urgent swirling soundtrack of native music, declare the exoticism of the piece before the mournful brass chords of the lament/slow march *The Minstrel Boy* (the Irish air *The Moreen*) introduce the European presence and herald the credits. The choices that Huston made in the rest of the film transformed the piece into what looked very like a tribute not only to the Kipling of literature, but the Kipling of the screen and specifically, George Stevens' *Gunga Din*. Huston's version makes much more of his character's military past than Kipling's original – their scarlet jackets were one of the major visual motifs of the film. Like *Gunga Din* the film included a represen-tation of Kipling within the action, moreover Christopher Plummer played

Kipling not as the young journalist of the original story but as the mature writer seen in *Gunga Din*. The scene in which Carnehan (Michael Caine) bullies an Indian railway passenger (Mohammad Shamsi) and throws him out of a moving train is played wholly at the expense of the Indian, assumes the complicity of the audience, and turns on an implicit racism unusual even in 1970s Hollywood. Saeed Jaffrey's native translator character – Billy Fish – ran parallel to Sam Jaffe's water bearer in his devotion to the British army, though Billy Fish is allowed rather more dignity. There are parallel sequences, such as the attempt to teach natives to drill. In Kipling's original Carnehan is impressed by how swiftly they learn. In *Gunga Din* and Huston's film, the scenes are played for laughs. The two films even share certain motifs like the action revolving around the rope bridge. The hidden city and fabulous treasure are outgrowths of *Gunga Din*'s secret temple and Huston's own fancy rather than Kipling's story. But above all it was in the exuberant friendship of the protagonists that the old spirit of *Gunga Din* rides high. The myth of male friendship is fully celebrated and the imperial project is shown to be, for the most part, tremendous fun, and the audience is left with the suggestion that but for the intrusion of a woman, Carnehan and Dravot could have kept their kingdom and ruled till doomsday.

The pre-publicity for the film aimed squarely at its connection to the imperial adventure genre. The poster promised: 'Adventure in all its glory!' Copy on a major advertisement ran:

> Danny Dravot and Peachy Carnehan have just been cashiered out of the British army for flouting a few regulations about larceny, brawling, boozing, and the sanctity of maidenhood. So now they're a two man army of their own, battling their way through the Khyber pass, across the barbaric Afghan Plains, over the frozen peaks of the Himalayas and into the fabled land of Kafiristan. Where men fight. Women love. And treasure glitters in the streets.[37]

The film premiered as Britain's entry at the Teheran film festival on 26 November 1975 and at a royal charity performance on 18 December.[38] It did disappointing business at the box office. It failed to show on *Variety*'s list of the year's best earners, and contributing to the decline of Allied Artists, earning only $8 million in its first year and a half. Caine and Connery were forced to sue the company for their share of the takings. An indignant Connery told *The New York Times*: 'I've never stolen from anybody in my life. To work in good faith and be cheated is wrong. I'm tired of being robbed. I think they should be in jail.' Allied introduced a counter suit for defamation, but eventually settled. The poor performance of the film and the settlement contributed to the studio's decline into bankrupt-cy.[39] Compensation came in Oscar nominations for editing, art direction, costume design and adapted screenplay, but it lost to *Jaws* in the first of these categories, *Barry Lyndon* for art and costume and *One Flew over the Cuckoo's Nest* for the script. Further near misses followed at the BAFTAs and Writers Guild of America awards. Most critics enjoyed the ride that Huston provided. Pauline Kael commented on the anti-imperial implications of the plot. Others had their doubts. Scholar Sarah Kozloff has noted the echoes of *Gunga Din*, and saw the wedding at the film's denouement as revealing both Huston's misogyny and playing to Hollywood's traditional phobia of inter-racial unions.[40] Fans of the film included the New York-based religious group 'The Christophers', who presented Huston with a special award hon-ouring the film's moral compass.[41] Its severest critics were in Afghanistan where the government objected to the child-like representation of its inhab-itants and banned the film outright.[42]

The Man Who Would Be King stands as a film somehow out of time: a tribute to the golden age of imperial adventure movies, which made it to the screen because of the dogged determination of its creator and its ser-endipitous intersection with a fad for buddy films. There was much on the screen to please, but something also to unsettle. In the last analysis Huston's critique of imperialism was that it was bad for the conqueror. A full critique of imperialism must also consider whether it is also bad for the conquered.

Notes

1   Gideon Bachmann, 'How I Make Films: An Interview with John Huston', in Stephen Cooper (ed.), *Perspectives on John Huston* (New York: G. K. Hall, 1994), p.100; Axel Madsen, *John Huston* (New York: Doubleday, 1978), p.244; Stuart Kaminsky, *John Huston: Maker of Magic* (Boston: Houghton Mifflin, Boston, 1978), pp.91, 197. Contrary to Kaminsky's claim he cannot have read *Treasure of the Sierra Madre* as a boy, as the novel did not appear until 1927 when Huston was 21 years old.

2   Rudyard Kipling, 'The Man Who Would Be King', in *The Phantom Rickshaw and Other Erie Tales* (Allahabad: A. H. Wheeler, 1888). The hymn has Anglo–Indian significance as it is the work of the Bishop of Calcutta, and martyr to the Indian climate Reginald Heber (1783–1826).

3   For a biography of Josiah Harlan (1799–1871) see Ben McIntyre, *Josiah the Great* (London: Harper-Perennial, 2004).

4   Jim Beckerman 'The Man Who Would Be King: On Adapting the Most Audacious Thing in Fiction', in Michael Klein and Gillian Parker (eds), *The English Novel and the Movies* (New York: Ungar, 1981), p.180.

5   Huston's radicalism was plainly on display in his 1949 film *We Were Strangers* which deals with the Cuban revolution of 1933.

6   Peter Viertel, *Dangerous Friends: At Large with Huston and Hemingway in the Fifties* (New York: Doubleday, 1992), pp.180–3, 210; Herrick Library, Huston Papers: 28–f.274, Script: ManKing-Viertel, 19 July 1954.

7   Madsen, *John Huston*, p.239.

8   Huston Papers: 31–f.297, ManKing Correspondence, 1953–6. For Huston's account of the tiger hunt see John Huston, *An Open Book* (New York: Knopf, 1980), pp.346–8.

9   Huston Papers: 31–f.297 Correspondence 1953–6, Huston to Paul Kohner (Allied Artists), 31 July 1955.

10 Huston's intent to emphasize spectacle was borne out by associated negotiations with the Huston Papers: 31–f.300, Mirisch, Harold, 1953–4, Mirisch to Huston 2 December 1954 regarding negotiations with Mike Todd to use the Todd-AO wide screen process on the film.

11 Huston Papers: 28–f.275 Script: writer's report by Aeneas MacKenzie with sample screenplay pages; 4/24/56. 'Izzat' was a local term apparently introduced by the Moguls referring to a rulers reputation or honour.

12 Huston Papers: 28–f.275 Script: writer's report by Aeneas MacKenzie with sample screenplay pages; 4/24/56.

13 Kaminsky, *John Huston*, p.107.

14 Huston Papers: 31–f.297 Correspondence 1953–6, Huston to Ernst Scheidegger, 3 April 1956.

15 Huston interview with Joseph McBride, *Variety*, 1975 in Robert Emmet Long, *John Huston Interviews*, University of Mississippi, Jackson, 2001, p.56.

16 University of Southern California, Los Angeles, Doheny Memorial Library: Cinematic Arts Library, Clarke Gable papers, 101, box 2, file: *The Man Who Would Be King*, George of MCA artists to Gable, 17 September 1957; Huston Papers: 31–f.298, Correspondence 1959–66, including Cary Grant to Paul Kohner, 26 July 1960.

17 Madsen, *John Huston*, p.239.

18 Huston Papers: 28–f.277, Script: screenplay by Aeneas MacKenzie, 1959. This was not part of the 1975 screenplay.

19 Huston Papers: 32–f.307 ManKing Research: Notes and Sketches: *The Man Who Would Be King*, also to be found in the Clark Gable Papers, Item 101/2.

20 Huston Papers: 29–f.280 Script: draft by Aeneas MacKenzie; 2 May 1960; 29–f.281 Script: no date; 29–f.282 Revised screenplay; 27 April 1961.

21 Huston Papers: 29–f.281 27 April 1961, p.130.

22 These scripts are located in Huston Papers: 29–f.283 through to 30–f.287.

23 Huston Papers: 29–f.385 ManKing script, 22 February 1964.

24 Huston Papers: 30–f.287.

25 Huston Papers: 32–f.309, Stark to Huston, 21 December 1964; Stark to Huston 14 May 1965; Stark to Martin Baum at Ashley Famous Agency, 23 September 1965. Kaminsky, *John Huston*, p.170, dates Huston's plan to make the film with Burton and Peter O'Toole to 1966. On the Burton/Caine pairing see p.198. Madsen, *John Huston*, pp.215–25.

26 'Ritt to direct produce "King" for WB-7 Arts', *Variety*, 22 March 1968; 'Ritt Taking a Year Before Starting First W-7 Film', *Variety*, 7 June 1968.

27 Gerald Pratley, *The Cinema of John Huston* (London: Tantivy Press, 1977), p.187. Madsen, *John Huston*, p.239.

28 Huston, *An Open Book*, pp.151–2.

29 Huston Papers, 31–f.303, Miscellaneous, 1974: Gladys Hill diary, entries October 1973–June 1974.

30   Huston Papers: 30–f.288 ManKing script 25 June 1974. The double death scene is p.127.

31   These scripts are to be found in Huston Papers: 30–f.288 to 30–f.295.

32   Huston Papers: 30–f.292 ManKing discards 7/5/74 to 13/1/75.

33   Huston Papers: 30–f.292 ManKing battle revisions.

34   Huston Papers: 31–f.299 Correspondence, 1974–7, including Huston to Dahl family, 2 June 1975. Huston, *An Open Book*, pp.352–8.

35   Pratley, *Cinema of John Huston*, p.187; Madsen, *John Huston*, p.244 and Bachmann interview in Cooper (ed.) *Perspectives on John Huston*, p.100.

36   Kaminsky, *John Huston*, p.199.

37   Huston Papers: 32–f.306.

38   'Kipling to Iran', *Variety*, 12 November 1975, p.28.

39   See *Variety*, 7 January 1976, p.52; 'Critics of the Movie Business Find Pattern of Financial Irregularities', *The Man Who Would Be King*. *New York Times*, 29 January 1978, pp.1, 39; 'Allied-Artists Counter-Sues Sean Connery, Michael Caine', *Variety*, 8 March 1978, p.5; 'AA Pays Actors Connery and Caine; Terms Are Locked', *Variety*, 2 August 1978, p.5; 'Sean Connery: "I Don't Even Get Alphabetical Billing in AA Fade', *Variety*, 24 October 1979, p.7.

40   Sarah Kozloff, 'Taking Us along on the *Man Who Would Be King*', Cooper, *Perspectives on John Huston*, pp.187–90.

41   Huston Papers: 31–f.299, Correspondence, 1974–7, Christophers to Huston, 3 February 1976.

42   Kaminsky, *John Huston*, p.202.

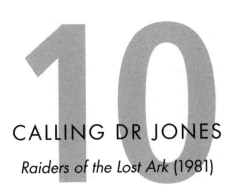

CALLING DR JONES

Raiders of the Lost Ark (1981)

The three 'Indiana Jones' adventures of the 1980s – *Raiders of the Lost Ark* (1981), *Indiana Jones and the Temple of Doom* (1984) and *Indiana Jones and the Last Crusade* (1989) – represent par excellence the style of the New Hollywood blockbuster so indelibly associated with their director Steven Spielberg and executive producer George Lucas. In the late 1970s and 1980s the films of Spielberg and Lucas broke box office records and redefined the nature of popular cinema. Spielberg's *Jaws* (1975) became the first film to earn rentals of over $100 million in North America alone (in fact it returned $129 million) – an achievement that in the words of film historian Thomas Schatz 'recalibrated the profit potential of the Hollywood hit'.[1] This was surpassed by Lucas's *Star Wars* in 1977 ($193 million) and Spielberg's *E.T.: The Extra-Terrestrial* in 1982 ($210 million). By 1989 Spielberg and Lucas were responsible, either singly or jointly, for eight of the top ten all-time box office hits. *Raiders of the Lost Ark* ($116 million), *Indiana Jones and the Temple of Doom* ($109 million) and *Indiana Jones and the Last Crusade* ($115 million) were surpassed only by *Jaws*, *E.T.*, *Star Wars* and its sequels *The Empire Strikes Back* ($142 million) and *Return of the Jedi* ($165 million), and by the non-Spielberg–Lucas *Batman* ($150 million) and *Ghostbusters* ($127 million).[2]

The popular success of the Spielberg–Lucas films is all the more significant given the state of the US film industry at the time. The extraordinary returns of individual films such as *Jaws* and *Star Wars* disguised the underlying economic reality that the late 1970s was a time of recession for Hollywood. The effects of a declining cinema audience were escalated by the increasing fragmentation of the leisure market due to competition from cable television and video cassettes. At the same time production costs were spiralling. This was partly the result of inflationary pressure and partly due to the industry's profligacy as it gave successful film-makers greater control over their films. The most expensive films of the late 1970s were Spielberg's overblown comedy *1941*, Francis Ford Coppola's Vietnam

War epic *Apocalypse Now* and Michael Cimino's sprawling Western *Heaven's Gate*. The last was the most catastrophic flop since *Cleopatra*: it lost $40 million and forced United Artists into a shotgun marriage with MGM. An indication of the chronic uncertainty of the film industry at this time is that *Raiders of the Lost Ark* was 'offered to every single studio in town – and they all turned it down. All except Paramount'.[3] Spielberg's previous three films (*Jaws, Close Encounters of the Third Kind, 1941*) had all gone over schedule and over budget. *Raiders*, in contrast, was brought in ahead of schedule and within its $20 million budget.

It was this background of economic uncertainty that in large measure accounts for the reception of *Raiders of the Lost Ark*. Most critics greeted it ecstatically as a return to the sort of traditional genre film that had all but disappeared from Hollywood during the 1970s. In particular it was praised for its entertainment qualities and production values. *Variety*, for example, called it 'a cracker jack fantasy-adventure ... exhilarating escapist entertainment' and felt that 'the film is among the best-crafted ventures of its kind'.[4] Vincent Canby of *The New York Times* thought it 'a wildly paced, nonstop adventure movie that recalls the delights of movie serials and Grade-Z adventure movies of the 30s and 40s, but in a manner that was forever beyond the artistic and economic reach of the people who once turned out those pictures by the yard'.[5] And for Richard Schickel in *Time* it was 'an exemplary film, an object lesson in how to blend the art of storytelling with the highest levels of technical know-how, planning, cost control and commercial acumen'.[6] It is significant that reviews dwelt upon the technical qualities of the film rather than its plot or characterizations. It has been argued that the film's narrative is really just an excuse for showcasing state-of-the-art technology. Steve Neale, for example, avers that *Raiders* 'uses an idea (the signs) of classic Hollywood in order to promote, integrate and display modern effects, technologies and production values'.[7]

The most common way of reading *Raiders of the Lost Ark* is to see it as an homage to the 'old' Hollywood with its many allusions to and quotations from classic Hollywood films. Appropriately for two film-makers steeped in movie lore, *Raiders of the Lost Ark* is replete with narrative and visual references to other films. The film and its sequels chronicle the adventures of an American archæology professor who travels the world in search of historical artefacts of great symbolic value and possessing supernatural power: the Ark of the Covenant (*Raiders of the Lost Ark*), the Sankara Stones (*Indiana Jones and the Temple of Doom*) and the Holy Grail (*Indiana Jones and the Last Crusade*).[8] This formula recalls adventure stories such as *King Solomon's Mines* (filmed in 1937 and 1950, with another version in 1985) and *She* (filmed in 1935 and 1965).[9] It references 'B' movies such as Universal's

Zanzibar (1940), in which agents of competing European powers had fought over the skull of an African chief whose possession (according to the Treaty of Versailles!) would give control over the region. The principal reference points for Indiana Jones, however, are the serials or 'chapter plays' of the 1930s and 1940s. The serial represented an alternative mode of film practice to the dominant classical cinema of Hollywood. It was a 'cinema of attractions' based on action (stunts, chases, fights, breathless escapes) and the non-closure of narrative.[10] Republic Pictures specialized in adventure serials such as *Perils of Nyoka* (1942), in which rival teams of archæologists seek the Lost Tablets of Hippocrates, and *Secret Service in Darkest Africa* (1943), in which an American special agent thwarts a Nazi plot to acquire the sacred Dagger of Solomon. The latter, with its German villains and their Arab henchmen, has been cited by Lucas as the template for *Raiders of the Lost Ark*.[11]

The narrative structure of *Raiders*, certainly, is rather like episodes of a serial laid end to end. In contrast to, say, *North West Frontier*, which uses the device of the train journey to provide a coherent linear narrative, *Raiders* is really a series of self-contained set pieces that are linked by mechanical plot contrivance. The opening of the film, for example, has Indiana Jones overcome a series of fiendish booby traps to retrieve a golden idol from a lost temple in South America. This is merely a prelude, however, unconnected to the events that follow, except for the introduction of the villain Belloq. Thereafter the film moves from one climax to another every reel or so: a shootout in a burning tavern, a foot chase through the casbah, a descent into a pit of snakes, an exploding aeroplane and a sustained chase sequence along a desert road as Jones leaps from horse to truck and steals the Ark from a German convoy. The film gleefully draws attention to its contempt for narrative logic ('I'm making this up as I go' Jones remarks at one point) and its refusal to explain plot loopholes (when the heroine, presumed dead in an explosion, turns up alive, her survival is glossed over with a throwaway line: 'I thought you were dead – they must have switched baskets'). The episodic construction is further highlighted by the ease with which sequences planned for *Raiders* which proved surplus to requirements were incorporated into its sequels.[12]

There are further specific visual references in *Raiders of the Lost Ark*. These can be understood both as a strategy for anchoring it within genre conventions and as a commentary on its own status as a fictional text. In the opening shot of the film, for example, the famous mountain logo of Paramount Pictures dissolves into a similarly shaped mountain somewhere in South America – a device repeated in subsequent films. Indiana Jones's journey from America across the Pacific Ocean to Nepal and then on to

Cairo is illustrated by the device of a red line moving across a map – a quaintly dated form of narration that refers to the style of the films of the period in which it is set. The work of the legendary Hollywood stuntman Yakima Canutt is acknowledged in the superbly staged desert truck chase where Jones falls under the moving vehicle and allows it to pass over his body before climbing on the back.[13] Jones's outfit of battered leather jacket and snap-brim fedora recalls Charlton Heston's in *Secret of the Incas* (1954) – one of Paramount's exotic melodramas of the 1950s – while his expertise with a bullwhip is an inheritance from Douglas Fairbanks in *The Mark of Zorro* (1920) and *Don Q, Son of Zorro* (1925). The apocalyptic climax in which Belloq opens the Ark and unleashes a lightning storm that vaporizes the watching Nazis recalls the end of Robert Aldrich's *Kiss Me Deadly* (1955). And the final scene, where the Ark is sealed in a crate and stored in a vast warehouse, is nothing if not an homage to *Citizen Kane*.

These references to other movies have led some critics to see *Raiders of the Lost Ark* as nothing more than a pastiche.[14] The reading of *Raiders* as a tribute to the craftsmanship and history of Hollywood was further promoted in a 'making of' television special narrated by star Harrison Ford aired to coincide with the film's theatrical release.[15] It has been argued that the publicity discourse of the film represents an attempt to overlay a particular meaning onto it as 'entertainment' and 'escapism' and in so doing to disguise its deeper ideological mechanisms. Patricia Zimmermann, for example, argues that 'the public sphere surrounding the film – reviews, production notes, behind-the-scenes information and television interviews – functioned to eradicate any political reading of the film's jingoism, Third World exploitation, spectacle and backlash against feminism'. The effect of the publicity machine was to 'direct the film as pure entertainment, free from ideology, and simultaneously erase it as a social practice imbued within and referring to a current social and historical context'.[16]

What, then, was the social and historical context of *Raiders of the Lost Ark*? The film was released early during the presidency of Ronald Reagan, whose tenure in the White House is associated with an assertive foreign policy that sought to restore American influence and prestige following the débâcle of Vietnam and the siege of the US Embassy in Tehran. The 'new conservatism' of Reaganite America was characterized by a hawkish foreign policy and by its attempt to forge consensus in domestic policy in response to the increasing militancy of women's rights and gay rights protestors. It has been suggested that the narrative of *Raiders* 'put the film in the ideological position of spokesperson for the new Reagan administration's policies in the Middle East, Central and South America, as well as the new regime's positions on women's rights, laissez-faire capitalism, CIA covert operations, the Moral Majority, and America's renewed stature in the world of nations'.[17] A cautionary note should be sounded here against the too-easy temptation of reading *Raiders* as a 'Reaganite' film: it had been in development since the latter years of the Carter presidency and the cameras had rolled in the summer of 1980 several months before the US presidential election. *Raiders* should be seen, rather, as a transitional film between the uncertainty of the 1970s and the renewal of American confidence in the 1980s. It is less assertively patriotic than mid-1980s Reaganite films such as *Red Dawn, Rambo* and *Top Gun*.[18] It even satirizes the glib confidence of the American abroad: 'You can't do this to me, I'm an *American!*' protests the heroine as she is bundled ignominiously into a laundry basket by her Arab kidnappers.

Raiders explores the anxieties that attended America's role as a global superpower and the threat to its national security from a highly ideological enemy seeking the ultimate weapon. Indiana Jones is recruited by US Army Intelligence to find the legendary Ark of the Covenant before the Nazis can lay their hands on it. America's interest in acquiring the Ark is not for its significance as a religious artefact but for its military value ('An army which carries the Ark before it is invincible').[19] The quest for control of a super weapon was a recurring theme of early 1980s films, including the 'Genesis' device in *Star Trek II: The Wrath of Khan* and the supersonic stealth plane in *Firefox*.[20] This identifies the films as products of the Cold War. The early 1980s was a period of renewed Cold War tension, following the détente of the 1970s, prompted by the Soviet invasion of Afghanistan (1979) and the escalation of the nuclear arms race that saw Soviet SS-20 and US Cruise and Pershing missiles stationed in Europe. The Ark is clearly a metaphor for the atomic bomb: we are told that it is capable of 'levelling mountains and laying waste to entire regions'. In this context the film's ending, sometimes read as a reference to a Watergate-style conspiracy (the US government officially denies possession of the Ark), might also be seen as offering a sense of reassurance (America controls the most powerful weapon on earth).[21]

In reading *Raiders* as a narrative of US foreign policy and power projection, a useful comparison can be made with the James Bond films.[22] The Bond movies offer a fantasy of British power in which the decline of the British Empire never took place. Bond functions as an agent of the *Pax Britannica*: Bond movies such as *The Spy Who Loved Me* and *Tomorrow Never Dies*, for example, are replete with references to British seapower.[23] Indiana Jones is an agent of the *Pax Americana*: he travels the world to spread the doctrine of 'Manifest Destiny'. Bond, the first of the cinema's cynical, saturnine modern heroes, is the symbolic 'father' of Indiana Jones – a link that was made explicit when Sean Connery was cast as Indy's father in *Indiana Jones and the Last Crusade*.

There are ideological similarities between Bond and Indiana Jones. Tony Bennett and Janet Woollacott have argued that the Bond stories are structured around a set of narrative codes which regulate relations between characters.[24] The 'imperialist code' regulates relations between Bond and his allies, usually loyal colonial and/or pro-British characters who are in a subordinate power relationship to him. The 'sexist code' determines relations between Bond and 'the girl', who is often in the service of the villain and therefore needs to be repositioned, sexually and ideologically, to Bond's side. And the 'phallic code' governs relations between Bond and secret service chief M (who endows Bond with lethal authority – his 'licence to kill') and between Bond and the villain (who threatens him with symbolic castration through torture). Similar narrative codes inform the Indiana Jones films. For example, Jones is aided in two of the films (*Raiders* and *Last Crusade*) by Sallah, 'the best digger in Egypt', who is characterized as a pro-Western 'wog' with a penchant for Gilbert & Sullivan. His loyalty and affection for Indy is reminiscent of Bond's allies such as Quarrel (*Dr No*), Kerim Bey (*From Russia with Love*) and Vijay (*Octopussy*). Sallah's role is taken in *Temple of Doom* by Short Round, a Chinese orphan boy and martial arts prodigy. And, just as the Bond stories rehearse familiar racist stereotypes about non-Western races (such as the Afro–Chinese villains of *Dr No* or the brutal Bulgar killers of *From Russia with Love*), so do the Indiana Jones films with their Arab assassins (*Raiders*) and Chinese gangsters (*Temple of Doom*). The racist discourse of *Raiders* is even embedded in the script, where minor villains are labelled by their ethnicity such as 'ratty-looking Nepalese', 'mean Mongolian' and a whole gang of 'Bad Arabs'.

The relations between Jones and the heroines of the films – particularly the feisty Marion Ravenwood (*Raiders*) and the scatterbrained Willie Scott (*Temple of Doom*) – follow the same trajectory as the Bond films as their initial resistance to the hero's sexual charisma is overcome and the women are repositioned ideologically and sexually. (*Last Crusade* is a partial exception to this rule: Indy seduces Dr Elsa Schneider but does not detach her from her Nazi allegiance.) Robin Wood has argued that the core ideological project of Reaganite cinema is 'the restoration of patriarchal order'.[25] This process is evident in the Indiana Jones films where women are invariably subordinated: at one point in *Raiders* Indy stuffs a gag into Marion's mouth and tells her to 'sit still and keep quiet', while at the end of *Temple of Doom* he uses his whip to pull Willie into an embrace. In *Raiders* this process is also represented by Marion's changing costumes. She is introduced wearing masculine garb of trousers and shirt, but acquires more traditional feminine attire

19. Marion (Karen Allen) is menaced by a Mean Mongolian, a ratty-looking Nepalese and a nazi wielding a hot poker in *Raiders of the Lost Ark* (1981).

when she is provided with a white dress by the villain Belloq ('I would very much like to see you in it'). Marion is literally repositioned, therefore, by the forces of patriarchy which want to get her into a dress.

The phallic code is most evident in *Last Crusade*, where Indy is very much in awe of his father and where the revelation that both of them have slept with Elsa adds an unusual œdipal twist to the narrative that is not fully explored. There are also elements of this in the relationship between Indy and Belloq in *Raiders*. Belloq represents Indy's dark side ('I am a shadowy reflection of you') and competes with him for the possession of material artefacts ('Again we see there is nothing you can possess which I cannot take away') and by extension Marion ('Where'd you get *this*?' Indy enquires sarcastically when he sees the dress.) That the film is entirely knowing about its code of phallic authority is suggested by Indy's line when he discovers that his enemy has made a mistake in his calculations to find the Well of Souls where the Ark is hidden: 'Belloq's staff is too long. They're digging in the wrong place.'

It has been suggested that the period settings and comic-book Nazi villains of *Raiders of the Lost Ark* represent a form of nostalgia: that the film constructs a mythical past of moral certainties and innocence before America's reputation was tarnished by the Vietnam War. This, however, is to ignore the film's politics. *Raiders* is a narrative of US intervention in the Third World. It is significant that the action takes place in South America (identified as an area of US influence since the Monroe Doctrine of 1824) and the Middle East (a region of strategic interest since the end of the Second World War). It was during Reagan's presidency that the United States provided military support for a right-wing regime in El Salvador, aided anti-communist rebels in Nicaragua and invaded the island of Grenada following a communist *coup d'état*. And in the Middle East there were serious challenges to American authority such as the prolonged hostage crisis in Tehran (1979–80) and the bombing of the US Marine base in Beirut (1983). In this context the narrative of *Raiders* is no comforting retreat into nostalgia, but is informed by very contemporary concerns about America's relations with the Third World.

The politics of *Raiders* are explicitly colonialist. The film easily lends itself to a Marxist critique in that it effectively endorses the plundering of the religious artefacts and cultural treasures of the Third World to support the geopolitical interests of the United States. Jones's moral right to acquire the Ark for America is taken for granted and he glibly ignores warnings that 'it is something that man was not meant to disturb'. The sequels would respond to this criticism: in *Temple of Doom*, for example, Jones is accused of being a grave robber by his Indian hosts. In *Raiders*, however, the rivalry between Jones and Belloq is presented as a contest between First World nations played out in the Third World.

20. 'I am a shadowy reflection of you.' Indiana Jones (Harrison Ford) and his foe Belloq (Paul Freeman) in *Raiders of the Lost Ark* (1981).

21. America and the Third World: Indy and the Arabs in *Raiders of the Lost Ark* (1981).

The assertion of American power in the Third World is best dem-onstrated in one of the film's most memorable scenes. Searching for the abducted Marion in the casbah, Jones is confronted by a tall Arab war-rior wielding a huge scimitar. The Arab twirls the sword in a threatening manner and the scene seems set for a confrontation between the sword and the whip – whereupon Jones simply draws his pistol and casually shoots the swordsman. The film's publicity averred that a duel had been planned and the scene was improvised on set because Harrison Ford was running a high temperature and did not feel up to the physical demands of shooting the fight sequence. The scene always draws a laugh from audiences due to the inherent comedy of the situation: the Arab's excessively elaborate gesturing undercut by the matter-of-fact simplicity of Jones's reaction. But it also lays bare the technological advantage of the American who ruthlessly employs his superior firepower in an unequal contest. It amounts to nothing less than an assertion that (American) might is right.

The film's affirmation of American values is also suggested through its symbolism. It is surely no coincidence that the headpiece to the Staff of Ra – a 'MacGuffin' which reveals the location of the Well of Souls – resembles the Great Seal of the President of the United States. This sug-gests an association between God's Law (the Ark is supposed to contain the original stone tablets on which the Ten Commandments were written) and the American Constitution. The film's coda, following the spectacular special effects climax where the Ark is opened, is set in the US capital and opens with an establishing long shot of the Washington Monument. Jones is therefore associated on a symbolic level with American history and with political figures including its first president.

In the sequels the narrative of American imperialism which informs *Raiders* is partially displaced onto a theme of Western imperialism more generally. The Indian setting of *Indiana Jones and the Temple of Doom* required that it acknowledge the British presence in India (the film is set in 1935) which provides the opportunity for a limited critique of colonialism. 'The British worry so about their empire', remarks Chattar Lal, prime minister to the Maharajah of Pankot, when faced with a 'routine inspection' by the British army. There are also barbed references to the Indian Mutiny of 1857. In Hollywood's narrative of the twentieth century it is significant that British colonialism is de facto a bad thing by the 1980s whereas America represents the acceptable face of imperialism. For its villains *Temple of Doom* resurrects the Thugs who had previously seen service in *Gunga Din* and in the Hammer horror film *The Stranglers of Bombay* (1959). The Thugs were a real murder cult who existed in India in the early nineteenth century. The film is hardly less racist than *Gunga Din* in its stereotyping of Indian characters who are either simple peasants or religious fanatics. In *Temple of Doom* the Thugs, who worship the goddess Kali and practice human sacrifice, are associated with the Indian aristocracy, brutally exploiting the local population by stealing the sacred stone of a small village, thereby destroying its crops and condemning its people to starve.

Temple of Doom is generally regarded as the darkest of the films. It certainly includes more horrific and violent scenes than *Raiders*, prompting the creation of a new PG-13 rating by the US Classification and Rating Administration. This was due in large measure to Indy's capture and torture by the Thugs who feed him a mind-altering potion and force him to participate in human sacrifice. The brutal nature of his treatment anticipates *Rambo*, where the hero is captured and tortured by the Vietcong and their Russian 'advisers'. In both films the injury inflicted upon the body of the all-American hero by the colonial 'other' is so cruel and excessive that it legitimates intervention in the local conflict. In *Temple of Doom*, Indy's ordeal also turns into a process of ideological conversion. He has initially agreed to help the peasants because he sees the recovery of the sacred stone as providing an opportunity for the 'fortune and glory' he craves. After experiencing the evil of the Thugs at first hand, however, he resolves to rescue the children imprisoned in their mine and returns the stone to the village. The film therefore posits a dual motive for Indy's actions – hard-nosed economics masked by heroic altruism – that reflects US foreign policy in the Third World.[26]

Temple of Doom is the most inventive of the films in its use of genre conventions, suggesting that Spielberg and Lucas were confident enough with their formula to explore its boundaries. Willard Huyck and Gloria Katz wrote the script, utilizing some set pieces left over from Lawrence Kasdan's original screenplay for *Raiders*. It opens in unexpected fashion with a Busby Berkely–style dance extravaganza in a Shanghai nightclub as *chanteresse* Willie Scott (Kate Capshaw) performs Cole Porter's 'Anything Goes' in Mandarin. This sums up the narrative that follows as surely as Indy's 'I'm making this up as I go' describes the plot of *Raiders*. Like its predecessor, *Temple of Doom* is really a series of set pieces, culminating in a thrilling mine-car chase and a climax on a collapsing rope bridge.

Indiana Jones and the Last Crusade, written by Jeffrey Boam, is essentially a remake of *Raiders*. It revives some of the same characters (Marcus Brody, Sallah), reintroduces Nazi villains ('Nazis! I hate those guys!') and resurrects Belloq in the form of Walter Donovan (Julian Glover). It also replays many of the set pieces, including what Spielberg called the 'phobia sequence' (rats and snakes), the extended desert chase and the final melting of the villains who are destroyed by the power of the holy artefact.[27] The structural similarity between *Raiders* and *Last Crusade* means that the interventionist narrative and the sexist cultural politics of the first film are rehearsed again. On this occasion, however, the neocolonialist implications of Indy's quest for a vastly significant religious artefact in the Middle East (this time a fictitious Sultanate presided over by an unlikely-cast Alexei Sale) are displaced onto his search for his missing father. Indy initially refuses Donovan's commission to find the Holy Grail, changing his mind only when it is revealed that his father, an expert in Grail lore, has disappeared in Europe. 'I didn't come for the Cup of Christ, I came to find my father', Indy tells Khazim, leader of a secret brotherhood dedicated to preserving the secret of the Grail. He is forced to enter the Grail temple when Donovan shoots his father – Indy needs the healing powers of the Grail to save his life – but the Grail itself cannot be removed from the temple.

What distinguishes *Last Crusade* is the relationship between Indy and his father. It is a more light-hearted film than the previous two, largely on account of the by-play between Ford and Connery ('Our situation has not improved' Connery's Henry Jones Sr remarks dryly as they find themselves in another tight spot). The relationship also provides a warmth that is not evident in the other films. Indy blames their estrangement on his father's obsession with the Grail ('What you taught me was that I was less important to you than people who had been dead for five hundred years in another country, and I learned it so well that we've barely spoken for twenty years'). The absent father was a recurring motif of 1980s cinema including Spielberg's *E. T.* and films such as the fantasy *Field of Dreams*, while surrogate father figures abound in characters such as Obi Wan Kenobi (*Star Wars*), Doc Brown (*Back to the Future*) and Mr Miyagi (*The Karate Kid*). It is Henry Sr who first realizes Elsa's treachery ('I'm sorry – but you should have listened to your father') and who possesses the knowledge necessary to find the Grail. At the end of the film Indy accepts the authority of his father who tells him to leave the Grail, calling him by his preferred name of 'Indiana' for the first time. Indy loses the Grail (and the girl) but gains a father. The last shot of the film has the all-male quartet of Indy, Henry, Sallah and Brody riding off into the sunset – and into myth.

Last Crusade opens with a 'prequel' sequence in 1912 as a teenaged Indy, separated from a Boy Scouts expedition in Utah, comes across a gang of villains plundering a mine and daringly retrieves a gold cross from beneath their eyes. The ensuing chase along a circus train explains Indy's trademarks, including his scar, whip, hat and phobia about snakes.[28] It was this sequence that inspired Lucas to produce a series of television films under the collective title of *The Young Indiana Jones Chronicles* in the early 1990s. The series was shot over two years on locations around the world and the directors included Nicolas Roeg, Mike Newell, Gillies MacKinnon, Joe Johnston and Terry Jones. Two actors played the young Indy: Corey Carrier as a 10-year old in 6 episodes and Sean Patrick Flanery as a teenager and young adult in a further 26 adventures. The series was characterized by its high production values and authentic period detail. It was broadcast on the ABC network between 1992 and 1994. The original one-hour episodes were later edited to feature-length and released on video in 1999 (and again on DVD in 2008) as *The Adventures of Young Indiana Jones*.

The advertisements for *Young Indiana Jones* declared: 'Before the world discovered Indiana, Indiana discovered the world.' The premise of the series was that Indy would have adventures in various locations (principally Africa and Europe, but also including Mexico, Arabia and India) during which he would encounter famous historical figures from the early twentieth century. Thus the younger Indy, accompanying his academic father on a lecture tour in 1908–9, meets T. E. Lawrence on an archæological expedition in Egypt ('My First Adventure'), goes on safari with Theodore Roosevelt in East Africa ('Passion for Life') and in Vienna debates the meaning of love with Sigmund Freud and Carl Jung ('The Perils of Cupid'). In 1916 the teenaged Indy, after an encounter with Pancho Villa during the Mexican Revolution ('Spring Break Adventure'), stows away on a ship to

Dublin where he befriends Sean O'Casey and witnesses the Easter Rising ('Love's Sweet Song'). Indy and his friend René enlist in the Belgian army and see active service on the Western Front and in Africa. Indy is captured at Verdun but escapes from a German prisoner-of-war camp with a young Charles De Gaulle ('Trenches of Hell'). He enjoys his first sexual relationship with Mata Hari while on leave in Paris ('Demons of Deception'). He is promoted to lieutenant and sent to Africa where he leads a commando raid to destroy a German naval gun ('Phantom Train of Doom'). In 1917 he joins the Lafayette Escadrille – an American volunteer squadron of the French air force – and is shot down by Manfred Von Richtofen ('Attack of the Hawkmen'). Other adventures see him caught up in the Russian Revolution ('Adventures in the Secret Service') and serving in the French Foreign Legion ('Tales of Innocence'). After the war he returns to America where he crosses the path of Al Capone in 1920s Chicago ('Mystery of the Blues') and Erich Von Stroheim in Hollywood ('Hollywood Follies'). Amongst the other characters whom Indy encounters at various times are Norman Rockwell, Pablo Picasso, Leo Tolstoy, Giacomo Puccini (who nearly succeeds in seducing his mother), Thomas Edison, Winston Churchill, Sylvia Pankhurst, Siegfried Sassoon, Robert Graves, Jan Smuts, Paul von Lettow-Vorbeck, Charles Lindbergh, Anthony Fokker, Vladimir Lenin, Ernest Hemingway, Kemal Ataturk, Lowell Thomas, Edith Wharton, Woodrow Wilson, Eliot Ness and Louis Armstrong. In an ingenious piece of inter-textuality he works as a movie extra and stuntman for director John Ford on the set of a silent Western, where he performs the 'transfer' stunt that Ford would use in *Stagecoach* and would later be recycled in *Raiders of the Lost Ark*.

The ideological project of *Young Indiana Jones* is to narrate the early years of the 'American Century' from the perspective of a fictional observer and participant. Its historical background indicates an educational remit: it was repeated on the History Channel, where it was accompanied by specially made documentaries about the various historical characters and events featured in the series. But the historical narrative of *Young Indiana Jones* is very much one told from the perspective of the late twentieth century and informed by the values of its time. Thus the series is highly didactic in its adherence to the 'correct' values. Young Indy is associated with progressive causes. In 'Passion for Life', for example, he pleads with Theodore Roosevelt not to shoot any more zebra ('If they're so rare, why do you kill so many of them?') and causes the former president to rethink his attitude towards the environment ('Mankind has the power to destroy the wilderness. That is something we should never be allowed to do'). And in 'The Winds of Change' his friendship with Paul Robeson is used to examine racism and prejudice. The unsympathetic characterizations of General Pershing as a belligerent nationalist and a young Lieutenant George Patton as a trigger-happy killer in 'Spring Break Adventure' prompted one critic to ask rhetorically: 'Hey, what's going on here? What are the America First multitudes going to make of this history lesson?'[29]

The ideology of *Young Indiana Jones* is most apparent in the series' attitude towards imperialism. This is invariably represented as a bad thing. Indy finds his youthful idealism stirred by the Mexican rebels and joins them in their struggle against political and economic oppression. Villa tells him that his men are fighting 'to save crops and feed our children ... We are slaves in our own land. They sold off half our country to the gringos'. But he is disappointed to see Villa's men looting and stealing from those for whom they are nominally fighting. An old peasant tells him:

> It is always the same. In a revolution it is the people who suffer. Years ago I rode with Juarez against Emperor Maximilian. I lost many chickens, but I thought it was worth it to be free. When Porfirio became president, I supported him – but he stole my chickens. Then came Huerta and he stole my chickens. Then it was Carranza's turn and he took my chickens too. Now Pancho Villa has come to liberate me and the first thing he does is steal my chickens.

Indy decides that 'This isn't my war' and, after seeing a newsreel of the battle at Verdun, resolves to fight against German expansionism in Europe: 'That's the war that has to be fought. And it has to be won. The alternative is unthinkable.'

The key episode in the representation of colonialism is 'Oganga, the Giver and Taker of Life'. A newly promoted Indy is serving in the Belgian Congo, believing that the war aims of the Allies are 'to get the Germans out of Africa so that your people can have a future'. His black sergeant is sceptical, however, telling Indy: 'The Belgians are not here for my people's future. Belgians are here for white people's future. When this war is over, will the Belgians go home, leave Africa to my people? No! The Belgians want to own African soil. Same as the Germans, no difference.' In the same story Indy meets German doctor Albert Schweitzer, who cures him of fever, and is touched by Schweitzer's humanitarianism and pacifism. Again there is a moral lesson to be drawn. As Schweitzer tells Indy: 'Civilization is collapsing all around us. The war is not a cause, merely a symptom. Society doesn't want thinking men who arrive at their own convictions, it wants servants who do as they are told ... The hope for human future lies not in nations or governments or religions. It lies in the human heart.'

The most historically revisionist episode is 'The Winds of Change'. In 1919 Indy, an accomplished linguist, is working as a translator for the American delegation at the Paris Peace Conference. He meets his old friend T. E. Lawrence, British historian Arnold Toynbee and journalist Gertrude Bell. Indy believes that the age of the great European empires is over ('Colonialism is dead. There must be dozens of countries competing to become free nations.') and is inspired by Woodrow Wilson's vision of an international 'brotherhood of man' which will resolve future conflicts between nations. Indy meets a waiter from French Indo–China (later identified as Ho Chi Minh) and secures him a hearing at the conference. But Wilson is outmanœuvred by Clemenceau ('a dinosaur') and Lloyd George ('no vision or morality'). Thus Arabia is carved up by the British and French, with Prince Feisal bought off with the kingdom of Iraq. The Indo–Chinese appeal is politely rebuffed. Indy's sympathy for the Arabian and Indo–Chinese delegations once again asserts his progressive credentials. It also reminds audiences of later trouble spots in the Middle East and Vietnam. To this extent the episode lays the blame for America's later problems in these regions squarely at the doors of European imperialists.[30] A revisionist perspective is also apparent in the suggestion that the harsh settlement imposed upon the defeated Germany in the Treaty of Versailles sowed the seeds of another war. Toynbee remarks: 'Those who forget the lessons of history are doomed to repeat it ... What happened will happen again for better or worse.'[31]

Young Indiana Jones, then, offers a progressive late twentieth century narrative of the years that saw the first stirrings of America as a global power. Its anti-imperialist, liberal politics and its sympathy for social and cultural outsiders (Africans, Arabs, Black Americans) differ significantly from the pro-interventionist narrative and reactionary social politics of the Indiana Jones films. This can probably be explained by the changing historical contexts as well as by the different political and cultural economies of the film and television industries. If the Indiana Jones films reflected the assertive foreign policy of the Reagan administration, *Young Indiana Jones* was a product of the liberal social values and multiculturalism that characterized domestic policy during the early years of the Clinton presidency.

A fourth film, *Indiana Jones and the Kingdom of the Crystal Skull*, marked a belated addition to the franchise in 2008. 'Indy IV' had been promised for over a decade and its long-delayed production has become part of movie folklore. At various times it was rumoured that Indy would be searching for the Lost City of Atlantis or that the story would involve Martians in an homage to 1950s sci-fi movies such as *Invaders from Mars*. Amongst the writers attached to the project at different times were Jeffrey Boam,

M. Night Shyamalan and Tom Stoppard. In 2004 Frank Darabont (*The Shawshank Redemption*) delivered a screenplay that reportedly pleased Spielberg but not Lucas. The final script was by David Koepp, writer of Spielberg's *Jurassic Park* and *War of the Worlds*, from a story by Lucas and Jeff Nathanson. The movie was shot under conditions of great secrecy and released worldwide in May 2008.

The long gestation and problematic development of *Crystal Skull* are evident from the finished film. It is a mixture of themes and styles that do not meld into a coherent whole. The film is set in 1957 and follows Indy's quest for a mythical crystalline skull of alien origin that contains the key to an untold power source. The villains this time around are the Russians, led by Agent Irina Spalko (Cate Blanchett). The anti-communist rhetoric and humourless Soviet automatons seem like nothing so much as a throwback to the Cold War propaganda of the 1950s. However, this is undercut by references to the McCarthyite witch hunts (the late Marcus Brody was a victim of HUAC) and US government duplicity. The opening sequence, for example, takes place in the vast warehouse seen in the last shot of *Raiders*, which turns out to be in the restricted 'Area 51' in New Mexico. This locates *Crystal Skull* in the realm of the television series *The X Files* (1993–2001) with its paranoid conspiracy narratives. Indy is reunited with Marion Ravenwood (Karen Allen) and discovers that he has a teenaged son called Mutt (Shia LaBeouf). The inclusion of this character – a leather-jacketed motorcycle-riding college drop-out who seems to have strayed in from a 1950s social problem film – was supposed to attract the core teenage demographic who had not experienced the original films and who might not otherwise have been attracted to a movie featuring an ageing action hero (Harrison Ford was 65 when the film shot, while Indy is supposed to be in his late fifties).

The critical reception of *Crystal Skull* was decidedly mixed, but its popular success demonstrates the irrelevance of critics in the age of the corporate blockbuster. *Crystal Skull*, which cost a reported $185 million, was made at a time of escalating budgets and inflated box office returns that had seen twenty-first century movie franchises such as *Harry Potter*, *Lord of the Rings* and *Pirates of the Caribbean* establish new benchmarks for the industry. In 1981, *Raiders of the Lost Ark* had opened on 1,078 screens in North America before it was seen overseas. *Crystal Skull*, in contrast, was released worldwide on some 15,000 screens.[32] This release strategy reflects the increasing economic significance of the international market (which now accounts for around 60 per cent of the total box office revenue for a major studio release) and the imperative of saturating the market to maximize publicity and get audiences into cinemas before the film becomes available on pirate DVD and illegal Internet downloads. *Crystal Skull* proved that Indiana Jones still possessed the old box office alchemy: within 12 weeks it had grossed $776 million worldwide.[33]

At the start of the twenty-first century the US film industry is more than ever in a position of economic and cultural hegemony throughout the world. Its markets have expanded following the fall of the Communist regimes in Eastern Europe and with the growth of mass consumerism in the emerging economies of Asia. Hollywood has aggressively sought out new markets whilst consolidating its position in established markets. Its control of the distribution sector – the majority of distributors are US-owned – ensures that its films are privileged over the domestic product. The world première of *Crystal Skull* was at the Cannes Film Festival, once a showcase for European art movies and independent cinema, now an outpost of Hollywood's overseas empire colonized by the major producer–distributors as a high-profile launching pad for their global blockbusters. To this extent Indiana Jones also represents another kind of empire – the empire of Global Hollywood.

Notes

1   Thomas Schatz, 'The New Hollywood', in Jim Collins, Hilary Radner and Ava Preacher Collins (eds), *Film Theory Goes to the Movies* (London: Routledge, 1993), p.17.
2   The rentals are the amounts returned to the distributor after exhibitors have taken their share of the total taken at the box office (the gross). Usually the rental is between 45–55 per cent of the gross. In terms of North American grosses *Raiders of the Lost Ark* was the fifth biggest film of the 1980s with $242.4 million (which includes two re-issues, in 1982 and 1983), *Indiana Jones and the Last Crusade* ninth with $197.2 million and *Indiana Jones and the Temple of Doom* tenth with $179.9 million. Peter Cowie (ed.), *Variety Almanack 2000* (London: Boxtree, 2000), p.71.
3   William Goldman, *Adventures in the Screen Trade: A Personal View of Hollywood and Screenwriting* (London: Macdonald, 1984), pp.40–1. George Lucas confirms this story in the documentary *Indiana Jones: Making the Trilogy* on the 'Bonus Material' DVD (VFC 49139) included in *The Adventures of Indiana Jones: The Complete DVD Movie Collection*.
4   Anon., 'Raiders of the Lost Ark', *Variety*, 10 June 1981, p.18.
5   Vincent Canby, 'Mixed Adventures', *The New York Times*, 21 June 1981, S2, p.17.
6   Richard Schickel, 'Slam! Bang! A *Movie* Movie', *Time*, 15 June 1981, p.74.
7   Steve Neale, 'Hollywood Corner', *Framework*, 19 (1982), p.37.
8   The production order of the films does not reflect their chronological sequence. *Raiders* is set in 1936, *Temple of Doom* in 1935 and *Last Crusade* in 1938.
9   *She* was filmed by RKO in 1935 (dir. Irving Pichel) and by Hammer Films in 1965 (dir. Robert Day). *King Solomon's Mines* had been filmed by Gaumont British in 1937 (dir. Robert Stevenson) and by MGM in 1950 (dir. Compton Bennett). *King Solomon's Treasure* (dir. Alvin Rakoff, 1978) was a television movie actually based on Haggard's sequel *Allan Quatermain*. The success of the Indiana Jones films prompted Cannon to cash in with *King Solomon's Mines* (dir. J. Lee Thompson, 1985) and *Allan*

Quatermain and the Lost City of Gold (dir. Gary Nelson, 1986). There was also a two-part US–German television version of *King Solomon's Mines* in 2003, starring Patrick Swayze and Alison Doody.

10   The phrase 'cinema of attractions' was coined by Tom Gunning in respect of early chase and stunt films. Gunning, 'The Cinema of Attractions: Early Cinema, Its Spectators and the Avant-Garde', *Wide Angle*, 8: 3–4 (1986), pp.63–70. 'Clearly,' Gunning writes, 'in some recent spectacle cinema has reaffirmed its roots in stimulus and carnival rides, in what might be called the Spielberg–Lucas–Coppola cinema of effects'. Lucas used a similar comparison when he said: 'My films are closer to amusement park rides than to a play or a novel. You get in line for a second ride.' Quoted in Schickel, 'Slam! Bang!', p.75.

11   R. M. Hayes, *The Republic Chapterplays: A Complete Filmography of the Serials Released by Republic Pictures Corporation, 1934–1955* (Jefferson NC: McFarland, 1991), p.73.

12   The screenplay for *Raiders of the Lost Ark* held by the British Film Institute (Unpublished Script Collection S18398), dated 3 August 1979 and credited to Lawrence Kasdan, features two extensive sequences that were dropped before principal photography. In this version the headpiece of the Staff of Ra is in two parts, one with Marion Ravenwood, the other in a museum in Shanghai belonging to General Tengtu Hok. Jones breaks into the museum, fights two samurai warriors and makes his escape behind a giant rolling gong while Hok shoots at it with a tommy gun. There is also an additional sequence on the secret island where Indy and Marion escape with the Ark via an underground mine railway. The escape from the Shanghai museum and the mine-car chase were both included in *Temple of Doom*.

13   This type of stunt is known as a 'transfer'. In *Stagecoach* Canutt plays the Apache attacker who jumps onto the leading horse and is shot by Ringo (John Wayne). The horse and stage pass over the prone body of Canutt, who can be seen getting to his feet at the end of the shot. Canutt improved on the stunt in the Republic serial *Zorro's Fighting Legion* (1939) where, doubling for Zorro, he climbs onto the back of the stagecoach after it has passed over him. The stunt in *Raiders* – requiring a trench to be dug under the truck, which is clearly visible on screen – was performed by Terry Leonard. The boulder sequence of *Raiders* and the nightclub fight in *Temple of Doom* are analysed in Charles Deemer, 'The Rhetoric of Action: Five Classic Action Scenes', *Critical Screenwriting*, 2: 4 (1995), pp.95–105.

14   See, for example, Fredric Jameson, 'Postmodernism, or the Cultural Logic of Late Capitalism', *New Left Review*, 165 (1984), pp.53–92 .

15   *The Making of 'Raiders of the Lost Ark'* (tx 28.11.1981). Another documentary focused on the stunt work: *Great Movie Stunts: Raiders of the Lost Ark* (tx 5.10.1981).

16   Patricia Zimmermann, 'Soldiers of Fortune: Lucas, Spielberg, Indiana Jones and *Raiders of the Lost Ark*', *Wide Angle*, 6: 2 (1983), p.34.

17   Frank P. Tomasulo, 'Mr Jones Goes to Washington: Myth and Religion in *Raiders of the Lost Ark*', *Quarterly Review of Film Studies*, 7: 4 (1982), pp.331–2.

18   *Red Dawn* (MGM-United Artists, dir. John Milius, 1984) was probably the most paranoid anti-communist film since the early 1950s: it posited a Russian and Cuban invasion of the USA defeated by an underground movement of Hollywood 'Brat Pack' actors. *Rambo: First Blood Part II* (Carolco, dir. George Pan Cosmatos, 1985) was a revisionist Vietnam combat movie in which a special forces veteran rescues American prisoners still held by the Vietcong. *Top Gun* (Paramount, dir. Tony Scott, 1986) is an

homage to male homoeroticism as elite pilots posture their way through training and combat.

19   It is the villain, Belloq, who appreciates the religious significance of the Ark, describing it as 'a transmitter – a radio for speaking to God'.

20   *Star Trek II: The Wrath of Khan* (Paramount, dir. Nicholas Meyer, 1982); *Firefox* (Warner/ Malpaso, dir. Clint Eastwood, 1982).

21   The idea of the Ark as a metaphor for the atomic bomb was suggested in a review of *Raiders* by R. J. Thompson in *Cinema Papers*, 35 (November–December 1981), pp.500–3. Major Eaton tells Indy that the Ark is in a 'safe place' and that 'we have top men working on it'. In the late 1930s the US government secretly set up the Manhattan Project – code name for the atomic bomb programme based at Los Alamos, New Mexico – led by 'top men' such as physicists Julius Oppenheimer and Enrico Fermi.

22   According to the publicity, *Raiders* originated when Spielberg, on vacation in Hawaii with Lucas, mentioned that he had always wanted to direct a James Bond movie and Lucas replied that he had 'something better'.

23   See James Chapman, *Licence To Thrill: A Cultural History of the James Bond Films* (London: I.B.Tauris, 2nd edn, 2007).

24   Tony Bennett and Janet Woollacott, *Bond and Beyond: The Political Career of a Popular Hero* (London: Macmillan, 1987), pp.99–141.

25   Robin Wood, *Hollywood from Vietnam to Reagan* (New York: Columbia University Press, 1986), p.

26   Joseph Sartelle, 'Dreams and Nightmares in the Hollywood Blockbuster', in Geoffrey Nowell-Smith (ed.), *The Oxford History of World Cinema* (Oxford: Oxford University Press, 19950, p.524.

27   The screenplay for *Indiana Jones and the Last Crusade* by Jeffrey Boam, dated 1 March 1988 (BFI Unpublished Script Collection S17980), again differs in detail from the finished film. Here it is Elsa rather than Donovan (Chandler in the script) who shoots Henry to force Indy to enter the Grail cave and who dies when she drinks from the wrong cup. It seems a shame that the film omits the sequence in Berlin where Leni Riefenstahl has problems choreographing Hitler and his aides and declares 'No more propaganda film!'

28   Young Indy is played by River Pheonix, who previously had played Harrison Ford's son in *The Mosquito Coast* (1986).

29   John O'Connor, 'Meeting Indiana Jones as a Boy and a Teen-Ager', *The New York Times*, 4 March 1992.

30   On the politics of *Young Indiana Jones*, see Mimi White, 'Indy & Dr Mike: Is Boy to Global World History as Woman Is to Domestic National Myth?', *Film & History*, 30: 1 (2000), pp.24–37.

31   There were of course some commentators even in 1919, including Marshal Foch and Jan Smuts, who predicted that the Treaty of Versailles would store up future problems with Germany. Foch called it a 'twenty-year armistice'. For a summary of the historiography of Versailles, see Anthony Lentin, *The Versailles Peace Settlement: Peacemaking with Germany* (London: Historical Association, 1991); and Alan Sharp, *The Versailles Settlement: Peacemaking in Paris, 1919* (London: Macmillan, 1991).

32   William Booth, 'The World Can't Wait for Indy? It Won't Have To', *Washington Post Mobile*, 19 May 2008.

[33] http//:www.boxofficemojo.com/movies/indianajones4.htm (15 August 2008). *Crystal Skull* had the second highest Memorial Day Weekend opening in the USA, taking $126.9 million in its first four days at 4,260 sites. (The record is currently held by *Pirates of the Caribbean: At World's End* in 2007.) After 12 weeks it had grossed $314.8 million in North America and $461.5 million in overseas markets. The 'foreign' gross accounted for 59 per cent of the total, again reflecting the importance of global release. When adjusted for inflation, however, *Raiders of the Lost Ark* remains the most successful of the series and currently stands at number 16 in the inflation-adjusted list of all-time domestic box office champions. See http//:www.boxofficemojo.com/alltime/adjusted.htm (7 July 2008).

THE RAJ REVIVAL
Gandhi (1982)

In March 1983 *Gandhi* surpassed the record set for a British film by *Lawrence of Arabia* when it won eight Academy Awards including Best Picture. Its success represented a personal triumph for its producer–director Sir Richard Attenborough, who had spent 20 years trying to make the film and who also collected the Oscar for Best Director.[1] There are some instructive comparisons between *Gandhi* and *Lawrence*. Both are biopics told on an epic scale; both feature stellar casts in support of a relatively unknown lead; both begin with the death of their protagonist followed by the main narrative in flashback; and both introduce an American journalist who acts as a commentator on the action. The long production history of *Gandhi*, furthermore, echoes that of *Lawrence*, with David Lean, Fred Zinnemann and Joseph Losey all in the frame to direct at one time or another, and treatments from screenwriters including Emeric Pressburger and Robert Bolt, before Attenborough fulfilled his ambition to bring the life story of Gandhi to the screen.[2]

Mohandas K. Gandhi (1869–1948) – known to his followers as Mahatma ('great soul') – was a London-educated barrister who first came to public notice in South Africa where he led a popular opposition movement to discrimination against the Indian population. In 1915 he returned to India and became a leading figure in the Congress Party. Gandhi advocated a policy of non-violent protest and passive resistance. Revered by his followers, Gandhi was often held in contempt in Britain. Winston Churchill notoriously called him 'a seditious Middle Temple lawyer, now posing as a fakir of a type well-known in the East', and said that he found 'nauseating' the sight of Gandhi 'striding half-naked up the steps of the Vice-regal palace, while he is still organising and conducting a campaign of civil disobedience, to parley on equal terms with the representative of the King-Emperor'.[3] It is in light of such views that we need to understand the suggestion of making an anti-Gandhi film as early as 1923. D. W. Griffith, who had made the patriotic melodrama *Hearts of the World* (1918) at the invitation of the British government, was approached. The magazine *Photoplay* reported: 'The effective answer to Gandhi, and the effective appeal to the potential colonists of the white world can, these British leaders feel, be more forcefully phrased in the motion picture than in any of the other media of modern propaganda.'[4] Perhaps fortunately nothing came of the idea.

It was following Gandhi's assassination, by a fanatical Hindu nationalist in 1948, that interest in his life story grew in the West. An American biographer, Louis Fischer, published *The Life of Mahatma Gandhi* in 1951.[5] Gabriel Pascal, like Alexander Korda another East European impressario who settled in Britain, tried to interest Indian maharajahs in backing a film in 1953.[6] David Lean was also attracted to the subject after reading Fischer's biography. In 1958 Lean travelled to India to undertake research with Emeric Pressburger. Pressburger, as was his wont, wrote a treatment in the style of a novel entitled 'Written in the Stars' which told Gandhi's life story through the eyes of an American doctor and an English policeman in India. Pressburger approached it from a humanist perspective. He prefaced his treatment: 'Gandhi has often said that his life was an experiment in Truth. I think it was richer than that. I would call it an experiment in human values. Our film should be the same.'[7] Lean – who had wanted Alec Guinness as Gandhi with William Holden as the American doctor – disliked Pressburger's treatment and went on to make *Lawrence of Arabia* instead.[8]

Attenborough became involved in 1962. According to his account, he was approached by Motilal Kothari, a follower and devotee of Gandhi born in the same state of Gujarat, who was 'determined to find a means of promoting the Mahatma's life and all he stood for' and felt this could best be achieved through film.[9] Attenborough was then best known as an actor but had moved into production in the late 1950s through his partnership with Bryan Forbes in Beaver Films and his involvement in the consortium Allied Film Makers. He read Fischer's biography and found himself 'totally enthralled from the word go'.[10] He resolved to make the film, despite never having directed before. He solicited the support of Earl Mountbatten who, as the last Viceroy of India, had known Gandhi and was able to provide an introduction to the Indian Prime Minister Jawaharlal Nehru. He asked Robert Bolt to write the screenplay – this was shortly after Bolt had finished working on *Lawrence of Arabia* – though Bolt was unable to commit to the project at this stage. Attenborough then turned to Irish writer Gerry Hanley, whose novel *The Consul at Sunset* examined British colonial policy in Africa.[11]

In 1963 Attenborough met Nehru and his daughter Mrs Indira Gandhi.[12] Nehru told Attenborough: 'Whatever you do, do not deify him – that is what we have done in India – and he was too great a *man* to be deified.'[13] Having secured the support in principle of the Indian authorities, Attenborough returned to London to put together the finance for the film. John Davis, the managing director of the Rank Organization, despite having little faith in the film, provided £5,000 development money.[14] But American producer Joseph E. Levine, who had just hit the box office jackpot with *Zulu*, agreed to back it. In December 1964 Levine held a press conference at the Savoy to announce that *Gandhi* would roll in October 1965.[15]

That it did not happen was due to several factors. Levine disliked Hanley's script, but Attenborough was unable to find a recognized writer willing to tackle it. Levine also wanted a star name to play Gandhi. Attenborough preferred to cast an unknown, as Lean had done with *Lawrence of Arabia*. Paramount, with whom Levine had a distribution arrangement, was unwilling to commit to the film without a writer and star in place. Neither would United Artists or Twentieth Century-Fox. Attenborough took a number of acting roles in the interim in *The Flight of the Pheonix* and *The Sand Pebbles*. The film appeared to have stalled. Then Robert Bolt, who had refused several previous overtures to write the script, announced that he would do so provided he could approve the director. That Bolt was able to make such a demand was down to his two successive Academy Awards for *Doctor Zhivago* (1965) and *A Man for All Seasons* (1966). Bolt nominated Fred Zinnemann, the director of *A Man for All Seasons*, and when Zinnemann withdrew turned instead to David Lean. Attenborough, now in danger of being sidelined, spoke to Lean during the production of *Zhivago*:

> Although David was now showing great interest, I felt dubious about his ultimate involvement. Some years beforehand, I had flown to Madrid to visit him, to make certain that the interest he had previously shown in the project was no impediment to my going ahead ... My purpose in going to see him had been that, if there really was a chance of this master of the cinema making this particular subject, it should be in his hands rather than mine.[16]

In the event, however, Lean and Bolt decided to make *Ryan's Daughter* instead.[17] With the Gandhi film still uncertain, Attenborough accepted an offer from John Mills to direct the film version of the satirical anti-war play *Oh! What a Lovely War* (1969).[18]

The uncertainty around *Gandhi* continued throughout the 1970s. Bolt wrote a script, entitled *Gandhiji*. Amongst those approached to direct it were Joseph Losey and, once again, David Lean.[19] As with *Lawrence of Arabia*, Bolt was more interested in the psychology of the character than in the political background. In the preface to one treatment he wrote:

> I have tried to show the steady flowering of the rigidly correct moralist into the carefree and compassionate Saint. I hope I have caught some of the emotion I felt in writing it. I have tried to lay the moral, personal and political foundations early so that the film accelerates from start to finish. I have necessarily telescoped many events into fewer. Other historical figures whose persons are still remembered I have introduced only briefly and in such a way that they need not even be named. This is to facilitate casting and to help the audience to suspend disbelief.[20]

For this reason, Bolt rarely mentions characters by name – exceptions are General Dyer, the officer responsible for the Amritsar massacre, and *The New York Times* journalist Walker (a composite of several journalists including Louis Fischer, Vincent Sheean and William Shirer) – and instead uses archetypes to represent the various politicians and authority figures.

The fullest version of Bolt's script is a complete screenplay dated October 1973. This was the version sent to Joseph Losey.[21] Bolt starts with the incident in South Africa where Gandhi, then a practising barrister, is thrown out of a first-class train compartment for being a 'coolie'. As he waits on a deserted platform with a thunderstorm brewing, a sequence of flashbacks reveal incidents from Gandhi's early life, including his wedding to Kasturbai at the age of 13, the death of his father, and his first triumph as a barrister, winning a case on behalf of an Indian client against an Englishman. These incidents – presented in non-linear fashion – recall, somewhat ironically, Michael Wilson's screenplay for *Lawrence of Arabia*. The script then follows Gandhi's role in the campaign to abolish the discriminatory pass laws and his advocacy of passive resistance. Gandhi is arrested but released when Indian workers go on strike: a government official manipulates him into voluntarily re-registering for a pass card in return for the extension of the vote to the small Indian minority. This right is later withdrawn. Gandhi leads a general strike to reclaim it. Gandhi's return to India is paralleled with the arrival of a young Englishman called Jones, who is taking up a post in the Indian civil service. Gandhi takes up the cause of unjust rents. His campaign is reported by Walker. Following the Amritsar massacre, when troops fire on a crowd of peaceful demonstrators, Gandhi calls for a campaign of civil disobedience. He is imprisoned and falls ill. Once released Gandhi leads a protest against the salt monopoly. He opposes Indian participation in the Second World War. Independence in 1947 marks the partition of India and Pakistan – opposed by Gandhi – and is followed by communal violence between Hindus and Muslims. Godse, a young Hindu fanatic, is appalled when Gandhi tells a repentant Muslim who has killed Hindus in retaliation for the death of his son to raise a Hindu child. Godse shoots and kills Gandhi. The screenplay concludes with the spectacle of Gandhi's funeral.

The Bolt screenplay is characteristic of the author's work. It resembles his script of *Lawrence of Arabia* in several respects. There are indicators of Bolt's anti-imperial politics throughout. He uses pointed phrases like 'the absurd grandiosity of the Imperial Ministries' to describe the folly of the British Raj. He takes every opportunity to portray the British as reactionaries ('I ask you, can you imagine this lot ruling themselves?') and racists (Indians, Hindu and Muslim alike, 'are essentially primitive people, self-deceived by mumbo-jumbo'). It is also, in parts, highly cinematic. Bolt brilliantly condenses the Second World War into a short sequence that cuts between a pacifist speech by Gandhi with images of the dropping of the atom bomb on Hiroshima. It is impossible not to be reminded here that Bolt was a long-standing supporter of the Campaign for Nuclear Disarmament.

At this point Attenborough was still hopeful that Joseph Levine would produce the film. In 1972 he had directed *Young Winston*, for Carl Foreman, which proved that he could handle complex production logistics. In April 1973 he assigned all rights in the Gandhi film to Levine's company Avco Embassy, who 'committed themselves to finance *Gandhi* with a budget limit of $6 million'.[22] The film was due to start shooting in January 1974.[23] In late 1973, however, Levine pulled out, citing 'political factors and ... financial complications'.[24] In 1975 Levine persuaded Attenborough to direct *A Bridge Too Far*, based on the book by Cornelius Ryan. *Bridge* cost $25 million and involved 12 months of pre-production and a 6-month shoot. It was followed in 1978 by *Magic*, a psychological thriller based on a novel by William Goldman, who had written the screenplay of *Bridge*. Attenborough returned once again to *Gandhi* at the end of the decade, now working with American writer John Briley.

Briley, originally employed to revise Bolt's script, did what Bolt had done when hired to revise Michael Wilson's *Lawrence of Arabia*: he wrote it as an original screenplay from scratch. Attenborough thought that 'it seemed to me much the most successful of the scripts so far written'.[25] Briley followed Fischer's example by starting with Gandhi's assassination and funeral and then telling the story in flashback. He maintained many of the same incidents as Bolt – including Gandhi's expulsion from the first-class carriage, his campaign against the pass laws, his return to India, Amritsar – and added others such as the March to the Sea and his attendance at the Round Table

Conference in London in 1931. Briley dispensed with the character of Jones, replacing him with a clergyman called Charlie Andrews. He also beefed up the parts of the American journalist, Walker, and Margaret Bourke-White, the celebrated *Life* magazine photographer who had befriended Gandhi towards the end of his life and who appeared in one scene towards the end of Bolt's script. There is a fuller sense of the political background in Briley's screenplay – to that extent it is closer to Wilson's *Lawrence of Arabia* – though it would be fair to say that it less well structured, particularly in the second half which becomes very episodic between Amritsar (1919) and independence (1947).[26]

Now with a satisfactory script in place – Attenborough had never been entirely happy with Bolt's treatment – *Gandhi* was finally nearing fruition after two decades in development. Yet raising the finance still proved a huge problem. Levine, a Jew, finally withdrew for good when the Indian government officially recognized the Palestine Liberation Organization.[27] In the meantime Attenborough had secured the personal support of Indira Gandhi, now Prime Minister of India, who had a long-standing interest in the project. After reading the script, she arranged that the National Film Development Corporation of India – an organization set up to promote investment in quality film-making as distinct from commercial 'Bollywood' fare – would support the film.[28] Goldcrest Films, a London-based company set up by Canadian Jake Eberts to provide 'seed money' for project development, provided the £1 million needed for Attenborough to buy the rights back from Levine.[29] The final budget of £9.5 million was provided by Goldcrest (60 per cent), the NFDC (30 percent) and a consortium of private investors (10 per cent) that included various merchant bankers and investment trusts.[30] *Gandhi* finally went into production in the autumn of 1981. Columbia, after seeing early rushes, agreed to distribute it and to spend $12 million on promotion.[31]

How *Gandhi* came to be made in the early 1980s was the result of two related factors. This was a time of renewed prestige for the British film industry when, following a lean time during the 1970s, a number of British films won international acclaim and put British cinema back on the map. The mood was caught by the success of the modestly budgeted *Chariots of Fire* in 1981 which earned over $36 million in the United States and won Academy Awards for Best Picture and Best Screenplay – the latter prompting its screenwriter, Colin Welland, to wave his Oscar aloft and declare: 'The British are coming!' *Chariots of Fire* was followed by a cycle of ambitious (and increasingly expensive) British films including *Gandhi*, *The Killing Fields* and *The Mission* and by a cultural attempt to promote interest in a 'British Film Year' (1985) just as the Thatcher government was finally winding down the last vestiges of state support for the film industry by abolishing both the Eady Levy and the National Film Finance Corporation.[32] Goldcrest had also supported *Chariots of Fire*, and it was the commercial success of *Chariots* and *Gandhi* that persuaded Eberts to move into direct production.

The early 1980s was also the period of what has been called the 'Raj revival' when British culture suddenly became obsessed with India. *Gandhi* needs to be seen in the context of films such as Merchant-Ivory's *Heat and Dust* (1982), David Lean's *A Passage to India* (1984) – even the James Bond film *Octopussy* (1983) – and television mini-series such as Granada's *The Jewel in the Crown* (1984) and HBO's *The Far Pavilions* (1985).[33] These productions (the Bond movie excepted) demonstrated a cultural fascination with the last days of the Raj that, a generation after independence, could be represented with a degree of historical and critical distance. They can be seen as vehicles for both the cultural and economic export of Britishness and in large measure they were successful. But some right-wing commentators accused them of promoting a negative image of Britain. A leader in the *Sunday Telegraph* attacked Attenborough for 'turning the film into a piece of straight political propaganda for India, at the expense of his own country's imperial past which is grossly traduced. If pandering shamelessly to America's anti-colonial prejudices is the only way to save the dying British film industry, then perhaps its resurrection is not such a good idea after all'.[34]

The filming of *Gandhi* in India had given rise to a rather different sort of controversy. There were protests against the film, which provoked hostility for a variety of reasons. Some objected to the fact that a foreign director, and a British director at that, was making a biopic of the 'father of the nation' instead of an Indian. Others felt that the government should not have invested in the film. There was controversy that the local crew were paid less than their British counterparts. Others still thought it sacriligeous to make a film about Gandhi at all.[35] It is a tribute to Attenborough's diplomatic abilities that the shooting, logistically one of the most complex since *Lawrence of Arabia*, proceeded largely without incident.[36]

The casting of *Gandhi* followed the same principle as *Lawrence*. Attenborough tested John Hurt for the title role but eventually settled on Ben Kingsley, an Anglo–Indian character actor with no previous film experience. The supporting cast comprised a veritable who's who of international acting talent. British stalwarts John Mills, Trevor Howard, John Gielgud and John Clements all made cameo appearances. The American contingent consisted of Candice Bergen as Margaret Bourke-White and Martin Sheen as Walker. Leading Indian actors Saeed Jaffrey, Roshan Seth and Amrish Puri also played important supporting roles.

Released in December 1982, *Gandhi* met with muted approval from the critics. It tended to be seen as a very worthy film but not as great cinema. It certainly suffered in comparison to *Lawrence of Arabia* – and to Lean's *A Passage to India*, which followed it two years later and was very warmly received, perhaps to make up for the scorn heaped upon *Ryan's Daughter*. Philip French in the *Observer* thought it an 'honourable, honestly affecting, carefully crafted film' which 'recalls those solid, inspirational Hollywood biographies of the 1930s associated with Paul Muni'.[37] Derek Malcolm in the *Guardian* described it as 'Gandhi for beginners – a big film with a cast of thousands that treats complicated, controversial things as simply and clearly as it can'.[38] Nigel Andrews in the *Financial Times* complained that it was 'like an endless series of illustrated Sunday School tales simplified and pre-digested (but not, Heaven knows, shortened) for our moral improvement'.[39] In contrast David Robinson in *The Times* admired its 'uncompromising simplicity' and praised it as 'a model of old, conservative, and in this case admirable virtues of the British cinema'.[40] The American response was along much the same lines. Vincent Canby described it in *The New York Times* as 'a big, amazingly authentic-looking movie, very sincere and aware of its responsibilities'.[41] Andrew Sarris, however, thought it 'a lumbering masto-don of a movie' and called Attenborough 'a poor man's David Lean'.[42]

Other commentators focused on the politics of the film. *Gandhi* was criti-cized, for different reasons, by both the intellectual right and the intellectual left. Paul Johnson, acting as a spokesman of the former, complained about 'the misrepresentation of British rule' and in particular that the Amritsar massacre was 'seriously misrepresented'. Johnson proceeded to defend the actions of General Dyer (played in the film by an icy Edward Fox) on the grounds that he 'was not put on trial and so never had a proper chance to defend himself with the assistance of counsel'.[43] It is entirely characteristic of the response of the right to what it sees as the inaccuracies of historical cinema that Johnson's review of *Gandhi* actually says very little about the film itself. Equally typical was the response of a commentator in the left-wing journal *The Leveller*, which averred that the film distorted the histor-ical record in order to whitewash British rule:

> More surprising is the way the British come across as obstinate and out of touch, but basically benevolent. The British Army offi-cer, who personally supervises the massacre of about a thousand Indians peacefully gathered at a protest meeting, is presented as slightly mad, an object of pity, not as a typical case that went too far ... While colonial oppression is excused as a series of moral misjudgements, the colonial attitude persists in the plot. Minor

> British and American characters are blown up out of all pro-
> portion and share Gandhi's most intimate moments. In contrast
> Nehru, Gandhi's lifelong friend and a major historical figure, has
> a relatively minor role, though his is the largest given to an Indian
> besides Gandhi.[44]

In fact 379 were killed at Amritsar and 1200 wounded, but facts are rarely
allowed to get in the way of polemic.

The criticisms of *Gandhi* from both right and left miss the point. *Gandhi* is
neither an indictment nor an apologia for British rule in India. It is a biopic. It
adheres to the conventions of the biopic in placing its protagonist at the centre of the narrative and treating other characters as secondary. It is not called
Gandhi and Nehru. The charge has always been levelled against historical biopics that they represent the past in terms of individual agency rather than historical process. The fact is, however, that very few film-makers have ever been
able to find a successful formula for dramatizing historical processes. Those
that have done so tend to work in documentary and other non-mainstream
film practices.[45] Any historical omissions or elisions in *Gandhi* – and there are
numerous examples – are due as much to the form of the biopic genre than to
any deliberate attempt to distort the historical record.

And in most respects *Gandhi* is a very conventional biopic. Gandhi is
characterized as the special individual whose actions succeed in bringing
about change. As an Indian critic, Ashish Rajadhyaska, remarks: 'The film
generates an interest in the individual – or rather, the Individual – and the
events are little more than dramatic props with which to highlight their
greatness.'[46] *Gandhi* is characterized by an extreme reverence for its subject: despite Nehru's advice it does tend towards deifying its protagonist.
It omits any mention of Gandhi's unconventional habit of laying naked
amongst young girls to test his vow of celibacy. And it emphasizes his moral
and spiritual beliefs – his ethos of pacifism and non-violent resistance – but
downplays his political and economic beliefs that were not shared by other
Congress leaders. It almost certainly attributes to Gandhi greater significance in the independence movement than he probably warranted.

Like all films *Gandhi* was the product of its own time and circumstances.
It interprets the past through the lens of the present. *Gandhi*, in common
with the other Raj films of the 1980s, exemplifies what has been called a 'liberal, neocolonialist historiographic project'.[47] It attempts not to whitewash
colonialism, but rather to present the end of empire as altruistic and progressive. The British withdrawal from India is presented as an acceptance
of the inevitable rather than as a capitulation to Indian nationalism. When
Mountbatten arrives as Viceroy he remarks that his job is 'to ensure that I

am the last British official to enter India in this capacity'. He is absolved of any blame for the bloody consequences of partition, which is laid squarely at the door of rival Hindu and Muslim factions. This is a narrative that, *pace* Paul Johnson, is tailored to make it palatable for British audiences.

Another criticism that has been made of *Gandhi* is that it is told from an Anglocentric perspective. This is undoubtedly correct. Again, however, it misses the point: it would be entirely unrealistic to expect a commercial film made by a British producer–director and an American writer within the institutional and ideological contexts of the British and American film industries to be anything else. The fact of *Gandhi*'s parentage is significant. It is a rare example of an Anglo–American film which privileges the perspective of the colonized subject. This fact alone is sufficient to suggest that *Gandhi* may be understood from a postcolonialist perspective. That it is postcolonial in the historical sense is unquestionable: it looks back on a period of imperial history from a post-imperial perspective. Its grand narrative is the end of empire and the emergence of Indian nationhood. Here the film's representation of internal divisions within the Congress Party is more nuanced than has sometimes been allowed. It sets up a difference between political nationalism (represented by Nehru) and Gandhi's spiritual nationalism ('Two countries and two religions. But one people – one God').

On an ideological level, moreover, *Gandhi* explores several postcolonialist themes. It explores social exclusion and racial discrimination against minorities, especially in the early scenes in South Africa – which, dramatically, are amongst the best in the film. (Here it should be noted that the seeds of Attenborough's next-film-but-one, *Cry Freedom*, a dual biopic of the anti-apartheid activist Steve Biko and the white journalist Donald Woods, were sown when he learned that *Gandhi* would be shown to segregated audiences in South Africa.) The film also explores issues of cultural identity. It charts Gandhi's transformation from a Westernized professional (he is first encountered wearing a suit) into an Eastern holy man in sandals and *dhoti*. In India Gandhi criticizes the Western lifestyle of the Congress Party elite. Through his spiritualism and asceticism Gandhi represents the 'Orientalist' tradition identified by theorists such as Edward Said – except here it is an identity he has created for himself.

Gandhi also demonstrates a characteristically postcolonialist fascination with how the colonial subject is constructed through the Western gaze. Thus Gandhi becomes an object both for the newsreels (his visit to London in 1931 is represented through pastiche newsreel footage – a device that Attenborough would employ again in *Grey Owl* in 1999) and for the camera of *Life* photographer Margaret Bourke-White. The sequence of the March to the Sea borrows a device from *Lawrence of Arabia* as we see it being recorded

22. A young Mohandas Gandhi (Ben Kingsley) campaigns for equal rights for Indians in South Africa in *Gandhi* (1982).

by Walker and a film crew. The sequence of Gandhi's funeral, finally, was shot on the Rajpath in Delhi, the scene of the great imperialist Durbars, and similarly represents a form of orientalist spectacle.[48]

The postcolonialist characteristics of *Gandhi* – also evident in the other Raj films of the 1980s, particularly *Heat and Dust* and *A Passage to India* – need to be understood in the context of 1980s Britain. There was much debate at the time about their ideological import. Salman Rushdie, for example, argued that the Raj films were 'the artistic counterpart to the rise of conservative ideologies in modern Britain'.[49] He saw them as exercises in nostalgia, lamenting the loss of Britain's imperial heritage. Other commentators, however, have seen the Raj films as offering a liberal critique of British society and values. Farrukh Dhondy, in a review of *The Jewel in the Crown*, pointed out that the Raj cycle allows 'the British to be self-obsessed and self-examining'.[50] The early 1980s was a period of acute racial tension in Britain, which erupted into violence in the riots in inner-city areas such as St Paul's (Bristol), Brixton (South London), Handsworth (Birmingham), Toxteth (Liverpool) and Moss Side (Manchester). These were caused by a variety of factors, including high unemployment and the sense of exclusion felt by many members of the Black and Asian communities. One part of the

23. An elderly Mahatma Gandhi (Ben Kingsley) and photo-journalist Margaret
Bourke-White (Candice Bergen) in *Gandhi* (1982).

ideological project of Thatcherism was to reconfigure a sense of national
identity that placed nationhood above race and class. An election poster
of 1983, for example, featured a picture of a Black male with the slogan:
'Labour say he's Black; Tory say he's British.' Yet, despite some evidence
that the Thatcherite creed of self-reliance and enterprise chimed with the
aspirational outlook of some immigrant groups, the Thatcherite heartland
was in the white, middle-class south of England.

Thatcherism was a divisive ideology that provoked mixed cultural
responses. The Raj cycle was one example. It was characterized by a revisionist interpretation of empire that can be seen as a strategy for coming to
terms with Britain's postcolonial experience. But there were other forms of
cultural production at the same time that offered different perspectives on
colonialism and race politics. The British cinema revival of the 1980s also
included films such as *My Beautiful Laundrette* (1985), focusing on the experiences of British Asians in Thatcherite Britain. Written by Hanif Kureishi,
a British-born writer of Pakistani descent, *My Beautiful Laundrette* represents the voice of the postcolonial subject more authentically than films like
Gandhi could ever hope to do. Elsewhere, the work of collectives such as

Sankofa, the Black Audio Film Collective and the Birmingham Film and Video Workshop examined the experiences of the Caribbean and Asian diasporas in Britain. Documentarists such as Isaac Julien (*Territories*, 1984) and John Akomfrah (*Handsworth Songs*, 1986) explored what it meant to be Black and British in contemporary Britain. It is to these films and film-makers that we should look for the most challenging representations of post-colonial Britain.

Notes

[1] *Gandhi* won Academy Awards for Best Picture, Best Director (Attenborough), Best Actor (Ben Kingsley), Best Original Screenplay (John Briley), Best Cinematography (Billy Williams, Ronnie Taylor), Best Costume Design (John Mollo, Bhanu Athalya), Best Art Direction (Stuart Craig, Bob Laing) and Best Editing (John Bloom).

[2] Attenborough's own account of his long quest to make the film can be found in his book *In Search of Gandhi* (London: The Bodley Head, 1982).

[3] Quoted in Martin Gilbert, *Prophet of Truth: Winston S. Churchill 1922–1939* (London: William Heinemann, 1976), p.390.

[4] *Photoplay*, August 1923, p.27.

[5] Louis Fischer, *The Life of Mahatma Gandhi* (London: Jonathan Cape, 1951).

[6] Charles Drazin, *The Finest Years: British Cinema of the 1940s* (London: André Deutsch, 1998), p.232.

[7] Quoted in Kevin Macdonald, *Emeric Pressburger: The Life and Death of a Screenwriter* (London: Faber and Faber, 1994), p.369.

[8] Kevin Brownlow, *David Lean* (London: Richard Cohen, 1996), pp.393–401.

[9] Attenborough, *In Search of Gandhi*, p.9.

[10] Ibid., p.43.

[11] Ibid., p.56.

[12] Nehru's daughter was the widow of Feroze Gandhi, whom she married in 1942 and who died in 1960. She was no relation to Mohandas Gandhi.

[13] Attenborough, *In Search of Gandhi*, p.111.

[14] Ibid., p.80.

[15] *Daily Cinema*, 16 December 1964, p.1.

[16] Attenborough, *In Search of Gandhi*, p.137.

[17] Brownlow, *David Lean*, p.543.

[18] Attenborough, *In Search of Gandhi*, p.139.

[19] David Caute, *Joseph Losey: A Revenge on Life* (London: Faber and Faber, 1994), p.287; Brownlow, *David Lean*, p.589.

[20] BFI David Lean Collection 17/2: *Gandhiji*. A film treatment by Robert Bolt. The treatment is undated but is accompanied by a letter dated 27 January 1976 from Bolt's agent Margaret Ramsay to Lean. As an aside the letter mentions the novel *Heat and Dust* 'by a young woman by the name of Jhabvala' and reports that 'Ishmael [sic] Merchant is coming to see me because he and James Ivory want to buy Jean Rhys' *Good Morning Midnight* and he wants Madam Jhabvala as Screenwriter'. Merchant-Ivory did indeed film *Heat and Dust*. Ruth Prawer Jhabvala was a Polish émigré married to an Indian doctor whose association with Merchant-Ivory dated back to *The Householder* (1963)

and included *The Guru* (1969), *The Europeans* (1979) and *The Remains of the Day* (1993). The 'young woman' was 48 in 1976.

21   BFI Joseph Losey Collection 131: *Gandhi. A Screenplay by Robert Bolt*, October 1973. This screenplay, like the *Gandhiji* treatment, bears the imprint of Indo–British Films Ltd, the company Attenborough had set up for the film.

22   Attenborough, *In Search of Gandhi*, p.151.

23   'Attenborough to Make Film on Gandhi', *The Times*, 30 August 1973.

24   Quoted in Attenborough, *In Search of Gandhi*, p.152.

25   Ibid., p.167.

26   BFI Unpublished Script Collection S14493: *Gandhi. A Screenplay by John Briley*, November 1979. The shooting script was published as *Gandhi: The Screenplay* (London: Duckworth, 1982).

27   Attenborough, *In Search of Gandhi*, p.173.

28   ' "Gandhi" dream nearer for Attenborough', *Daily Telegraph*, 22 August 1980.

29   Jake Eberts and Terry Ilott, *My Indecision Is Final: The Rise and Fall of Goldcrest Films* (London: Faber and Faber, 1990), p.41.

30   'Attenborough outlines 20-year crusade to realize "Gandhi"', *Variety*, 17 November 1982.

31   'Col commits $120 mil to "Gandhi" global launch', *Variety*, 25 November 1981.

32   *Chariots of Fire* (Twentieth Century-Fox/Allied Stars/Enigma, dir. Hugh Hudson, 1981); *The Killing Fields* (Goldcrest/Enigma, dir. Roland Joffe, 1984); *The Mission* (Goldcrest/ Kingsmere/Enigma, dir. Roland Joffe, 1986).

33   *Heat and Dust* (Merchant-Ivory, dir. Ismail Merchant, 1982); *A Passage to India* (ColumbiaEMI, dir. David Lean, 1984); *Octopussy* (MGM-United Artists/Eon, dir. John Glen, 1983); *The Jewel in the Crown* (Granada, 14 epis, dirs Christopher Monahan, Jim O'Brien, tx 09.01.1984–03.04.1984); *The Far Pavilions* (HBO/Goldcrest, 3 epis, dir. Peter Duffell, tx 03.01.1985–03.03.1985).

34   'Oscars won by knocking Britain', *Sunday Telegraph*, 17 April 1983.

35   'Indians Fear Film May Diminish Gandhi's Image', *The Times*, 14 October 1980; 'No Smooth Sailing for Attenborough's Gandhi Pic in India', *Variety*, 31 December 1980; 'Resentment Wanes, so "Gandhi" Speeds Up Indian Lensing', *Variety*, 28 February 1981.

36   See Sunil Seth, 'The Making of "Gandhi"', *India Today*, 16–31 December 1980, pp.84–94; and Marie Seton, 'Filming the Life of Gandhi', *Films and Filming*, 339 (December 1982), pp.8–13.

37   'Seductive Mahatma', *Observer*, 5 December 1982, p.31

38   'Gandhi for beginners', *Guardian*, 1 December 1982, p.11.

39   'Gandhi goes to Sunday School', *Financial Times*, 3 December 1912, p.19.

40   'A simplicity worthy of the Mahatma', *The Times*, 1 December 1982.

41   'Ben Kingsley in Panoramic "Gandhi"', *The New York Times*, 8 December 1982.

42   'It's Only a Movie, Mahatma', *Voice*, 14 December 1982, p.79.

43   Paul Johnson, 'Gandhi Isn't Good for You', *Daily Telegraph*, 16 April 1983, p.12. A similar case is made on behalf of Dyer's actions at Amritsar by Andrew Roberts, *A History of the English-Speaking Peoples since 1900* (London: Weidenfeld & Nicolson, 2006), pp.148–53.

44   'Propagandhi', *The Leveller*, February 1983, p.33.

45   Examples include *The Battle of Algiers* (Italy/Algeria, Casbah Films, dir. Gillo Pontecorvo, 1965), *Winstanley* (GB, British Film Institute, dirs Kevin Brownlow & Andrew Mollo, 1975), and *Hitler: A Film from Germany* (West Germany, dir. Hans-Jürgen Syberberg, 1977).

46　Ashish Rajadhyaska, 'Gandhiana and Gandhiology', *Framework*, 22/23 (1983), p.60.

47　See Shailja Sharma, 'Citizens of the Empire: Revisionist Historiography and the Social Imaginary in *Gandhi'*, *The Velvet Light Trap: A Critical Journal of Film and Television*, 35 (1995), pp.61–8.

48　The scene was shot on 31 January 1981, the 33rd anniversary of Gandhi's actual funeral. It is believed that over 200,000 volunteers responded to a general call in newspapers and on television and radio. There were a further 94,560 contracted performers. Patrick Robertson (ed.), *The Guinness Book of Film Facts and Feats* (London: Guinness, 1985), p.81.

49　Salman Rushdie, 'Outside the Whale', in *Imaginary Homelands: Essays and Criticism, 1981–1991* (Harmondsworth: Penguin, 1991), pp.91–2.

50　Farrukh Dhondy, 'All the Raj', *New Socialist*, 16 (March/April 1984), p.46.

12

IMPERIAL ADVENTURE REDUX

Three Kings (1999)

On the night of Thursday 14 October 1999 President Bill Clinton hosted a small gathering in the White House screening room to view a recently released feature film. His choice for that evening was *Three Kings*, a stylish war film set in the days following the end of the first Gulf War, written and directed by David O. Russell and starring George Clooney. Clinton had caught the 'making of' documentary on HBO and wanted to see the film. The story was a classic Imperial Adventure plot – a small group of American soldiers seek treasure in a foreign land – but its Iraq War setting and the plot twists resulting from a collision of the soldiers' plan with the post–Desert Storm chaos and tragedy gave the movie a biting satirical edge. It seemed amazing that a major Hollywood studio should back such a film, but Warner Brothers had done so. Guests for the screening included Russell, co-stars Spike Jonze and Nora Dunn, and members of the Arab–American community. Despite the deficiencies of the White House sound system, the audience was plainly delighted and moved by the film. Clinton rounded off the evening by launching into an extended seminar on the development and flaws of American foreign policy in the region.[1] With columnists already tipping *Three Kings* for Oscar glory, it seemed like a milestone in the representation of America's role in the modern world.[2]

The Plot

Three Kings was quite a ride. Its opening scene depicts the final confused moments of the First Gulf War as an American reservist, Troy (Mark Wahlberg), shoots an Iraqi soldier dead. As the victorious American armed forces throw a wild party in the Iraqi desert, Troy and two friends Vig (Spike Jonze) and Chief Elgin (Ice Cube) discover a map concealed in the backside of a prisoner of war. It shows the location of secret bunkers containing material looted from Kuwait. Archie Gates (George Clooney), a Special Forces Major assigned to assist an American TV journalist Adriana Cruz (Nora Dunn), learns of the map. He guesses that it gives the location of missing Kuwaiti bullion and takes command of the men's plan to steal it. He diverts Cruz by sending her on a wild goose chase with a dim solider named Norm (Jamie Kennedy) and leads the three men off in a humvee to find the bunker and steal the treasure.

The Americans enter a Shi'a village near Karbala and after some mis-direction locate not only the bunker and the gold but also an Iraqi government torture chamber. They liberate a prisoner Amir (Cliff Curtis) but as they are leaving the bunker Iraqi reinforcements loyal to Saddam Hussein appear to crush the anti-Saddam Shi'a uprising. The Iraqi reinforcements help load a van with the gold and try to hurry the Americans away so they can begin repression of the Shi'as. When an Iraqi soldier executes Amir's wife the Americans intervene. A stand-off leads to a fire fight in which Iraqi soldiers are killed. The Americans leave with the gold and a number of Shi'ite civilians but when mortared with tear gas they crash in the desert. Troy is captured and taken to another bunker while the others are rescued by locals and given refuge along with the loot in an underground refuge.

Hiding underground Amir strikes a deal with Gates whereby they will help him if he escorts them across the Iranian border. They acquire a fleet of looted luxury vehicles and drive to the bunker where Troy is held. Meanwhile Troy is undergoing torture at the hands of Captain Saïd (Saïd Taghmaoui). During the course of the torture Troy begins to understand something of the Iraqi point of view, and when rescued, Troy refuses to shoot Saïd. During the rescue Vig is killed and Troy seriously wounded. Gates radios Norm and arranges a rendezvous with Teebaux (Christopher Lohr) an accomplice from French Special Forces to supply the necessary trucks to transport the now sizeable group of Shi'a refugees across the border into Iran. He also arranges for the journalist Cruz to witness the whole thing. Gates gives some gold to the refugees and buries the rest. He, Chief and Troy lead the refugees across the desert towards the rendezvous point. But the US army has learned of Gates' plan and intercepts the whole group at the border. As American military police arrest Gates, Troy and Chief, the refugees are penned by the Iraqis for imminent execution. With the consent of Troy and Chief, Gates reveals the location of the missing gold as a bargaining chip to secure the safe passage of the refugees, who cross the border to safety. Titles reveal that Troy, Gates and Elgin were honourably discharged from the army because of the reporting of Cruz. We see their later lives as Troy opens a carpet shop in Torrance, California and Elgin leaves Detroit to work with Gates as a military adviser in Hollywood. Titles

24. Kings of the New Frontier: Poster for the British release of *Three Kings* in 2000.

explain that Saddam is still in power, the refugees are still in Iran and that Iraq returned the gold to Kuwait but some of it was missing. The credits roll over the ironic music: 'In God's Country'.

The Origins of *Three Kings*

It was an oft heard criticism of the generation of film-makers who emerged in the 1990s that their work was not so much engaging life as other movies. *Three Kings* was different. Its beginnings lay not in David O. Russell's adolescent viewings of *Gunga Din* or *The Man Who Would Be King* – indeed he had no particular recollection of having liked or even seen those films – but rather in the real world and an adventure of his own. In 1982, fired by interest in the revolution then underway in Nicaragua, Russell and his college girlfriend travelled to that country. They spent three months working in a literacy campaign run by the Sandinistas. Russell recalls:

> You could say I was having an anti-imperialist imperialist adventure, that is, I was the guy from the rich country that had bought

and sold Nicaragua through its years of poverty and dictatorship, and I had been preceded by many like me who had worked for Howard Hughes or the CIA or were soldiers of fortune...only I was there with my (at the time) young do-good socialist heart wanting to fight the historic injustices of imperialism while having an adventure myself.

Ironically, with his girlfriend working in another part of the country, he soon became intensely homesick and sought solace at what was one of the few functioning movie houses in the nation. The film he watched over and over again was *Raiders of the Lost Ark,* which he noted 'I never would have been into at all as a young alternative-minded young man' but in the circumstance while recognizing the 'backdrop of dark skinned people used mainly for a white man's heroic exploits' as 'offensive' he rather enjoyed.[3]

Russell's experiences in Nicaragua planted a desire to address the issue of America's role in the world and Indiana Jones provided a model of consequence-free adventuring to be subverted. The incongruous overlapping influence of American culture and foreign policy – in the jargon of international relations – America's soft and hard power – would surface as a prominent theme in *Three Kings*.[4]

In the early 1990s Russell emerged as a major talent in independent film making. His first two films, *Spanking the Monkey* (1994) and *Flirting with Disaster* (1996) were hailed by critics. Eager to harness his talent, Warner Brothers offered Russell the opportunity to direct a major feature. The studio handed him a list of properties owned by the studio with plot summaries and his eye fell of *The Spoils of War,* a heist thriller set during Desert Storm written by an emerging African–American writer and humorist John Ridley, which the studio had purchased but shelved. The set-up alone was enough to spark Russell's imagination and he embarked on a year of reading and research to create a screenplay of his own which would comment on issues dear to his heart in an innovative manner. Russell warned the studio executives that his approach would be idiosyncratic: 'I said I want to do the film in this freaky way, and I don't want to go write this freaky script if you're not going to let me make the film that way.' Pointing to Oliver Stone's *JFK*, 'they said they'd made freaky films before'.[5]

The precise debt of *Three Kings* to *The Spoils of War* has been a matter of dispute. Despite an on-screen credit for 'story' and 'executive producer', John Ridley complained bitterly about what Russell did to 'his' script and blocked Russell's later attempt to publish the screenplay. Russell maintains that he did not read beyond Ridley's plot summary. A comparison of the two screenplays supports Russell's version of events; there are none of the overlaps or borrowings so obvious in the Michael Wilson/Robert Bolt dispute over *Lawrence of Arabia*. Ridley's story was a standard 'shoot'em up' war movie with little attempt to probe the politics around the Iraq War and no sympathy for the Iraqis. The tenor may be gauged from script directions like:

> Jaeger whips around at the same time pulling his M-16. He jerks back hard on the trigger spraying back and forth, back and forth. Dig it: The Iraqis do a death dance in the strobe light of the muzzle flashes. They do the twist, they do the jerk, then they all fall down.

Three American soldiers – described as 'looking like the Three Musketeers' – buy a puzzle box in a Saudi bazaar, finding a treasure map inside and set off in pursuit of buried Ottoman gold. There are vague echoes of *Three Kings* in that they set off in a humvee and banter about buying cars with the loot, but American soldiers of the era would hardly set off in a Dodge mini-van and banter about house prices. They duel with a helicopter and encounter Shi'a rebels, but little else overlaps. The Shi'a are reduced to mere action movie devices, appearing on horseback and described as 'like Apaches' 'out of an old John Ford western'. The film had nods to the imperial adventure – one character jokingly calls another 'Bwana' – and the script was essentially a turbo-charged update of John Huston's *Treasure of the Sierra Madre*, with a heavy handed moral about money corrupting friendship. All three characters are destroyed by their greed. One is killed by a booby-trap, one is vaporized trying to save the loot on the 'Highway of Death' and the last man is convicted for desertion and jailed. While certainly spirited, Ridley's script was the merest shadow of Russell's final work.[6]

The casting of *Three Kings* presented problems. Russell approached Nicolas Cage for the lead role (he declined because of his commitment to work on Martin Scorsese's *Bringing out the Dead*) and also considered Tom Cruise or Brad Pitt. George Clooney courted Russell for the part in a movie he saw as a mix of *Lawrence of Arabia* and *Schindler's List*.[7] Clooney eventually convinced Russell that he was more than a TV actor turned romantic lead. Russell recalls: 'After meeting him, I was persuaded that he really got the whole thing, and had a deadpan sensibility for it. Also he has, I think, a grizzled maturity that Brad Pitt or Tom Cruise or even Cage don't exactly have.'[8] Mark Wahlberg seemed like an excellent fit for the role of Troy but Warner raised an eyebrow at Russell's desire to cast fellow film director Spike Jonze as Vig and former New York Yankee third baseman Charlie Hayes as the character eventually called Chief. Russell observed: 'I like stunt casting ... When you put a real person in a movie it stirs it up.' In the end the part of Chief went to rapper Ice Cube, who shone in the role.[9]

The film was a challenge to shoot, the most immediate problem being the need to recreate Iraq in an accessible location. A lake bed in Mexico provided the distinctive flat terrain for the opening scene, while the rest was shot at an abandoned copper mine near El Centro, Arizona, where the ingenious production designer Catherine Hardwicke recreated an Iraqi village. Hardwicke mixed old and unfinished new architecture and ubiquitous Saddam portraits while Iraqi refugees from Phoenix recreated the authentic graffiti of the period. The Iraqi torture chamber was precisely reconstructed from pictures taken in the aftermath of the war and a number of photos were smuggled out of Iraq to help the general design. Other problems include complex effects and crowd scenes and pressure of time. Despite a script that would need an estimated 80 days to shoot Warner insisted on a 68-day schedule. Clooney had to commute from the set of his TV drama *ER* in Los Angeles for three-and-a-half months of shooting, and fell ill. As the pressure mounted, with the director and star both working at the limit of their experience, Russell's relationship with Clooney became strained, flaring into what Clooney described as 'about three good screaming matches', but the final film and Clooney's performance bore out Russell's vision.[10]

Three Kings very nearly did not happen. In the midst of production a nervous Warner Brothers executive attempted to sink the whole movie. When the head of production Lorenzo di Bonaventura was out of town for a trip Jim Miller – the president of worldwide business operations – attempted to persuade Clooney to pull out of the project saying that 'the controversy, nationally and internationally would mean trouble'. Clooney refused to be dissuaded and the palace coup failed.[11] He also defended the integrity of the script when executives attempted to soften some of its harsher moments.[12] It was an early flowering of a political sensibility that would become a Clooney trademark.

Three Kings as a War Film

At its most basic level, *Three Kings* was a war story. Un-intimidated by the extent to which *Saving Private Ryan* and *The Thin Red Line* had raised the bar for the representation of war, Russell struck out into new territory. There had been no other major films about the Gulf War, but more than this Russell was able to bring a new edge to the depiction of combat. Like other directors seeking realistic performances, he put his actors through military training. His military adviser – Sgt. Major Jim Parker – had not only served in Vietnam and the Gulf War but confessed that he had attempted to steal a six-foot gold Buddha in Vietnam but had lost it while attempting to cross the Perfume River.[13]

Russell imagined action that flipped between the dramatic and the mundane: at the height of one of the combat scenes Vig gets a splinter in his finger. He went to immense trouble to research the 'look' of Desert Storm, taking his visual queue from Kenneth Jareke's 1992 collection of his own war photographs *Just Another War*, a book famous for its unflattering picture of the American military. Russell meticulously recreated the mass frat party celebrating the end of the war, a scramble for trophy photographs of a dead Iraqi and the racist language of some of the American troops. He also chose and manipulated his film stock to heighten the desert feel and contrasting collision with colour in the town.[14] Above all Russell sought to 'resensitize' his audience to violence and make the impact of bullets 'a truly traumatic thing'.[15] There were visceral set pieces of sudden violence as impactful as anything in the work of Sergio Leone or Sam Peckinpah – the explosion of a cow by a landmine, the slow-motion execution of the Iraqi woman and subsequent shootout – but the real innovation was to actually follow the bullet into the body and show it spilling green bile inside the wound cavity or causing a lung to collapse. The effect was so dramatic that Russell mischievously told *Newsweek* that he had used a real cadaver for the shots. A flurry of overwrought comment on movie ethics followed.[16]

No film about the First Gulf War could ignore the role of the media. The media was a battlefront in the conflict as tangible as the border between Iraq and Kuwait. Both the coalition and Saddam attempted to manipulate coverage of the war and some have argued that television pictures of the 'Highway of Death' accelerated the allied rush to ceasefire.[17] *Three Kings* delivers a prescient portrait of the media, with its cutaways to the frustrated CNN reporter Cruz desperate for a new and different story, finding herself passed over because she is no longer as pretty as her young rivals. Significantly, it is the fact of media coverage which changes the conclusion of the movie. It is Cruz's reporting which saves the Three Kings from a long spell in the stockade.

Three Kings as Imperial Adventure

The imperial adventure dimension is hardly less evident than the war theme in *Three Kings*. The film was – after all – constructed as a critique of America's imperial adventure in the Middle East: its rescue of oil-rich

Kuwait and tragic abandonment of the Shi'a people, who rose up with the encouragement of the president only to be slaughtered by the Saddam regime's helicopter gun-ships. Russell was impressed by testimony of American veterans who spoke of weeping in frustration at their being unable to help the Shi'a or finish the job and be rid of Saddam. If *Three Kings* is taken as an allegory in the manner of Kipling's *The Man Who Would be King* – with the four Americans standing in for their country – it makes the same important point about the initial motivation being greed. It is fascinating to note, however, that while Russell's characters suffer for their endeavour they are not destroyed by their hubris in the manner of Kipling's Danny and Peachy or John Ridley's protagonists. Rather, because of their willingness to become the leaders that the people need, they escape and find personal redemption.

Three Kings played like an updating of *Gunga Din*, with the same basic set-up of three heroes and a comic 'wannabe'. It was a sign of the shift in American culture that the comic figure had moved from being a black character to being the poor Southern white man: Vig. Vig is amazingly dense. When Gates first mentions bullion, Vig asks: 'You mean those little cubes you put in water to make soup?' He is also the character who uses racist language to describe Iraqis and is corrected by his peers, and who assumed that an Iraqi's education in America must have been 'some king of terrorist training'. He satirizes the ignorant American. There is a humorous cutaway to his life at home – we see him blasting soft toys off the roof of a rusty car – 'don't really have a day job' he says. His trajectory brings him to reconciliation with the African–American character, Chief Elgin, and sees him even develop an admiration for Islam. In the end his dying wish is to be buried at a Shi'a shrine to ensure his passage to paradise. Like Gunga Din his gets his wish in death and is carried to his rest by the departing column of refugees.

Arabs in *Three Kings*

Three Kings paid a remarkable level of attention to the representations of the Iraqi enemy and Shi'ite civilians. The film undercut the traditional imperial adventure movie by giving the Iraqis a voice. Where Hollywood films before and after had delivered a succession of outrageous stereotypes of Arab people, the Iraqis in Russell's film were presented in a balanced way, whether civilian victims or Saddam's loyal troops. They were given the dignity of speaking their own language and in the appropriate local accent and the scope to develop their own view of the events depicted. There is a remarkable respect shown for the Islamic religion by the American characters; this

25. An Image of Understanding: Chief (Ice Cube) joins Shi'a refugees in prayer in *Three Kings* (1999).

is apparent from Vig's request to be buried at the Shi'a shrine but also from the attitude of Chief. Chief Elgin's idiosyncratic Christianity – his belief in the protective 'ring of Jesus fire' around him – is established early in the movie, but he moved naturally into shared experience with the Shi'a, joining them in prayer in their underground hiding place. His understanding of the Arab position is reflected in his wearing an Arab scarf from this point onwards.

The sensitivity to the Arab experience was no accident. Early drafts of the script were circulated within the Arab–American community and consultants included Dr Jack G. Shaheen, author of the landmark indictment of Hollywood's depiction of Arabs: *Reel Bad Arabs: How Hollywood Vilifies a People*. Shaheen commented on several drafts of the script and visited the set during production. He was delighted to see how the rough edges and stereotypes of the earliest drafts were removed and replaced by genuine consideration and insight into the Arab and Iraqi condition. The characters in the film wanted real and believable things, like the brothers whose plan is to open a hair salon.[18] Credited cultural consultants the Iraqi technical adviser, Sermid Al'Serrif an Iraqi–American attorney who had been at school with one of Saddam's sons; Iraqi religious adviser, Sayed Moustafa Al-Qazwini, a Karbala-born Shi'ite Imam and founder of the Islamic Educational Center of Orange County; and Al No'mani a refugee Iraqi filmmaker who served as the Arabic language dialect coach, whose later work included the 2009 film *Mr. Sadman* in which he starred as an unemployed Saddam Hussein impersonator adrift in Los Angeles. The cause of authenticity was helped by the fact that the cast was full of refugees who had lived the events depicted or Iraqi–Americans who knew the culture well. The hairdressers were played by former teachers Jabir and Ghanem Algarawi. Saïd Taghmaoui, who played the interrogator, was French-Moroccan. One of the few actors cast against their personal experience was Cliff Curtis, who played the dissident Amir, who was a New Zealander of Maori descent, but even so excelled in the role.[19]

The key scene for exploring the Iraqi point of view was the torture sequence. This scene went beyond either Troy poetically suffering to level the score for his shooting of an Iraqi in the opening of the film, or presenting the nightmare of an invader experiencing invasion, realized so vividly in the 'rape' sequence of *Lawrence of Arabia*. First, there is the irony of the Iraqi having been trained to torture by Americans during the Iran-Iraq War. Beyond this, Troy's torturer, Saïd, tells him the story of his experience in the war and how an American bomb crippled his wife and killed his baby son. Vivid cutaways show the moment when the concrete ceiling collapsed on Saïd's baby's crib and Troy's imagining of a bomb killing his own wife and baby. When Troy protests that they are trying to Kuwait from trouble, Saïd snaps back: 'A lot of people in trouble and you don't fight no fahking war for them.' Troy's explanation of America's motive as being securing 'stability' draws a scornful response 'this is your stability my main man' as Saïd begins to force feed Troy with crude oil.

Popular Culture and America's Empire

In keeping with his experience in Nicaragua, Russell took pains to demonstrate that American power is not merely projected militarily. The power of American popular culture is visible throughout the film from the Bart Simpson doll tied to the front of the Americans' humvee to the language used by the Iraqis they meet. The four American protagonists continually encounter American consumer goods, cars, TV (including *Happy Days* and the Rodney King beating) and music. An Iraqi is able to settle a dispute between Troy and Chief over the availability of a Lexus convertible and the drive towards Troy's bunker is accompanied by the car stereo playing 'If you leave me now, you take away the biggest part of me'. This is different to the presence of American popular culture in *Apocalypse Now* where it appeared as a sort of crass bubble around the American soldiers. Here it is part of the world in which the Iraqis live providing the music they listen to and even structuring their careers and dreams. The dissident Amir has attended an American business school. In terms of *Apocalypse Now,* in this war Charlie DO surf.

The presence of popular culture is again nowhere more vivid than in the torture scene. Captain Saïd begins his interrogation with the question: 'What is the problem with Michael Jackson'. He points to the troubled singer's plastic surgery as evidence of the sickness in American society:

> SAÏD: A black man make the skin white and the hair straight. You
>   know why?"
> TROY: 'No.'
> SAÏD: 'Your sick fahking country make the black man hate hisself,
>   just like you hate the Arab and the children you bomb.'

The original screenplay had the Iraqi raise Jackson's alleged sexual interest in children but Russell was obliged to change this for legal reasons.[20] The interrogation is punctuated with American slang, as Saïd calls Troy 'bro' and 'my main man'. When he attempts to force oil into Troy's mouth he uses a CD case as a funnel.

The interaction of the Iraqis and the Americans carries its own satire. The American characters are frequently brought up short as their motives are called into question or Iraqis remind them that they are stealing the gold. There is humor when Iraqi troops attempt to bribe the Americans with consumer goods. Even more interesting is the scene when Gates tries to use idealistic rhetoric typical of the United States in the era to persuade some Iraqi guards to donate their cache of captured cars to his cause. As patriotic music swells on the soundtrack he pulls the guard and Chief together into a hug. 'Many races, many nations', he proclaims, 'George Bush wants you…Make the fight for freedom on your own' and then 'God bless America and God bless a Free Iraq'. When the guard still says 'Can not give car', Gates changes gear, abandons the soft power of persuasion for cold, hard cash: 'Then I guess we'll have to buy them'.

Exploring the Title

Russell's choice of title for *Three Kings* is revealing. Russell explained: 'I wanted to have a title that sounded cool and was, like the film, evocative without being exactly on the nose.' *Three Kings* could have referred to playing cards, but Russell's intent was to allude to the Magi of the Christian nativity story. For many Westerners representations of the three wise men on innumerable Christmas cards and in crib scenes serve as the point of entry into thinking about deserts, camels and traversing the Middle East in general. Developing the barest bones in the Gospel of Matthew, in which only their gifts are recorded, centuries of church tradition gave these characters names (Caspar, Melchior and Balthasar) and developed a fairly stable representation as three kings drawn – like the protagonists of Russell's film – from different races.[21] Within the film the allusion to the Magi is first made by the essentially comic character Vig (Spike Jonze) who sings – in parody of the Christmas carol – 'We three kings be stealing the gold'. In this initial use he is referring to himself, Troy and Chief, perhaps in his Red-Neck way reaching for a positive example of an inter-racial team. As the movie develops Vig becomes peripheral to the action and the three kings who are left standing at the end of the film (and depicted on the film's poster) are Gates, Troy and Chief. By the end of the film these three have come to realize that kingship is about more than just making off with the loot, but brings with it responsibility for one's people – they assume responsibility for the Shi'a refugees and sacrifice their own interests to secure their escape to safety. In this spirit the draft shooting script included a scene in which the three, while leading the refugees across the desert, find a store room containing snow globes with figures of the magi inside posed next to a gas station. The idea was that these were holiday gifts created by an oil company and looted as a job lot from Kuwait. Desperate for water, the three drain the water from the globes, straining out the snow fragments and passing the salvaged liquid between members of their party. The scene was filmed and appears as an 'extra' on the DVD. It is a touching moment of bonding between the Americans and the Shi'as, but Russell was obliged to cut the scene for reasons of budget as part of his deletion of a sub-plot about the shortage of water.[22]

The Response and Afterlife

Critics generally responded well to *Three Kings*.[23] Arab–Americans were especially impressed. Hala Maksoud, President of the American–Arab Anti-Discrimination Committee, told the *Hollywood Reporter* that the film 'shows the Arab and the Muslim in their complexity with feelings and normal aspirations'.[24] Audiences were initially respectable, with a gross of $16,000,000 on its opening weekend in the United States.[25] Multiple awards at the Boston Society of Film Critics in December seemed like the prelude to success at the Academy Awards. But it was not to be. With Iraq back in the headlines following the US and UK bombing campaign the subject seemed uncomfortably relevant. Audiences tailed off swiftly.[26] The Hollywood establishment backed away from the film and wholly passed over *Three Kings* in that year's Academy Award nominations. Writing in the *Los Angeles Times,* Saul Halpert complained that the Academy could not deal with the reality revealed by *Three Kings*: 'Tell me it wasn't political', he declared.[27]

History would give *Three Kings* unexpected resonance. While completing the film Russell found himself at a gathering at the home of Warner Brothers chairman Terry Semel, where the guest of honour was a prospective Republican Party candidate for the presidency in 2000, George W. Bush. On meeting Bush Russell mentioned that he was 'cutting a film that would question his father's legacy in Iraq' to which the candidate immediately shot back, 'I guess we may have to go back there and finish the job, right?' Russell's contacts with the exiled Iraqi community had convinced him that there was still a job to be done, but he was unsure of the best way to accomplish the task, as Gates' commanding officer put it in the film: 'Occupy and do Vietnam all over again? Is that your brilliant idea?'[28] The terrorist attacks of 2001 knocked Hollywood back into its default representation of Arabs and started a new cycle of cinematic slanders. The studios backed away from criticism of American foreign policy and wrapped themselves in the flag. *Three Kings* now seemed like a relic of a former era and charged with an almost clairvoyant prescience: a lost moment of self-awareness. As one critic put it, *Three Kings* provided a reality check on the second Gulf War.[29]

Russell sought to comment on the new war in a short interview-based documentary: *Soldiers Pay* (2004). His witnesses included Sergeant Matt Novak, dishonourably discharged for his part in 'finding' several million dollars in currency and gold. Life was imitating art. Alarmingly, Novak's testimony in the documentary spoke of routine theft of Iraqi valuables by Americans. Warner declined to include the film as an extra on its DVD re-release of *Three Kings* as it was 'too political'. Russell was delighted that the film was screened on television on the eve of the 2004 election.[30]

In the last analysis *Three Kings* was a film ahead of its time. *Three Kings* had raised the problem of America's unfinished business in Iraq and shown that it was possible to make a movie about that region and allow its inhabitants to remain human beings. It seemed like a miracle that it had survived the studio system and Russell bore the scars to prove that it had not been easy.[31] The film had engaged and subverted the Imperial Adventure and war genre and made a string of observations relevant to the current political situation, and done it all while remaining vivid, compelling and entertaining. Perhaps the key had been to avoid lecturing and to put the entertainment dimension first, as Russell noted in 2000:

> The main proposition is to have a cinematic experience that grabs you and doesn't let go of you until the end, and constantly sur-prises you. And then at the end you realize jeez, there was this historical-political exposé along the way. You want to put people in spin cycle. Because if it doesn't work at that level, then you've made a boring film.[32]

It would be a long time before any other Hollywood film would comment as successfully on America's foreign policy or American audiences would be as open to hearing it, but David O. Russell had shown that it could be done.

Notes

1   Christian Moerk, 'Clinton Reflects at Kings Screening', *Variety*, 18 October 1999.
2   Nicole Keeter, 'Sand Dollars', *Time Out* (New York), 30 September–7 October 1999, p.93.
3   Russell to Cull, 30 June 2008. Russell's DVD commentary notes an allusion to Latin American revolutionary cinema in his use of child sniper in one of the rebellion scenes, borrowed from Mikhail Kalatozov's *I am Cuba* (1964).
4   On Soft Power see Joseph S. Nye Jr., *Soft Power: The Means to Success in World Politics* (New York: Public Affairs Press, 2004).
5   Nicole Keeter, 'Sand Dollars', *Time Out* (New York), 30 September–7 October 1999, p.93; Charles Roven commentary track on *Three Kings* DVD.
6   The two screenplays may be downloaded from the Daily Script.com website. For Ridley's *Spoils of War* (July 1995) see http://www.dailyscript.com/scripts/three-kings_unproduced.html, for Russell's June 1998 draft of *Three Kings* see http://www.dailyscript.com/scripts/three-kings_shooting.html, and for the final version of February 1999 see http://www.dailyscript.com/scripts/threekings_shootingdraft.pdf. For comment see Christine Divine, 'Two Visions: *Spoils of War* and *Three Kings*', *Creative Screenwriting*, 1: 1 (2000), pp.60–3 and producer Charles Roven's commen-tary track on *Three Kings* DVD.
7   Studio press packet for *Three Kings*, as filed in New York Public Library of the Performing Arts (ARLSV 68608) and at the Herrick.
8   Andrew Pulver, 'Exploding the Myth of Desert Storm', *Guardian* (UK) 1 March 2000, sec 2, p.12.
9   Keeter, 'Sand Dollars', p.93.
10 Pulver, 'Exploding the Myth of Desert Storm', sec 2, p.12. See also Clooney's corres-pondence with Russell reproduced as an appendix to Sharon Waxman, *Rebels on the Backlot: Six Maverick Directors and How They Conquered the Hollywood System* (New York: Harper-Perennial, 2005). Russell contests Waxman's reconstruction of events on the set.

11 Pulver, 'Exploding the Myth of Desert Storm', sec 2, p.12. Also recounted in Waxman, *Rebels on the Backlot*, pp.334.

12 Waxman, *Rebels on the Backlot*, pp.334–5.

13 Studio press packet for *Three Kings*, as filed in New York Public Library of the Performing Arts (ARLSV 68608) and at the Herrick. Parker died of cancer as the film was completed and is its dedicatee.

14 Russell's DVD commentary explains that he used the 'bleach bypass' technique in the early scenes to give a sense of the heat and light of Iraq, and then switched to Ektachrome – the stock used for 35mm still pictures – to provide 'big hits of colour' once the Americans reached the Iraqi village.

15 Russell, DVD commentary.

16 Lewis Beale, 'Dummy took bullet sez "Kings" man', *New York Daily News*, 28 September 1999, p.46.

17 For background on the media aspects of the Gulf War see Philip M. Taylor, *War and the Media: Propaganda and Persuasion in the Gulf War* (Manchester: Manchester University Press, 1992), John R. MacArthur, *Second Front: Censorship and Propaganda in the Gulf War* (Berkeley CA: University of California Press, 1992); W. Lance Bennett and David L. Paletz (eds), *Taken by Storm: The Media, Public Opinion and U.S. Foreign Policy in the Gulf War* (Chicago: University of Chicago Press, 1994) and Douglas Kellner, *The Persian Gulf TV War* (Boulder: Westview, 1992). The French philosopher Jean Baudrillard argued that the disjunction between the war as experienced by Iraq and the representation seen on US television screens was such that 'the Gulf War did not take place': Jean Baudrillard, trans. Paul Patton *The Gulf War Did Not Take Place* (Bloomington and Indianapolis: Indiana University Press, 1995).

18 Jack Shaheen's contributions included prevailing on Russell to actually show the moment when a bomb hits the interrogator's house and the concrete ceiling collapses into his baby's crib. Cull interview (telephone) with Shaheen, 16 June 2008. This sequence was in the shooting script for the film but it may have been one which Warner hoped to cut along with a number of other sidebars such Vig's fantasy of the American Civil War which was to have been included in the draft script to reflect his incomprehension of the existence of any civil war other than 'the war between the states'. When George Clooney set out to make *Syriana* he sought out Shaheen as an adviser.

19 Studio Production Information for *Three Kings*, as filed in New York Public Library of the Performing Arts (ARLSV 68608) and at the Herrick.

20 Russell to Cull, 30 June 2008. The original draft may be viewed at http://www.dailyscript.com/scripts/three-kings_shooting.html

21 The idea of Kings from many nations is probably an extrapolation of the prophesy in Isaiah 60:3, 'And the Gentiles shall come to thy light, and Kings to the brightness of thy rising'.

22 Russell DVD commentary.

23 For positive reviews see Gene Seymour, 'Middle East meets Western in *Kings*', *Newsday*, 1 October 1999, p.B3. Detractors included David Sterritt, 'Snazzy *Three Kings* Misses Chance for Insights on War'. *Christian Science Monitor*, 1 October 1999, p.15.

24 David Finnigan, Arab Americans Cheer 3 Kings', *Hollywood Reporter*, 1 October 1999.

25 http://www.imdb.com/title/tt0120188/business. The film was not among the big box office hits of the year, which were exclusively escapist fare: *Star Wars Episode One, The Sixth Sense, Toy Story II, Austin Powers: The Spy Who Shagged Me* and *The Matrix*.

26   Daniel Kimmel, 'Boston Bows Before Kings'. *Variety*, 20 December 1999, p.19.
27   Saul Halpert, 'The Academy Voters Can't Deal with Reality of Three Kings', *Los Angeles Times*, 28 February 2000.
28   Russell to Cull, 30 June 2008.
29   David Edelstein, 'On One Film, Two Wars, *Three Kings*', *The New York Times*, 6 April 2003, sec 2, p.1.
30   John Hartl, 'Russell Wants 'Soldiers Pay' to Make a Difference', article on MSNBC website, 4 November 2004 see: http://www.msnbc.msn.com/id/6349030/. See also Bernard Weintraub, 'In Baghdad, the Stuff of Movies: Did Four GIs Steal a Bundle?' *The New York Times*, 25 April 2003, p.A10.
31   Hollywood attorney Linda Lichter noted in 2003, Russell had managed to make a thoroughly personal film and to do it on his 'own terms' without being 'eaten alive by the system'. 'Whether anybody else can do it again' she concluded, 'I don't know'. Russell told Peter Biskind in October 2002: '*Three Kings* was my bottom. It was so stressful and unpleasant that I said, "I will never, ever do that big a movie again." I will only write things that are closer to my heart, that I can do on a smaller scale.' Peter Biskind, *Down and Dirty Pictures: Miramax, Sundance and the Rise of Independent Film* (London: Bloomsbury, 2004), pp.477, 480.
32   Pulver, 'Exploding the Myth of Desert Storm', sec 2, p.12.

Afterword

Part of the fun of film history is the discovery of what might have been. The cinema of empire has more than its share of tantalizing 'ifs'. The archives open a parallel world in which Leslie Howard or Dirk Bogarde played Lawrence of Arabia, Vivien Leigh starred in *Elephant Walk* and *Carry on Follow That Camel* included jokes about hashish. But the relevance of a book like this lies not in the 'what ifs' but in what it tells us about this world. Narratives have woven their way through this text: writers like Kipling, film-makers like Huston and Lean, and even actors like Douglas Fairbanks Jr recur in these pages. The genre unfolds as an Anglo–American conversation with ideas and even personnel moving backwards and forwards, and many films becoming Anglo–American co-productions, as if the representation of empire was one subject the two nations could agree upon, though transatlantic fault lines often remain visible. It is especially fascinating to see the blurring of America's 'Western' genre with Britain's imperial 'Eastern' and stories effectively being relocated from one empire to the other for their remakes.

Many of the themes which emerged from the research might have been predicted: the fixation with issues of race, masculinity and national identity. More surprising is the presence of religion within the genre, its special claims to depicting reality and the extent to which the genre was co-opted to serve interests beyond those of the immediate story teller. These themes provide fertile avenues for further research.

A religious dimension has always sat the heart of the concept of empire. In ancient times to be an emperor was to claim the authority of god to rule over kings. There could only be one. From Augustus to Napoleon, from Baghdad to Beijing the emperor was the channel of heaven. The European empires of the nineteenth century justified themselves in religious terms and missionaries were their shock troops. The cinema of empire has also engaged this concern with religion both in its representation of the colonial other and the self. Representations of indigenous religion are prominent in *Elephant Walk, Lawrence of Arabia, The Naked Prey* and *Three Kings*. In *The*

Four Feathers, Gunga Din, two of the *Carry On* films and *Indiana Jones and the Temple of Doom* the white characters face religious violence and full-scale religious rebellion. *Gandhi* is essentially a religious biopic. Indiana Jones seeks objects of religious power. The condition of the imperialist is frequently represented in religious terms, Danny Dravot in *The Man Who Would Be King* is destroyed by a potent blend of temporal and religious power. They become victims of their own propaganda and belief in their own destiny. In contrast with this foregrounding of religion, economics – also a major engine of empire – is seldom seen, the lust for wealth which drove European imperialism and its American analogue forward is sublimated into the symbolic quest for ivory in *The Naked Prey* and gold in *The Man Who Would Be King* and *Three Kings*.

Given the prominence of religion and attention to the supernatural it is perhaps curious to find a parallel concern with reality in the cinema of empire. Many of the films make specific claims to truth and realism in their representation of the colonial world by taking a true story, as with *Lawrence of Arabia*, *Gandhi* or the documentary *Burma Victory*, or real historical events as with *The Four Feathers* or by pursuing realism in their style as with *Three Kings*. History and myth were so intertwined that real historical characters T. E. Lawrence and Henry Morton Stanley were nearly featured in the *Carry On* comedies. Rudyard Kipling pops up to validate his own stories in *Gunga Din* and *The Man Who Would be King*. *Gunga Din* even opens with a claim that 'the portions of this picture dealing with the worship of the goddess Kali are based on historic fact'. Claims of ethnographic authenticity are made by fictional films including *The Naked Prey*. Implicitly these films were offered to audiences as a way of structuring their understanding of their world. *Gunga Din* was even made the subject of one of a series of special school textbooks to teach children about India.[1] One wonders if the same authors consider a primateology text based on *King Kong*. This blend of fact, fiction, myth, fantasy and even slander with the power of cinema to tell a story has made the imperial adventure a potent force for perpetuating imperial attitudes, which by extension makes its deconstruction in a movie like *Three Kings* all the more significant.

The third surprise is the use of the cinema of empire by the nations who experienced it for their own purposes. In the aftermath of the Second World War, as Hollywood looked to international locations as a route to spectacle and funds locked in unconvertible currency, the governments around the world were happy to oblige. Part of their motive was financial. American and British film-makers could provide a substantial boost to a local economy. Franco's Spain was ahead of the game and provided a convenient location for portions of *Lawrence of Arabia*. But more than this, these film projects were embraced as elements of public diplomacy or – more crudely, international propaganda policy – by their hosts. Hence Ceylon welcomed *Elephant Walk*, Jordan embraced *Lawrence of Arabia*, South Africa actively solicited *The Naked Prey*, India collaborated on *Gandhi* and was open to Huston's first attempt to film *The Man Who Would Be King*. In the end Morocco got the valued credit in the end titles. There are more agendas than that of the author present in many imperial adventures. Latterly the films have provided an opportunity to get the story right. The Iraqi–American community welcomed *Three Kings* as a mechanism for communicating something of the reality of their experiences and culture to a public used to outrageous Hollywood fantasy.

In recent years the genre has displayed certain absences. In the past the imperial adventure genre leant heavily on literature: *The Four Feathers*, *Gunga Din*, *Elephant Walk*, *Lawrence of Arabia*, and *The Man Who Would be King* were all literary adaptations. Even the *Carry Ons* included literary allusions. Over the past 20 years or so popular film has veered away from literature. Specifically, whereas the literary world has produced a fertile field of postcolonial literature in which the former empire has 'written back' to its erstwhile masters, these themes seldom reach the screen outside of their countries of origin. Compare the list of nominees for the Booker Prize with pictures recognized with BAFTA or Academy Awards and there is little correlation of titles, authors or even themes. The adaptations of Michael Ondaatje's *The English Patient* in 1996 and Giles Foden's *The Last King of Scotland* in 2006 represent some of the few points of overlap in the post-imperial field.[2] Hollywood has generally preferred to keep the imperial adventure as a comfortable space for reassuring escapism as with the Indiana Jones series or its successors like *The Mummy* franchise. The videogame industry has followed suit with imperial adventure themes evident in games like *Tomb Raider*.

Some things have moved. The shock of the genocide in Rwanda sparked an overdue reconsideration of Africa as a setting for movies, with a cycle of dark adventures which foreground the violence and tragedy of that continent, many of which feature protagonists who implicitly walk in the footsteps of the imperial adventurers. Prime examples include Bruce Willis as a Special Forces Lieutenant whose conscience calls him to action in Nigeria in *Tears of the Sun* (2003) or the white African mercenary played by Leonardo DiCaprio in *Blood Diamond* (2006). Escapism is nearer the surface in *Sahara* (2006), but even here African humanitarian issues are evident.[3] All these films have included benevolent female characters typically associated with non-governmental organizations but hope is sparse. Africans are represented with unremitting tragedy, as though predestined to suffer silent and wide-eyed at the hands of other Africans. Films like *Syriana* (2005) and *Babel* (2006) have addressed issues of the new interconnections that crisscross the terrain of T. E. Lawrence and *Beau Geste*. But critical silences remain.[4]

The deployment of American and British troops in Afghanistan and then Iraq rekindled thoughts of imperial adventure for observers and participants alike. While film was slow to reflect this, the stage was swift to comment on continuities. In the United States, Robert Schenkkan's play *Lewis and Clark Reach the Euphrates* fused an epic first act account of the first cross-country journey to the Pacific West with a second act plunging Lewis and Clark into America's subsequent imperial adventures, ending with scenes in Iraq, where the first act's villain, an evil French trapper, reappears as secretary of defence, Donald Rumsfelt and Clark's slave, York, becomes his dupe, secretary of state, Colin Powell.[5] In the UK there was a scene in Gregory Burke's script for the National Theatre of Scotland's wildly successful Iraq War drama *Black Watch* in which two Scottish squaddies – Cammy and Fraz – sweltering in the heat of Babel Province compare their experience with that of Lawrence of Arabia, noting that he had been there before them. Fraz asks: 'Do you think they'll make a film about this war?' Cammy replies: 'They'd fucking better. I didnay join the army for it not to be immortalized on the big screen.' Fraz then asks: 'You dinnay think it'll be ta fucking boring?' Cammy assures him that if necessary he will make the film himself on Fife's Kinghorn beach and call it 'Sweating Way Out Moving'. The play has been such a success that there is talk of adapting the film for the big screen. Just as the Anglo–American imperial adventure has re-emerged on the world stage, so variations on its fictional adaptations may be expected in films yet to come.[6]

Notes

[1] This text book has been preserved among the microfiche materials for *Gunga Din* in the Herrick Library core collection.

[2] *The English Patient* (Miramax, dir. Anthony Minghella, 1996); *The Last King of Scotland* (Fox Searchlight/Film 4, dir. Kevin MacDonald, 2006)

[3] *Blood Diamond* (Warner, dir. Edward Zwick, 2006); *Tears of the Sun* (Revolution Studios, dir. Antoine Fuqua, 2003); *Sahara* (Paramount, dir. Breck Eisner, 2005).

[4] *Syriana* (Participant, dir. Stephen Geghan, 2005); *Babel* (Paramount, dir. Alejandro González Iñárritu, 2006).

[5] *Lewis and Clark Reach the Euphrates* was performed at the Mark Taper forum in Los Angeles in spring 2006. For review see Irene Lacher, 'Go West, Young Playwright', *The New York Times*, 8 January 2006.

[6] On *Black Watch* see Nicholas J. Cull, *The National Theatre of Scotland's Black Watch* (Washington DC/Los Angeles: British Council/USC Center on Public Diplomacy, 2008). The text of the play is available as Gregory Burke, *Black Watch* (London: Faber, 2007).

Filmography

The Four Feathers

GB. London Film Productions. 1939.

Director: Zoltan Korda. *Producer:* Alexander Korda. *Associate producer:* Irving Asher. *Screenplay:* R. C. Sherriff. Based on the novel by A. E. W. Mason. *Additional dialogue:* Lajos Biro, Arthur Wimperis. *Director of photography:* Georges Périnal. *Location photography:* Osmond Borradaile, Jack Cardiff. *Technicolor consultant:* Natalie Kalmus. *Production designer:* Vincent Korda. *Editor:* Henry Cornelius. *Second unit director:* Geoffrey Boothby. *Music:* Miklos Rosza. *Military consultants:* Captain Donald Anderson, Lieutenant Colonel W. F. Stirling. *Running time:* 130 mins.

Cast: John Clements (Harry Faversham), Ralph Richardson (Captain John Durrance), June Duprez (Ethne Burroughs), C. Aubrey Smith (General Burroughs), Jack Allen (Willoughby), Donald Gray (Peter Burroughs), Frederick Culley (Dr Sutton), Allan Jeayes (General Faversham), Amid Taftazani (Karaga Pasha), Henry Oscar (Dr Harraz), John Laurie (Khalifa), Robert Rendel (Colonel), Hal Walters (Joe), Clive Baxter (Young Harry), Archibald Batty (Adjutant), Derek Elphinstone (Lt Parker), Norman Pierce (Sergeant Brown).

Gunga Din

USA. RKO Radio Pictures. 1939.

Producer and director: George Stevens. *Executive producer:* Pandro S. Berman. *Screenplay:* Joel Sayre & Fred Guiol. *Story:* Ben Hecht & Charles MacArthur. From Rudyard Kipling's poem 'Gunga Din'. *Director of photography:* Joseph H. August. *Art director:* Van Nest Polglase. *Costume designer:* Edward Stevenson. *Editors:* Henry Berman, John Lockert. *Assistant directors:* Edward Killy, Dewy

Starkey. *Special effects:* Vernon L. Walker. *Music:* Alfred Newman. *Technical advisers:* Sir Robert Erskine Holland, Captain Clive Morgan, Sergeant-Major William Briers. *Running time:* 117 mins

Cast: Cary Grant (Cutter), Victor McLaglen (McChesney), Douglas Fairbanks Jr (Ballantine), Sam Jaffe (Gunga Din), Eduardo Ciannelli (Guru), Joan Fontaine (Emmy), Montagu Love (Colonel Weed), Robert Coote (Higginbotham), Abner Biberman (Chota), Lumsden Hare (Major Mitchell).

Burma Victory

GB. Army Film and Photographic Unit. 1945.

Director: Roy Boulting. *Producer:* David Macdonald. *Commentary written by:* Frank Harvey, Roy Boulting. *Commentary spoken by:* David King-Wood, Ivan Brandt, Norman Claridge. *Editor:* Roy Boulting. *Music:* Alan Rawsthorne. *Running time:* 64 mins.

A documentary film compiled from actuality footage shot by British, American and Indian service cameramen of South East Asia Command.

Elephant Walk

USA. Paramount. 1954.

Director: William Dieterle. *Producer:* Irving Asher. *Screenplay:* John Lee Mahin. Based on the novel by Robert Standish. *Director of photography:* Loyal Griggs. *Art directors:* J. McMillan Johnson, Hal Pereira. *Costume designer:* Edith Head. *Editor:* George Tomasini. *Second unit director:* Alvin Gazner. *Special effects:* John P. Fulton, Paul Lerpae. *Music:* Franz Waxman. *Running time:* 104 mins.

Cast: Elizabeth Taylor (Ruth Wiley), Dana Andrews (Dick Carver), Peter Finch (John Wiley), Abraham Sofaer (Appuhamy), Abner Biberman (Dr Pereira), Noel Drayton (Atkinson), Rosalind Ivan (Mrs Lakin), Barry Bernard (Strawson), Philip Tunge (John Ralph), Edward Ashley (Gregory), Leo Britt (Chisholm), Mylee Haulami (Rayna), Jack Raine (Norbert), Victor Millan (Koru).

Lawrence of Arabia

GB. Columbia/Horizon Pictures. 1962.

Director: David Lean. *Producer:* Sam Spiegel. *Screenplay:* Robert Bolt [and Michael Wilson – uncredited]. Based on *The Seven Pillars of Wisdom* by T. E.

Lawrence. *Director of photography:* F. A. Young. *Production designer:* John Box. *Art director:* John Stoll. *Costume designer:* Phyllis Dalton. *Editor:* Anne V. Coates. *Second unit directors:* Andre Smagghe, Noel Howard, Nicolas Roeg. *Special effects:* Cliff Richardson. *Music:* Maurice Jarre. *Conducted by:* Sir Adrian Boult. *Running time:* 222 mins (cut to 202 mins in 1963, 185 mins in 1971, restored to 220 mins 1989).

Cast: Peter O'Toole (T. E. Lawrence), Alec Guinness (Prince Feisal), Anthony Quinn (Auda Aby Tayi), Jack Hawkins (General Allenby), Omar Sharif (Sherif Ali), Anthony Quayle (Colonel Brighton), Claude Rains (Dryden), Arthur Kennedy (Jackson Bentley), Jose Ferrer (Turkish Bey), Donald Wolfit (General Murray), I. S. Johar (Gasim), Gamil Ratib (Majid), Michel Ray (Farraj), John Dimech (Daud), Zia Mohyeddin (Tafas), Jack Gwillim (Club secretary), Howard Marion Crawford (Medical officer), Hugh Miller (RAMC Colonel), Jack Hedley (Reporter), Harry Fowler (Corporal Potter), Norman Rossington (Corporal Jenkins), Basil Dignam (Cavalry officer), Mohammed Habachi (Talal), Cher Kaoui (Khitan).

The Naked Prey

USA. Paramount. 1965.

Producer and director: Cornel Wilde. *Co-producer:* Sven Persson. *Screenplay:* Clint Johnston & Don Peters. *Director of photography:* I. A. R. Thompson. *Costume designer:* Freda Thompson. *Editor:* Roger Cherrill. *Music:* Andrew Tracy. *Running time:* 94 mins.

Cast: Cornel Wilde (The Man), Gert Van Den Bergh (2nd Man), Ken Gampu (Bold One), Horace Gilman (Young One), Bella Randels (Young Girl), Morrison Gampu (Chief), Patrick Mynhardt (Safari overseer/Slaver/Sergeant), Eric Mcanyan (The Brother), Jose Sithole (Gaunt One), John Marcus (Big Warrior), Sandy Nkomo (Broken Nose), Joe Dlamini (Bull Marked), Fusi Zazayoku (Other warrior).

Carry On ... Follow That Camel

GB. Rank. 1967.

Director: Gerald Thomas. *Producer:* Peter Rogers. *Screenplay:* Talbot Rothwell. *Director of photography:* Alan Hume. *Art director:* Alex Vetchinsky. *Costume designer:* Emma Selby-Walker. *Editor:* Alfred Roome. *Music:* Eric Rogers. *Running time:* 95 mins.

Cast: Phil Silvers (Sergeant Nocker), Jim Dale (Bertram Oliphant 'Bo' West), Kenneth Williams (Commandant Burger), Peter Butterworth (Simpson), Charles Hawtrey (Capitaine Le Pice), Joan Sims (Zig Zag), Bernard Bresslaw (Sheikh Abdul Abulbul), Angela Douglas (Lady Jane Ponsonby), Anita Harris (Corktip), John Bluthal (Corporal Clotski), Peter Gilmore (Captain Bagshaw), William Mervyn (Sir Cyril Ponsonby), Larry Taylor (Riff), William Hurndell (Raff).

Carry On Up the Khyber

GB. Rank. 1968.

Director: Gerald Thomas. *Producer:* Peter Rogers. *Screenplay:* Talbot Rothwell. *Director of photography:* Ernest Steward. *Art director:* Alex Vetchinsky. *Costume designer:* Emma Selby-Walker. *Editor:* Alfred Roome. *Music:* Eric Rogers. *Running time:* 88 mins.

Cast: Sidney James (Sir Sidney Ruff-Diamond), Kenneth Williams (Khasi of Kalabar), Charles Hawtrey (Private Widdle), Joa n Sims (Lady Joan Ruff-Diamond), Bernard Bresslaw (Bungdit Din), Peter Butterworth (Brother Belcher), Roy Castle (Captain Keene), Angela Douglas (Princess Jelhi), Terry Scott (Sergeant-Major MacNutt), Cardew Robinson (Fakir), Peter Gilmore (Private Ginger Hale), Julian Holloway (Major Shorthouse), Leon Thau (Stinghi), Michael Mellinger (Chindhi), Alexandra Dane (Busti), Patrick Allen (Narrator).

Carry On Up the Jungle

GB. Rank. 1970.

Director: Gerald Thomas. *Producer:* Peter Rogers. *Screenplay:* Talbot Rothwell. *Director of photography:* Ernest Steward. *Art director:* Alex Vetchinsky. *Costume designer:* Courtenay Elliott. *Editor:* Alfred Roome. *Music:* Eric Rogers. *Running time:* 89 mins.

Cast: Frankie Howerd (Professor Inigo Tinkle), Sidney James (Bill Boosey), Charles Hawtrey (Walter Bagley/King Tonka), Joan Sims (Lady Evelyn Bagley), Kenneth Connor (Claude Chumley), Bernard Bresslaw (Upsidaisi), Terry Scott (Ug the Jungle Boy), Jacki Piper (June), Valerie Leon (Leda), Reuben Martin (Gorilla), Edwina Carroll (Nerda), Banny Daniels (Nosha Chief), Yemi Ajibadi (Witch Doctor).

The Man Who Would Be King

USA. Allied Artists. 1975.

Director: John Huston. *Producer:* John Foreman. *Screenplay:* John Huston and Gladys Hill. Based on the story by Rudyard Kipling. *Director of photography:* Oswald Morris. *Production designer:* Alexander Trauner. *Art director:* Tony Inglis. *Costume designer:* Edith Head. *Editor:* Russell Lloyd. *Second unit director:* Michael Moore. *Stunt co-ordinator:* James Arnett. *Special effects:* Richard Parker. *Music:* Maurice Jarre. *Running time:* 129 mins.

Cast: Sean Connery (Danny Dravot), Michael Caine (Peachy Carnehan), Christopher Plummer (Rudyard Kipling), Saeed Jaffrey (Billy Fish), Jack May (District Commissioner), Doghmi Larbi (Ootal), Karoom Ben Bouih (Kafu Selim), Mohammad Shamsi (Babu), Albert Moses (Ghulam), Paul Antrim (Mulvaney), Shakira Caine (Roxanne).

Raiders of the Lost Ark

USA. Paramount/Lucasfilm. 1981.

Director: Steven Spielberg. *Producer:* Frank Marshall. *Executive producers:* George Lucas, Howard Kazanjian. *Associate producer:* Robert Watts. *Screenplay:* Lawrence Kasdan. *Story:* George Lucas, Philip Kaufman. *Director of photography:* Douglas Slocombe. *Production designer:* Norman Reynolds. *Art director:* Leslie Dilley. *Costume designer:* Deborah Nadoolman. *Second unit director:* Michael Moore. *Editor:* Michael Kahn. *Visual effects supervisor:* Richard Edlund. *Stunt co-ordinator:* Glenn Randall. *Music:* John Williams. *Running time:* 115 mins.

Cast: Harrison Ford (Indiana Jones), Karen Allen (Marion Ravenwood), Paul Freeman (Belloq), Ronald Lacey (Toht), John Rhys-Davies (Sallah), Denholm Elliott (Marcus Brody), Alfred Molina (Satipo), Wolf Kahler (Dietrich), Anthony Higgins (Gobler), Viv Tablian (Barranca/Monkey Man), Don Fellows (Colonel Musgrave), William Hootkins (Major Eaton) Fred Sorenson (Jock), George Harris (Katanga), Matthew Scurfield (Second Nazi), Pat Roach (Giant Sherpa/Second mechanic), Malcolm Weaver (Ratty Nepalese), Sonny Caldinez (Mean Mongolian), Anthony Chinn (Mohan), Christopher Frederick (Otto), Tutte Lemkow (Imam), Ishaq Bux (Omar), Kiran Shah (Abu), Souad Messaoudi (Fayah), Steve Hanson (Nazi agent), Terry Richards (Arab swordsman), Frank Marshall (Pilot), Tony Vogel (Tall captain).

Gandhi

GB. Columbia/Indo–British Films/Goldcrest/National Film Development Corporation of India. 1982.

Producer and director: Richard Attenborough. *Screenplay:* John Briley. *Executive producer:* Michael Stanley-Evans. *Co-producer:* Rani Dube. *Associate producer:* Suresh Jindal. *Directors of photography:* Billy Williams, Ronnie Taylor. *Production designer:* Stuart Craig. *Supervising art director:* Bob Laing. *Costume designers:* John Mollo, Bhanu Athaiya. *Second unit director:* Govind Hihalani. *Editor:* John Bloom. *Special effects supervisor:* David Watkins. *Music:* Ravi Shankar. *Additional music:* George Fenton. *Historical consultant:* Professor R. Puri. *Running time:* 188 mins.

Cast: Ben Kingsley (Gandhi), Candice Bergen (Margaret Bourke-White), Edward Fox (General Dyer), John Gielgud (Lord Irwin), Trevor Howard (Judge Broomfield), John Mills (The Viceroy), Martin Sheen (Walker), Ian Charleson (Charlie Andrews), Athol Fugard (General Smuts), Gunter Maria Halmer (Herman Kallenbach), Geraldine James (Mirabehn), Roshan Seth (Nehru), Amrish Puri (Khan), Saeed Jaffrey (Sardar Patel), Rohini Hattangady (Kasturba Gandhi), Alyque Padamsee (Jinnah), John Clements (Advocate General), Ian Bannen (Senior police officer), Michael Bryan (Principal Secretary), Richard Griffiths (Collins), Bernard Hepton (GOC), Shreeram Lagoo (Professor Gokhale), Virenda Razdan (Maulama Azad), Nigel Hawthorne (Kinnoch), Michael Hordern (Sir George Hodge), Richard Vernon (Sir Edward Gait), Om Puri (Nahari), Harsh Nayyar (Godse), Shane Rimmer (Commentator), Peter Harlowe (Mountbatten), Marius Wayers (Conductor), Winston Ntshona (Porter), Peter Cartwright (European passenger), (Harilal Gandhi), Avpar Jhita (Manilal Gandhi), Anthony Sagger (Ramdas Gandhi), Daniel Day Lewis (Colin).

Three Kings

USA. Warner Bros./Village Roadshow Pictures. 1999.

Director: David O. Russell. *Producers:* Charles Roven, Paul Junger Witt, Edward L. McDonnell. *Executive producers:* Gregory Goodman, Kelley Smith-Wait, Bruce Berman. *Associate producer:* Alan G. Glazer. *Screenplay:* David O. Russell. *Story:* John Ridley. *Director of photography:* Newton Thomas Sigel. *Production designer:* Catherine Hardwicke. *Supervising art director:* Derek R. Hill. *Costume designer:* Kym Barrett. *Second unit director:* Dan Bradley. *Stunt co-ordinator:* Dan Bradley. *Special effects co-ordinator:* Marty Bresin. *Music:* Carter Burwell. *Running time:* 115 mins.

Cast: George Clooney (Major Archie Gates), Mark Wahlberg (Sergeant Troy Barlow), Ice Cube (Sergeant Chief Elgin), Nora Dunn (Adriana Cruz), Spike Jonze (Private Conrad Vig), Cliff Curtis (Amir Abdulah), Jamie Kennedy (Walter Wogaman), Mykelti Williamson (Colonel Horn), Saïd Taghmaoui (Captain Sa'id), Holt McCallany (Captain Van Meter), Judy Greer (Cathy Daitch), Christopher Lohr (Teebaux), Jon Sklaroff (Paco), Marsha Horan (Amir's wife), Alia Shawkat (Amir's daughter), Liz Stauber (Troy's wife).

Index